LOCAL AND CENTRAL GOVERNMENT

LOCAL AND CENTRAL GOVERNMENT

A COMPARATIVE STUDY OF ENGLAND, FRANCE, PRUSSIA, AND THE UNITED STATES

BY PERCY ASHLEY, M.A.

LINCOLN COLLEGE, OXFORD

LECTURER AT THE LONDON SCHOOL OF ECONOMICS AND
POLITICAL SCIENCE IN THE UNIVERSITY OF LONDON

LONDON:

JOHN MURRAY, ALBEMARLE STREET

1906

TO

WILLIAM JAMES ASHLEY

AND

MARGARET ASHLEY

18*th July*, 1906.

CONTENTS

INTRODUCTION

CHAPTER I

LOCAL ADMINISTRATION IN ENGLAND

CHAPTER II

LOCAL ADMINISTRATION IN FRANCE

CHAPTER III

LOCAL ADMINISTRATION IN PRUSSIA

CHAPTER IV

THE GOVERNMENT OF AMERICAN CITIES

CHAPTER V

THE HISTORY OF LOCAL ADMINISTRATION IN ENGLAND SINCE 1832

CHAPTER VI

THE HISTORY OF LOCAL ADMINISTRATION IN FRANCE SINCE 1789

CHAPTER VII

THE HISTORY OF LOCAL ADMINISTRATION IN PRUSSIA SINCE 1806

CHAPTER VIII

ADMINISTRATIVE LAW

CHAPTER IX

LOCAL AUTHORITIES AND THE LEGISLATURE

CHAPTER X

THE ADMINISTRATIVE CONTROL OF LOCAL AUTHORITIES

CHAPTER XI

THE CONTROL OF LOCAL FINANCES

CHAPTER XII

THE COURTS OF JUSTICE AND LOCAL ADMINISTRATION

LOCAL AND CENTRAL GOVERNMENT

INTRODUCTION

SECTION 1

IN all European nations, whatever may have been Self-government and decentralisation. the previous course of their constitutional history, the persistent and rapid growth of the functions of the state, and the constant assumption of new and onerous duties and responsibilities in the last century, have rendered some attempts at decentralisation and some grants of self-government absolutely necessary, if the national administration is to be carried on with success. Experience, ancient and modern alike, has shown conclusively that a completely centralised bureaucracy—that is, a self-recruiting body of officials working from a single centre, and responsible only to itself— cannot carry on indefinitely the administration of a large country; it tends to ignore the varieties of local conditions, to become stereotyped in its ideas and methods, and overburdened; and sooner or later a breakdown becomes inevitable. And where the people have been discouraged from

A

taking an interest in the task of government, where they have not been habituated to the management of public affairs, the collapse, when the bureaucracy fails, is so much the greater, since there is nothing which can be substituted for the broken - down official organisation. For these practical reasons, amongst others of a more theoretical and political character, in all progressive states, during the last century, attempts have been made at decentralisation and the development of self-government in two ways:[1] (a) by entrusting the inhabitants of localities, or their chosen representatives, with the conduct (under greater or less control) of those matters of public interest and utility which concern the localities chiefly or entirely; and (b) by providing for the participation of unofficial citizens in the management of some at least of those other matters of administration which are supposed to belong particularly to the sphere of the central government. The systems of local administration in vogue, and the constitution and working of the authorities established for these purposes, have naturally been influenced greatly by the constitutional ideas and the forms of government of the different states; they reflect these, as they

---

[1] "Selbstverwaltung bedeutet zunächst die Verwaltung der eigenen Angelegenheiten öffentlicher Verbände durch selbstverwählte Organe . . . Eine fernere Bedeutung hat die Selbstverwaltung durch Heranziehung dieser Organe oder der von ihnen gewählten oder vorgeschlagenen Personen zu Geschäften der staatlichen Verwaltung erlangt." Hue de Grais, *Handbuch der Verfassung und Verwaltung*, (15th edition, p. 64, n. 1).

do also the political habits and social conditions of the citizens.

So far as Europe is concerned, the develop- *Local self-government in Great Britain.* ment of local self-government has gone furthest in Great Britain. No attempt has been made there to classify the functions of government into "central" and "local" on scientific grounds; the division actually in existence has been determined partly by administrative convenience (which is not necessarily the same as efficiency), and partly by our traditional political theories; and the result is a measure of decentralisation greater than can be found in any other European state. A certain number of functions are discharged by central departments (*i.e.*, by officials alone); but much the larger part of the national administration is carried on by local authorities, elected either for historical areas (the county, municipality, or parish), or for artificial areas (the unions and districts), but acting in either case under the control of the central government. Sometimes that control is exercised only by the Courts of Justice; in other cases the central departments are armed with powers of supervision and direction. But these powers are limited by law, and the departments in their turn are subject to the elected national assembly; so that the principle of self-government is supreme. And, moreover, we have in England traditional ideas as to the autonomy of local communities, which are the outcome of the particular course of our political

and constitutional history; and we are inclined
to regard the central power as something imposed
upon the localities often without their consent,
and for centuries extending its influence and
authority at their cost. Since the passing of the
first Reform Act, the enlargement of the sphere
of state action, and the multifarious character of
the work brought within it, have compelled the
central government either to create new local
authorities, or to extend the powers of those
already in existence. But even when the national
administration was most centralised in England,
and local government was most decrepit, the local
authorities never ceased to discharge some duties;
and so to-day they exercise two kinds of powers
—some which they are thought to possess by a
sort of immemorial prescriptive right, and others
which have been bestowed upon them by the will
of the central government.[1] In law, the local
authorities are simply the creatures of the legislature, set up and destroyed by it at its pleasure;
but the influence of the historical tradition is so
strong, that the English citizen probably has still
some conception of local self - government as a
right with which no central power may properly
interfere.[2]

[1] "Local government . . . may be defined generally as the carrying
out by the inhabitants of localities, or by their elected representatives
of the duties and powers with which they have been invested by
the Legislature, or which devolve upon them at common law."
Redlich and Hirst, *Local Government in England*, p. xxiv.

[2] "En résumé, les grands pouvoirs politiques en Angleterre ne
sont à aucun degré les créatures d'un pouvoir constituant, car leur

SECTION 2

Our Continental neighbours have approached the question from a very different standpoint. The history of both France and Prussia is the record of the building-up of a consolidated and powerful state by means of a great bureaucracy, directed from a single centre, and pursuing a uniform policy; and so, in both countries, the people became accustomed to look to that centre, to the monarch and his officials, for guidance in all their affairs. The local self-government, which had existed in the early days of the national history, slowly became almost extinct, and centralisation was complete. When the local institutions revived, it was at the will, and

Local self-government in France and Prussia.

existence est antérieure à quelque acte constituante que ce soit. Leur titre n'est pas une volonté expresse, manifesté regulièrement et distinctement à un jour donné, mais une antique possession de fait qu'aucune contestation n'a troublée depuis des siècles. . . . La condition des autorités subordonnées, locales ou speciales, n'est pas moins particulière. Les autorités subordonnées peuvent, en général, invoquer, comme en France, un titre exprès, une institution conférée à une date certaine; mais ce titre original est si incomplet, cette institution est si ancienne, qu'ils paraissent peu de chose en regard du crédit attaché au fait de la longue possession et des droits coutumiers qu'une pratique intense a greffés sur ce premier fonds statutaire. . . . Et leur passé est si long, leur origine est si voisine parfois de l'époque où le corps politique lui-même s'est formé; ils se sont si bien désaccoutumés de regarder comme une délégation la fonction sociale qu'ils remplissent de temps immémorial; ils se considèrent si naturellement et naïvement comme des associés de l'Etat et non comme des subordonnés, que le législateur anglais a besoin de réfléchir longtemps et de philosopher plus qu'il n'en à le goût, pour découvrir qu'ils sont en effet ses créatures et qu'ils doivent se plier à l'utilité commune." Boutmy, *Etudes de Droit Constitutionnel*, pp. 229-232 (edition 1885).

for the purposes, of the central authorities; and so, both in France and Prussia, local self-government is regarded rather as a gift from above than as an inherent right. Hence it is naturally weaker than in England; and its weakness is increased by the ineffectiveness of the authority exercised by the French and Prussian Parliaments over the national administration. In France and Prussia alike there is a careful classification of public services into "local" and "central." The former are left to the locally elected authorities, subject, however, in most cases to the more or less stringent control of the central government. "Central" matters (which include many things that we in England regard as primarily local, such as education, sanitary administration, and police), are administered in a few cases solely by central departments, but generally by territorial delegations of those offices—that is, by official agents acting singly, or in groups, within prescribed areas.[1] These delegations are formed in various ways. Sometimes they are purely official, consisting of a single member, or several members, of the bureaucracy; examples of this are the French Prefect and the Prussian *Regierung*. Sometimes they are composed partly of officials, and partly of unprofessional members selected by the local authorities and approved by the central

---

[1] French writers use the term "deconcentration" for this form of decentralisation. Bertélemy, *Droit Administratif*, p. 81.

government, as is the case with the Prussian *Bezirksausschuss*. And, finally, the local elected authorities, called into being for other purposes, may be made to act as agents for the central departments; the Prussian *Landrath* and *Kreisausschuss*, and to some extent also the French Mayor, are instances of the use of this method.

It might be supposed that where this third alternative is adopted, the effect is much the same as that already described for England, where the local authorities have so large a share in the national administration. But actually the result is very different. For in all the matters entrusted to them the English local authorities regard themselves as carrying out the law according to the will of, and in the manner desired by, the inhabitants of their localities, subject to the general supervision of the central government; whilst French and Prussian local authorities consider normally that their task is to carry out within their localities the will of the central government, even in those matters which are supposed to be of purely local importance. The causes of this difference of attitude have already been indicated; it is due chiefly to the historical part played by the bureaucracy, and the maintainance of its old influence; but the result is further promoted by the fact that whilst English local authorities are responsible only to the inhabitants of their areas so long as they obey the law, and even when they disobey or exceed the law are answerable in practice only to the Courts of Justice, the French and Prussian authorities, so far as they are agents of the central departments, are responsible to them, are counted as a part of the bureaucracy, and subjected to administrative control. And it is almost unnecessary to add that since they are bound to obey the central officials in a great number of matters, they become inclined to act in accordance with central ideas in all the questions with which they have to deal, even when some of these concern directly the localities alone. Thus in practice the whole of French and Prussian local government is still largely under the direction of the bureaucracies.

SECTION 3

The grant of powers to local authorities.

There are certain other important differences between the English and continental systems, which are indeed the outcome of the fundamental distinction which has been indicated, but need to be noticed here. One is in the manner in which powers are conferred upon the local authorities.[1] They may be permitted to do certain specified acts, and those alone; or they may be empowered to do anything which is not expressly forbidden. The first of these methods—the specific grant— has been adopted in England: a local authority

[1] These remarks apply, of course, solely to the functions of local authorities as representatives of their local communities.

may exercise only the powers conferred upon it either by the legislative enactment which created it, or by general Acts of Parliament applying to all authorities of a particular class, or by special Local Acts—these last being a peculiarity of the British system.[1] The second method—the grant of general powers—is employed in France and Prussia; there the local bodies are authorised to do anything that they may deem advisable in the interests of the community which they represent, subject to the necessity of obtaining the approval of the higher administrative authorities. The result of this difference in method is that in Great Britain Parliament determines what the local authorities may do, for any fresh powers they must have recourse to the legislature, and the task of the central departments is limited in some matters to enforcing the law, and in others to preventing the law being exceeded by the localities (though in this respect they have very little control over the municipalities); whilst in the two Continental states it is the business of the departments (*i.e.*, of an administrative body) to determine what the local authorities shall do. Consequently, although the legal powers of a French or Prussian municipality may be much wider than those of an English Town Council, the use made of them depends on the character

---

[1] Such special legislation is prohibited by the constitutions of many states of the American Union, though, as will be seen later (c. ix.), the prohibition can be avoided.

of the controlling bureaucracy. If it is enterprising and receptive of new ideas, as on the
whole it is in Prussia, then there is the fullest
and largest opportunity for municipal development; whilst if, as in France, the bureaucracy
is conservative and slow to move, the action of
the local authorities remains cramped and limited.

The methods of central control.

This brings us to another difference, which
has already been indicated, in the relative importance of the ways in which control is exercised by
the central government over the local authorities.
There are in fact only two ways — the judicial
and the administrative. Under the first of these
the local authorities are compelled to obey the
law (or restrained within its limits) by the Courts
of Justice, set in motion either by the government
departments or by private individuals. Under
the second form the local authorities are forced
to obedience by the higher authorities acting
by administrative or bureaucratic methods, *e.g.*,
fines, suspensions, dismissals, or supersession of a
negligent authority.

In Great Britain the control is almost entirely
judicial. The central departments, by means of
inspectors, watch and advise the local administration; by their power in respect to the parliamentary
grants for some services they can enforce a measure
of efficiency; they can bring pressure to bear
upon negligent authorities; but that is all. If
a local authority persists in its refusal to obey
the law, all a department can do is to invoke the

aid of the Courts of Justice;[1] and then the conflict is no longer between the local authority and a central administrative office, but between the recalcitrant authority and a legal tribunal. From the merely administrative standpoint, this is one of the weaknesses of the British system, that so long as the local bodies can make a show of obedience to the law in any matter, there is in most public services no means of compelling them to be really efficient or to attain the standard which may be desirable. In the United States of America, where local government is the concern of the separate states, the judicial control is the only one which exists, since there are no central departments authorised to exercise any power over the local authorities, or capable of doing so.

In France and Prussia, on the other hand, there is very much more administrative control, since (as already pointed out) for many purposes the local authorities are regarded as peculiarly the agents of the central government, and as such are part of the bureaucratic organisation and subject to the ordinary forms of official control; and also because of the system of grants of general power, and the constant necessity of approval from above for all acts of the local bodies.

[1] There are some powers of administrative action, but they are practically all left in abeyance.

The Courts of
Justice and
the adminis-
tration.

One other great and far-reaching difference need only be touched briefly here, since it will be discussed very fully in subsequent chapters. In Great Britain conflicts between the central departments and the local authorities, or between public authorities of any kind and private individuals, are determined by the ordinary Courts of Justice, which apply to them the principles of the ordinary law of the land. The citizen who considers himself aggrieved by the action of any public authority has precisely the same remedies against it, and against any of its officials who participated in the act of which he complains, as he would have if the act had been committed by another citizen. That is to say, an authority (central or local) has no protection from liability for a wrongful action (even if due to an honest mistake), and its official agents are personally responsible for their share in that action—they cannot plead obedience to orders as a defence. The same is true generally of the United States. In France and Prussia the position is altogether different ; there, disputes between authorities are seldom brought before a legal tribunal, but are usually determined by administrative decisions. Further—and this is the important point—all disputes between individuals and public authorities as such, are decided by a set of tribunals distinct from the ordinary Courts, constituted in a special way, and administering a body of law which aims at protecting the officials from any personal responsibility for acts done by them in their official character; the citizen has not the same remedies as against another citizen, and those which he has are by no means so effective. This system of "administrative courts" is obviously of very great importance in its effect upon the working of the national administration.

The continental official is then in a legally privileged position; he also stands in a relation to the elected local authorities altogether different from that which exists in England. With us the unprofessional administrators are supreme; they are the authorities, and the salaried experts are merely their agents and servants. It is true that the permanent officials (both of the central departments and of the local bodies) often exercise very great influence, and largely determine policy; but that fact is due to their skill, experience, and personal character, and not to their legal status. In Prussia the professional administrator, even when appointed and paid by the elected authority, is emphatically the head of that authority, and to a considerable extent directs and controls its action. In France the prefect occupies an even stronger position, for his appointment rests solely with the central government; he is its agent and also (and therefore only secondarily) the sole executive

Position of officials in local administration.

official of the locality. In England, then, the non - professional elected members conduct the local administration, with the aid and expert advice of a permanent professional staff: in Prussia and in the French departments the officials administer, subject to the supervision and financial control of the elected representatives.

The "separation of powers."

Finally, at once a cause and a consequence of this, there is a difference in the relations between the executive and deliberative powers in local government. The English system reflects the interdependence of the executive and the legislature which is a characteristic feature of the national constitution. The members of an English local council together form a deliberative body, but for administrative purposes they divide into committees; and so each member has a share in the determination of local policy, and also in the practical work of carrying the policy into effect. In France and Prussia, on the contrary, the deliberative and executive functions are kept more or less carefully distinct—a member of a local council has not commonly, as such, any share in the actual work of administration; whilst in the American cities, in imitation of the Federal and State constitutions, the separation of powers has been carried to an extreme.

The purpose of the following chapters is to endeavour to illustrate, by a description of the organisation and working of local institutions in England, France, and Prussia, and in some

American cities, the differences which have been thus briefly indicated; and to show how those differences have resulted from the national history, and from the influence exercised by forms of central government upon the local institutions.

CHAPTER I

LOCAL ADMINISTRATION IN ENGLAND

SECTION 1

Central departments.
THE English ministerial departments concerned in any way with local government are five in number, one of them being a branch of the Secretariat of State and the others offshoots of the Privy Council as an administrative authority. They are:—

(1) The Home Office, under a Secretary of State, assisted by a Parliamentary Under-Secretary (politician), and a permanent Under - Secretary (civil servant). It has the sole direction of the Metropolitan Police, inspects all other constabulary forces and gives a certificate of efficiency without which they cannot receive the grants from the central Exchequer; and its approval is required for all police bye-laws made by local authorities. It also controls the local sanitary authorities so far as they are entrusted with duties under the Factory Acts, which in the main are enforced by its own staff of inspectors. The department has a few other powers relating to local government, including the administration of the Burial Acts

and the inspection of reformatory and industrial schools.

(2) The Local Government Board is composed nominally of a number of Privy Councillors, but the work is actually done only by a President, with the help of a Parliamentary Secretary and a permanent Secretary.[1] The Board is the directing and controlling authority in all that relates to the Poor Laws, and for this it is armed with very extensive and complete powers; it supervises and guides the work of the local health authorities; it watches the financial operations of the various local bodies; it has a number of miscellaneous duties in regard to such matters as the alteration of boundaries, the constitution of authorities and the conduct of local elections; and it collects and publishes annually elaborate information as to the conditions, financial and other, of local government throughout the country. The amount of detailed work done by the department is enormous, and in many ways it is over-burdened; but no satisfactory scheme of devolution has yet been proposed.

(3) The Board of Trade is another and much older nominal committee of Privy Councillors, whilst in fact it has the same organisation as the Local Government Board. Its functions are very

---

[1] The Act of 1871, establishing the Board, directs that " all rules, orders, and regulations made by the Local Government Board shall be valid if made under the seal of the Board, and signed by the President or one of the *ex-officio* members, and counter-signed by a Secretary or an Assistant Secretary."

B

numerous and varied, but so far as the local bodies are concerned it deals only with what are known as their "trading" enterprises—that is, it sanctions, or enquires into, proposals for the supply by them of water, gas, tramways, electric light and power, and issues annual returns of these undertakings; and it constitutes harbour, dock, and pier authorities. Its approval is necessary for bye - laws made under the Weights and Measures Acts.

(4) The Board of Education resembles in form the Boards already described, and its duties are indicated by its title. It directs and supervises the whole of the education, in elementary schools, science and art schools, and evening schools, which is aided by public funds; it inspects training colleges similarly supported; and it advises the local education authorities upon their schemes for higher education. It is assisted by a consultative committee of experts, who however advise only upon questions submitted to them by the President.

(5) The Board of Agriculture differs from the others in that it has not a Parliamentary Secretary. It is brought into contact with the local authorities only with reference to the enforcement of the Diseases of Animals Acts, and to public markets.[1]

Methods of departmental action.
These departments, each in charge of a minister of Cabinet rank, are entrusted with the direction,

---

[1] The most recent account of the Central Departments concerned with local government is in Redlich and Hirst, *Local Government in England*, II., pp. 242-321. See also Traill, *Central Government*.

control, and guidance of the local authorities,
under the general supervision of the Cabinet,
and ultimately of Parliament. For the purposes
of direction they all possess what are called "sub-
legislative" powers; that is, they are empowered
by the legislature to issue orders and regulations
for the detailed application and enforcement of
its enactments. This is particularly the case with
the system of Poor Relief, which is the product
of a vast number of orders issued by the Local
Government Board and its predecessor, the Poor
Law Board; but the same plan has been adopted
in various degrees for almost all branches of
internal administration. Connected with this is
the discretional grant of powers to local bodies;
it is common for Parliament to bestow certain
powers upon all local authorities of a particular
class, but to make the exercise of them dependent,
in each particular case, upon the approval of
the department specially concerned. Thus, for
example, the Local Government Board may
confer on a rural district council any or all of
the powers of an urban district council, for the
whole or any part of its area; and in a number of
cases the central department may direct a local
authority to undertake some special duty.

Secondly, the central offices are controlling
authorities. Their approval is required for many
acts proposed to be done by local bodies, such
as the issue of bye-laws, dealings with municipal
property, housing schemes, loans, and many other

matters which the legislature has sanctioned in principle, but leaves to be determined in particular cases by the departments. It is their duty to see that the local authorities carry out the positive directions of the law, and (in the event of persistent neglect) to take the necessary steps to enforce obedience. As the local bodies are responsible only to the electors, and the departments have no powers of bureaucratic control over them, usually all they can do is to invoke the aid of the Courts of Justice to enforce the law; only in a very few cases have they the right to step in and do the work themselves, and they seldom make use of it.[1] The Local Government Board can dismiss any of the paid officials of the Poor Law authorities at any time, but this is not of much use in a conflict with the elected guardians. The local authorities (but not the councils of municipal boroughs) are restrained within the limits of the law to some extent also by the audit of their accounts by the Local Government Board and the powers which it exercises in connection therewith. In the cases of education, police, and, to a much smaller degree, public health, the departments can do something to secure efficiency by their right to give or withhold the Exchequer grants to those particular services; but in other cases all they can do is to try persuasion.

[1] The powers which the Education Department formerly possessed in this respect were abandoned by the Act of 1902.

The third function is guidance. It is the task of the ministries to collect and issue information, to give expert advice to any local authorities which may ask for it, or to issue advisory circulars on their own initiative.

In order to keep acquainted with the detailed work of the local administrators, to enquire into their various proposals, to watch their financial operations, to determine in the cases of education and police the grant or amount of the Exchequer contributions, and to give general advice and assistance, there are staffs of inspectors (Poor Law, medical, engineering, educational) attached to all the central departments which have been described. These officials are sometimes assigned to particular districts with which they become intimately acquainted; in other cases they are sent down from headquarters as occasion may require. The auditors (who are a kind of financial inspectors) may take decisions on their own responsibility, subject to appeal to the Local Government Board; in other cases the inspectors merely report to the central departments, which send down the consequent orders, or it may be only recommendations. The inspectorate renders it possible for the ministries to keep watch over local action, without forcing that action into too uniform a mould; and it also places a large amount of expert advice at the disposal of the localities.

Character-
istics of
English local
government.

Before we pass now to the consideration of the local authorities themselves, it may be useful to point out the general characteristics of the system which is to be examined.[1]   They may be summarised as—(*a*) the predominance throughout of the elected councils; (*b*) the participation of the elected councillors in both the deliberative and administrative work—by means of the committee system; (*c*) the subordination of the paid professional official to the unpaid elected amateur; (*d*) the constant recourse of the local authorities to Parliament for fresh powers; (*e*) the comparative weakness of the merely administrative control exercised by the central departments; and (*f*) the reference of all disputes, between central and local authorities, or between authorities and private citizens, to the ordinary Courts of Justice.

SECTION 2

The "ancient
county."

The largest of the local administrative areas in England and Wales is the ancient county, which exists now merely for the purposes of parliamentary elections, as the territorial basis for the militia, and for judicial affairs.   Its

---

[1] The sketch given in this chapter is intended only to bring out the general features of the English system for the purposes of comparison.   For detailed accounts see the small books of Ashley (1905) and Odgers (1899), the large work of Redlich and Hirst (2 vols.), and Maltbie, *English Local Government of To-day* (a study of the relations between central and local authorities).

authorities, all appointed by the Crown, are the
Lord Lieutenant, who is the head of the Commission of the Peace; the Sheriff, who has certain
duties connected with the administration of
justice; and the Justices of the Peace, who
formerly conducted the whole of the affairs of
the county in addition to their judicial functions.
They still have a few semi-administrative powers;
in Quarter Sessions they issue licences for private
lunatic asylums and for inebriate homes, appoint
visitors of prisons, by their representatives on
the Standing Joint Committee share in the
control of the county police, and now have to
administer the Act for the reduction of liquor
licences by compensation; in Special Sessions
they grant public-house licences; and in Petty
Sessions they may give certificates of exemption
from vaccination, and make various orders under
the Public Health Acts. Appeals against assessments for local rates are heard in Quarter Sessions.

But for the general purposes of local govern- The "ad-
ment the chief areas are the administrative county."
counties, which in most cases are practically
identical with the ancient counties,[1] and are
therefore in the main historical areas, with some
common life and sentiment. But ten of the
ancient counties are divided into two or (in the
cases of Yorkshire and Lincolnshire) three

---

[1] Actually the boundaries are exactly the same in six out of the
fifty-two counties of England and Wales. It may be noted here
that in Acts of Parliament the term "England" includes Wales,
unless otherwise stated.

administrative counties; and towns, which on 1st
June 1888, had a population of not less than fifty
thousand, or were "counties" by themselves (*i.e.*,
had sheriffs and special powers in regard to the
administration of justice), are excluded from the
areas of the administrative counties and from the
control of their authorities.   There are sixty-two
administrative counties,[1] and sixty - nine county
boroughs.

The County Council.   In each administrative county the authority
is the County Council, composed of ordinary
members elected for three years (women being
ineligible), and aldermen chosen for six years by
the whole council.   The number of councillors
was originally left to be fixed by the Local
Government Board, and so were the electoral
divisions, which were intended to be as nearly as
possible equal in population; and both the number
of members and the electoral divisions may be
varied from time to time by the Board on the
representation of the council.   The aldermen are
one-third of the number of councillors, and apart
from their longer tenure of office they have no
special privileges.   The council elects a chairman
and vice-chairman, who hold office for one year,
but are usually re-elected.   A strong chairman
may exercise very considerable influence (based on
his personal character and ability, and not on any

---

[1] Including the Administrative County of London, to which the
following description does not apply.   It will be considered in a later
section.

legal powers) upon the action of the council, and there are some cases in which the chairman is the real directing spirit of the whole county administration.

In the elections to the county councils the most striking fact is the absence of party feeling and the consequent infrequency of contested elections.[1] The persons elected are drawn very largely from the classes who supply the Bench of Justices—the large and small landowners, the large farmers, professional men, and clergy; representatives of the lower middle and working classes are comparatively rare. This is due partly to the maintenance of the old influence of social position, partly to the expense involved in travelling often some considerable distance to the county centre for the meetings of the council or its committees, and partly also to the fact that the administrative work was done quite well by the Justices under the old system. But in spite of this class predominance, particularly strong in the rural counties, the councils have aroused a considerable amount of popular interest, they have shown much enterprise and energy, and they have maintained the best traditions of English local administration.[2]

---

[1] In the first year (1889) in 3,240 districts there were 1,749 elections; in 1901 in 3,349 districts there were only 433 contests. There was a temporary increase in 1904, owing to education controversies.

[2] " Unsatisfactory and anomalous as the appointment of Quarter Sessions undoubtedly was, it is equally certain that the Justices of the Peace performed their duty with integrity and efficiency, and inspired such confidence that the inhabitants as a rule have been willing to leave the work in very much the same hands as before

The ordinary council meets only some four times a year, and so conducts its business chiefly by committees. These have charge of the administrative work and direct the permanent officials; the business of the council is to determine questions of policy, and control the action of the committees. But inasmuch as the councils meet ordinarily only once a quarter, and administrative questions often arise which cannot wait so long for a decision, a council may delegate all or any of its powers in a particular matter to the committee concerned, and in that case the committee may act without waiting for the council's approval;[1] but the power to levy a rate or raise a loan cannot be so delegated. Some committees are "statutory" (*i.e.*, required by law); such are the committees for finance,[2] asylums, education (with co-opted members), diseases of animals, allotments and small hold-

... What was good in the old Quarter Sessions administration —strict observance of law, abstention from political partisanship, and freedom from corruption—is no less characteristic of the new body; but in addition . . . the county councils have devoted themselves with discriminating zeal to important and useful public work which had previously been almost or entirely neglected." Redlich and Hirst, II., pp. 47-48.

[1] Local Government Act, 1888, sec. 82 (2).

[2] The Finance Committee has special duties: "Every county council shall from time to time appoint a Finance Committee for regulating and controlling the finance of the county, and an order for the payment of a sum out of the county fund . . . shall not be made by a county council except in pursuance of a resolution . . . passed on the recommendation of the Finance Committee and . . . any costs, debts, or liability exceeding £50 shall not be incurred except upon a resolution of the council passed on an estimate submitted by the Finance Committee." Local Government Act, 1888, sec. 80 (3).

ings. Others are optional, and joint committees of two or more councils may be appointed for special purposes.[1] There is also a Standing Joint Committee for the administration of the county police; it is composed of equal numbers of representatives of the County Council and Quarter Sessions, and is practically independent of the council, though it reports to it and receives from it the money which it requires.

The powers and duties of a council are many and varied. It is the highway authority, being responsible for all the roads within its area which it recognises as "main roads" (over 27,000 miles in all), and maintaining them either directly or through the district councils; it keeps up county bridges, and may construct or aid light railways. It has recently received a great addition of work in regard to education; it must secure an adequate supply of elementary education in the county, and in addition may supply or aid the supply of higher education. It is a public health authority: it supervises the sanitary work of the rural district councils, and for that and other purposes may appoint a medical officer; it administers the Acts relating to foods and drugs, diseases of animals, weights and measures, and river pollution; and it may establish isolation hospitals.

Powers of County Council.

---

[1] The committees of the Surrey County Council are for Asylums (2) Finance, Education, General Purposes (including Allotments and Small Holdings), Highways and Bridges, Public Health, Reformatory and Industrial Schools, Diseases of Animals, County Rate, and Selection.

It provides asylums for pauper lunatics, and, if
it so wishes, for lunatics who are not paupers;
in the former case the cost of maintenance of
the patients falls upon the Poor Law authorities.
The council administers county property, may
provide reformatory and industrial schools, makes
bye-laws for the county, and may exercise any
additional powers which it can obtain by means
of Private Bills promoted by it. Through its
representatives on the Standing Joint Committee
it has a share in the control of the police.
Finally, it has some powers of supervision over
the smaller rural authorities, as to the approval
of loans, changes in boundaries, etc., and these
powers could be greatly extended, since the Act
of 1888, as now amended, provides that the
Local Government Board may by order transfer
to any or all of the county councils any powers,
duties, or liabilities of any of the central departments concerned with local government. The
devolution of control intended by this would
however be resisted strongly by the councils of
non-county boroughs and urban districts.

Finance. The expenses of a county council are met by
(1) the proceeds of any county property that
there may be; (2) "general" or "special" county
rates (that is, rates levied upon the whole or part
of the county) made on the basis of the poor
rate; (3) Government grants from the Exchequer
Contribution Account,[1] for police, higher educa-

[1] For the Exchequer Contribution Account see Redlich and Hirst,

tion, and other services, and unassigned; (4) Government grants for elementary education; and (5) grants under the Agricultural Rates Act in relief of the rates upon agricultural land.[1]

The principal officers of a county council are the clerk (who is also clerk of the peace), medical officer, education secretary or director, coroners, surveyors (for highways, etc.), public analyst, inspectors under the Food and Drugs and Weights and Measures Acts, and a county treasurer. These officials are permanent (that is, they are untouched by changes in the composition of the council); they are the servants of the council, as are the permanent officials of all English local authorities, and so far as they influence the administration at all they do it by their knowledge and experience, and not because of their legal position. *County officers.*

The administrative county contains four different classes of local government areas— non - county boroughs, urban districts, rural districts, and rural parishes.[2] It will be convenient to take the two last - named here, and

---

II., pp. 92 - 97, and also the Memorandum on Grants - in - Aid by Hamilton in the Volume of Memoranda published by the Royal Commission on Local Taxation.

[1] The Act directs the payment from the National Exchequer to the local authorities of a sum equal to half the rates levied by them in 1895-96 upon agricultural land. Passed originally in 1896 for a term of years, it seems now to have become a permanent arrangement.

[2] The parishes in the boroughs and urban districts exist now only for some purposes of Poor Law machinery, and not for general matters of local government. They will be noticed later in the account of Poor Relief.

to leave the boroughs and urban districts to be discussed in the next section. This is justified also by the fact that the County Council exercises some control over the authorities of the rural district and the rural parish, but practically none over those of the other two areas.

The rural district.

A rural sanitary district was originally a Poor Law Union (*i.e.*, a group of parishes formed for purposes connected with the relief of the poor), or the rural portion of a Union, treated as an area for the administration of the Public Health Acts. The rural district is in fact still generally conterminous with the rural Poor Law Union, or with the rural part of a Union which is both rural and urban; but with the limitation that no rural district may lie in more than one county. There are six hundred and seventy-two such districts in England and Wales.

The District Council and its powers.

The authority of the district is the council, composed of persons (including women) elected in most cases triennially by the rural parishes according to population; the persons so elected are also representives of their parishes on the Board of Guardians. A council may elect its chairman from outside; he is *ex-officio* a Justice of the Peace during his year of office. The council must meet at least once a month; it may appoint whatever committees it thinks advisable, and co-opt outside persons to any of them;[1] and it may

---

[1] " A parish or district council may appoint committees consisting wholly *or partly* of members of the council." Local Government Act,

delegate to such committees any of its powers
except those relating to rates and loans. The
councils are the sanitary authorities for their areas,
and in fact the real responsibility for the public
health administration of rural England rests upon
them. They therefore have varied and extensive
powers and duties under the various Public
Health Acts — including sewerage and drainage,
water supply, etc. — and, moreover, the Local
Government Board may, by order, confer upon
a rural district council, for the whole or any part
of its area, all or any of the powers otherwise
exercised only by urban authorities. The councils
also have charge of all the roads (about 95,000
miles in length), which are not main roads, and
may take over from their county councils the
charge of the main roads in return for an annual
payment.[1] The rural district councils may provide allotments, carry out housing schemes, and
make use of other "Adoptive Acts" (such as
those for the provision of open spaces); and they
may take any action necessary for the protection
of public rights of way, and rights of common.
The chief salaried officials are the clerk, treasurer,

1894, sec. 56 (1). This power of co-optation seems to be used only
very infrequently.

[1] It is generally agreed that the highway administration of this
country is far from satisfactory. The roads, indeed, are usually well
made, but there are too many authorities; each county council and
each district council may organise its own system in its own way,
without regard to its neighbours. A co-ordinating authority is
badly needed; and, moreover, the revival of the use of the main
roads for long distance travelling seems to involve some readjust-
ment of the burden of maintenance.

medical officer, one or more sanitary inspectors and surveyor.

Finance. The expenditure is chiefly upon public health and highways, and is met by (1) general or special district rates, levied upon the same basis as the poor rate, but with the difference that agricultural land, railways, canals, tithes, and tithe - rent charges are assessed at only one-quarter of their poor rate valuation; (2) the state contributions under the Agricultural Rates Acts; (3) subventions from the Exchequer Contribution Account of one-half the salaries of medical officers and sanitary inspectors appointed on terms approved by the Local Government Board; and (4) the proceeds of any district property, such as waterworks.

The combination of the duties of rural district councillor and guardian, and the amount of work attached to both these offices, makes them sufficiently important to be attractive; and on the whole the average quality of the councils is good. There are doubtless a number of exceptions, and the sanitary administration is not always carried on with the energy which could be desired; but when all the conditions of rural England are taken into account, it may fairly be said that the councils have done their work well.

The rural parish. Each rural district consists of a group of poor law parishes, which indeed exist in urban areas also, but these are of no importance for general

local administration.[1] In each rural parish there
is a parish meeting of all persons on the local
government and parliamentary registers (including therefore women and lodgers); it elects its own
chairman, and also the overseers, who have certain
duties in regard to the poor rate, the assessment
and collection of other local rates, and the making
of electoral and jury lists. The further organisation of the parish depends upon its size ; every
parish with a population of 300 has a Parish
Council, parishes with populations of 100 may
have councils if they so desire, and parishes with
less than 100 inhabitants may have them by
agreement with the county councils. A county
council may group parishes, but in that case each
of the parishes in the group retains its separate
parish meeting. In the year 1902-3 there were
12,985 rural parishes ; and of these 7,250 were
entitled to have councils, 5,735 to have meetings
only.

Where there is not a council, the chairman of the
parish meeting generally conducts whatever administrative business there may be (though a parish
committee may be appointed), and the chairman
with the overseers forms a body corporate for the
holding of any parish property. Parish meetings
must be held in all parishes at least once a year,

Parish meeting and council.

---

[1] The "Poor Law Parish" is "a place for which a separate poor
rate is or can be made, or for which a separate overseer is or can
be appointed." It differs often from both the ancient civil, and
ecclesiastical parishes. Wright and Hobhouse, *Local Government and
Local Taxation* (2nd edition), p. 1.

but may be more frequent. The number of members of the parish council ranges from five to fifteen, and is fixed by the County Council; women are eligible, and so are any persons residing within three miles of the parish boundaries; the elections are usually triennial. A parish council may appoint committees, and co-opt outside persons to any of them.

Parochial
administra-
tion.

There is much work which these parochial authorities *may* do. A parish council or meeting may acquire rights of way, control or maintain footpaths, manage civil parochial property, apply the Adoptive Acts relating to allotments, recreation grounds, baths and wash-houses, lighting, and burial grounds; it may utilise wells or springs, provide protection against fire, and watch the sanitary conditions of the locality in order to keep the rural district council informed, and if that body neglects its work to invoke the aid of the county authorities. It appoints (wholly or in part) trustees of all civil charities in the parish, and is represented upon the managing bodies of all public elementary schools. But the exercise of these powers is crippled by the smallness of the great majority of the parishes; about nine-tenths of the total number have populations of less than 1,000, and 2,000 have less than 100 inhabitants each. There are certain obvious difficulties which result from this. One is the financial weakness of the authorities. The general rate (on the basis of the poor rate) which may be levied must not exceed sixpence in the pound, and the special rates under the various Adoptive Acts are all limited. In small parishes, therefore, sufficient money for any except a very few purposes cannot be obtained; and even if the rate limit were removed there would still be a strong disinclination to undertake any action involving much expenditure. Further, there is not much ability on which the parishes can draw, partly owing to their small size, and partly because the small amount and apparent unimportance of the work renders it in most cases unattractive.[1] The result on the whole is that the working of the Act of 1894 has disappointed its promoters. Something has been done in regard to lighting, allotments, and burial grounds (for which parishes may combine); there has been activity in the protection of rights of way and of commons and open spaces; and the representation of the inhabitants of the parishes in the management of elementary schools and charities is useful. But, speaking generally, the conditions of rural England do not promise much development or success for the parochial organisation of local government in the absence of considerable social changes; and the real work must come more and more into the hands of the authorities of a larger administrative area—the rural district.

[1] In 1902-3 out of 7,250 parishes entitled to councils, 6,531 had financial transactions of some kind; out of the 5,735 other parishes, only 390 had any receipts and expenditure. The parish authorities spent in all £228,917 (the largest item being £60,000 for lighting), and an additional £25,332 from loans.

SECTION 3

Coming next to the urban areas, we take first
the municipal boroughs, *i.e.*, urban communities
which have received a Charter of Incorporation and
therewith certain privileges from the Crown, and are
governed under the Municipal Corporations Act,
1882 — an amended version of the reforming Act
of 1835. The municipalities of England are
either historical communities remodelled in 1835,
or modern communities which have been
incorporated by a Royal Charter (granted by
the Crown in Council)[1] since that year; many of
the former were always very small, whilst charters
are now given only to fairly populous places.
Consequently the municipalities vary remarkably
in size, from Liverpool with 723,000 inhabitants
in 1901, to Hedon with only 1,020; there are 31
with populations of over 100,000, and 109 with
populations of less than 10,000 (whilst 66 of
these have less than 5,000 each). It follows from
this[2] that whilst the outline structure of municipal

[1] The charter is not given as a matter of course. An enquiry may
be held, either by the Privy Council, or by the Local Government
Board at its direction; and opponents are heard. Between 1888 and
1902, 55 applications for charters were made, and only 35 were
granted.
[2] And also from differences in social and economic conditions.
"No anatomical resemblances of outward structure can assimilate
the inner municipal life of quaint old cathedral cities with that of
new and fashionable watering-places, that of sea-ports with that
of inland towns, that of manufacturing or mining settlements with
that of market towns in the midst of agricultural neighbour-

government is everywhere the same, there are very great differences in its character and extent. The charters do not specify the powers to be exercised by the municipal authorities, but are concerned mainly with structure. The powers are derived from a number of sources:—(1) The Municipal Corporations Act, 1882; (2) general Acts, conferring powers on all authorities of particular classes, as the Public Health Act, 1875, and the Education Act, 1902; (3) "Adoptive Acts," i.e., Acts giving particular powers to any of specified classes of local authorities, which choose to "adopt" them; (4) Private (or Local) Acts promoted by the town councils or by any authorities whom they have superseded.

There are a number of differences between the municipal boroughs which must be noticed. Some are differences of status; a small proportion of the boroughs are "cities," and as such have a certain precedence due sometimes to the fact that they are the seats of bishops,[1] and in rarer cases (as Nottingham and Sheffield) to grants from the Crown; in a few instances the chief representative of the municipality bears by royal grant the title of Lord Mayor. Other differences of much greater importance are connected with the administration of justice; many boroughs

Differences between boroughs.

hoods." Brodrick, in Cobden Club's *Local Government and Taxation* (1875), p. 50.

[1] There are two cathedral "cities" which are not municipal boroughs—Ely (which is an urban district), and St David's (which has only a parish council).

have a separate Commission of the Peace; some have a stipendiary magistrate[1] appointed by the Crown; in a considerable number there is a separate Court of Quarter Sessions, in which justice is administered, not by a bench of justices, but by a legal officer, the Recorder, also appointed by the Crown; and a few boroughs are " counties of cities or towns," and possess their own sheriffs. The chief distinction, however, from our present standpoint is between " county " and " non-county " boroughs;[2] in the former, the town councils have most of the powers and duties of a county council; whilst the " non-county " boroughs send representatives to the county councils, which exercise some powers within the municipal boundaries.

The Town Council. In all the boroughs the municipal authority is concentrated in the Town Council, consisting of from nine to seventy-two (or in a few cases more) councillors elected for three years — one-third retiring every year — and of aldermen to the number of one-third of the councillors. The aldermen are chosen by the whole council, for six years, usually from amongst those members of the council who have the longest experience of municipal affairs;[3] women are not eligible as

[1] A stipendiary (police) magistrate can act alone, whilst there must be at least two justices.

[2] *Vide supra*, p. 24.

[3] The aldermen form a second Chamber, and are *ex-officio* Justices, only in the City of London, which will be described later. It shares with Winchelsea (a tiny Cinque Port), the distinction of being the only unreformed municipalities.

either councillors or aldermen. Party politics enter much into municipal elections, especially in the larger towns, and the local machinery of national parties is greatly used in municipal contests; but, nevertheless, there are very many cases of long and continuous membership of the councils. Experience seems to show that in spite of many efforts party loyalty cannot be relied upon in municipal elections in this country as it can be in the United States; and consequently our municipal government has, on the whole, not become a field for the rivalry of political factions.

The Town Council elects, annually in November, *The Mayor.* a Mayor who holds office for one year; re-elections are frequent in the small boroughs, but not in the larger. The Mayor, who is unpaid, is usually chosen from amongst the aldermen or councillors; but he may be elected from outside their ranks, and may be absolutely inexperienced in municipal affairs. He presides over the council meetings, and is generally an *ex-officio* member of all committees; he is *ex-officio* chairman of the borough bench of magistrates, where there is a separate Commission of the Peace; and he represents the municipality at all public ceremonies. He may be a mere figure-head; in any case his influence and authority depend solely upon his own personal character and energy, and not upon any powers attached to his office.

A town council has a two-fold character. It *Municipal functions.* is the representative authority of the municipality, and it is also the urban sanitary authority ; its functions in these two respects are distinct in law, and to some extent also in fact, but the distinction has come to be of small importance, except in regard to finance. As a municipal authority it administers corporation property and has powers in regard to police and education ; as an urban sanitary authority it carries out the Public Health Acts, and deals therefore with drainage and sewerage, water-supply, lighting, street improvements, housing schemes, markets, cemeteries, and isolation hospitals. Many of the " Adoptive Acts," for the provision of baths and wash-houses, parks and open spaces, museums and art galleries, may be used by a town council in either character ; and similarly as either a municipal authority or an urban sanitary authority it may promote Bills in Parliament to obtain additional powers.[1] There is a growing tendency to limit the powers of the smaller boroughs. Thus since 1882 no separate police force may be established in any borough with less than 20,000 inhabitants, and in 1888 the forces in boroughs with less than 10,000 inhabitants were transferred to the county authorities ; only boroughs with populations of

[1] The Borough Funds Act, 1872, as now amended lays down that municipal and urban district councils may promote a Bill, and spend money out of the rates for that purpose, only on the conditions that (1) a special resolution to that effect be passed by the council with special formalities, and that (2) the resolution be confirmed by the ratepayers either at a towns-meeting or poll. This is the nearest approach in England to the referendum which exists in some American cities, and in Canada (*e.g.*, at Toronto); instances of rejection by the ratepayers here are not uncommon.

not less than 10,000 can be separate areas for elementary education under the Act of 1902 ; and the same limit is applied for a number of other services, such as the administration of the Acts relating to the diseases of animals, weights and measures, and food and drugs—for these purposes the smaller municipalities are merged in the counties. It should be added that all county boroughs, and a number of Quarter Sessions boroughs, are required to provide accommodation for pauper lunatics.

In the last thirty years or so there has been "Municipal trading." a great development of the activity of town and urban district councils in regard to what is called "municipal trading"—waterworks, tramways, gas and electric lighting, electric power, and a number of other things, ranging from river steamers to sterilised milk for children. The increase in the apparent debt of local authorities, resulting from the heavy capital expenditure required for the provision of these services, and the action of the councils in taking to themselves services which would otherwise offer a field for private enterprise, have recently provoked much opposition and roused keen controversy.[1] It is not proposed to discuss the matter here, but only to point out the considerations which have had most weight with the local authorities. They seem to have been two—

[1] There is a very extensive literature, chiefly in pamphlets and articles, on "municipal trade." See L. Darwin, *Municipal Trade* ; Shaw, *Common Sense of Municipal Trading*; and the *Reports of the Select Committees of* 1900 *and* 1903.

first, the belief that practically all these services,
essential to the well-being of the inhabitants, tend
to become monopolies, and therefore should be
in the hands of authorities amenable to public
opinion and control, and not seeking merely a
financial profit; and, secondly, the desire to obtain
from these financially remunerative services something to set against the heavy unremunerative
expenditure rendered necessary by English sanitary
legislation.[1] These two ideas are not always held
together—there are many advocates of municipal
ownership who are opposed entirely to the alloca-
tion of profits to any purpose except the reduction
of charges; but nevertheless these two considerations, either separately or together, seem to have
determined municipal policy. It is, of course,
possible to adopt an alternative policy—private
enterprise under strict control; but this has not
hitherto been popular in England, in the United
States its results have been far from satisfactory
(especially in their indirect effects on civic life),
and in Germany the city administrators are moving
rapidly in the same direction as ourselves.

[1] "He held distinctly that all monopolies which were sustained in
any way by the state ought to be in the hands of the representatives
of the people, by whom they should be administered, and to whom
the profits should go. At present the council had inadequate means
for discharging all the obligations and responsibilities devolving upon
them, and he believed that the pressure of the rates would become
intolerable unless some compensation could be found in such a
proposal as that before the council. The purchase would help to
relieve the ratepayers of burdens which were every day becoming
more oppressive."—Mr Joseph Chamberlain as Mayor of Birmingham,
1874, on the purchase of the gasworks.

A town council determines its own procedure, Committees. and works chiefly by committees; the meetings of the council as a whole (which are held as often as may be necessary) are occupied chiefly by the receipt of the reports of the committees, the discussion of any questions raised by them, and the voting of the necessary resolutions. Some of these committees are statutory — those for police (the "watch committee"), education (with co-opted members, including women), diseases of animals, and asylums, in boroughs which are separate areas for these purposes. Others are appointed to the number which the council thinks necessary, and any committee may appoint sub-committees for special branches of its work. Unlike the county councils, town councils may not delegate any of their powers (except those relating to education) to their committees.[1]

The expenses of a town council as a municipal Finance. authority are met from the borough fund, which is formed from the proceeds of corporation property, fees, fines, etc., and of the borough rate, which is levied on the same basis as the poor rate. Its expenditure as a sanitary authority is met by the general district rate, levied on a slightly different

---

[1] "The council may from time to time appoint out of their own body such and so many committees, either of a general or special nature, and consisting of such number of persons, as they think fit, for any purposes which, in the opinion of the council, would be better regulated and managed by means of such committees; but the acts of every such committee shall be submitted to the council for their approval." Municipal Corporations Act, 1882, sec. 22 (2). Contrast the Education Act, 1902, sec. 17 (2).

basis; whilst the special rates which may be levied under some of the "Adoptive Acts" are limited in amount. It also receives Government grants for police, sanitary officers, and education. Dealings in municipal property, and loans (unless expressly authorised by Parliament), need the approval of the Local Government Board, but the accounts of municipalities (except those for education) are not subject to audit by that department. Officers. The chief permanent officers of a town council are the town clerk (who may exercise very great influence upon the municipal administration), treasurer, education secretary, medical officer, and sanitary inspectors, chief constable (where there is a separate police force), and the heads of the various administrative departments, which vary in number with the extent of municipal activity.

The urban district. The urban districts may be dismissed more briefly.[1] They are areas organised under the Local Government Act, 1894; and include (1) areas which prior to 1894 were Improvement Districts under Commissioners established by Local Acts; (2) Local Board of Health Districts formed under the Public Health Acts; (3) other areas since formed by the joint action of the county councils and the Local Government Board. In 1902-3 there were 812 such districts, ranging in population

---

[1] From the standpoint of the Public Health Acts, England is divided into rural and urban sanitary districts (the latter including boroughs). But the term "Urban Districts" usually means the areas under the Act of 1894.

from 300 to nearly 100,000 in a few cases.[1] The
authority in each is a council consisting solely *Council.*
of members elected either one-third every year,
or all every third year; women are eligible,
and there are no aldermen. Each council elects
its own chairman who (unless a woman) is a
Justice of the Peace during his year of office;
it must meet at least once a month, and may
appoint committees which may include co-opted
persons. To the committees entrusted with
sanitary and highway matters all the powers of
the council in regard to those services may be
delegated, with the usual exception as to rates
and loans.

The urban district council is the sanitary authority *Powers.*
for its area, and therefore has many powers and
duties under the Public Health Acts; it is the
highway authority, maintaining its local streets
and roads, and may take over from the county
council that portion of the main roads which lies
within its boundaries, in return for an annual payment; it may make use of any of the "Adoptive
Acts"; it may exercise any powers which it can
obtain under Private Acts promoted by itself, or
under provisional orders for tramways, water-supply,
gasworks, electric light and power, etc. An urban
district authority has not the status and ornamental
trappings of a municipal authority; but its powers

[1] It will be observed that population has little to do with the
classification of English areas. Many urban districts are larger
than most municipal boroughs; and some are smaller than most
rural districts.

are practically of equal importance and extent. Many urban district councils are much more important and active than the council of an average middle-sized borough ; and the general remarks made above as to the work of the municipalities apply equally to the urban districts. The main differences between a municipality and an urban district (apart from forms) are that the latter has no aldermen, has none of the privileges connected with the administration of police and justice which most of the boroughs enjoy, has its accounts audited by the Local Government Board, and is much more closely controlled by that body.

Finance. The expenses of the council are met by (1) the proceeds of district property, fees, and fines ; (2) the special rates levied under Adoptive Acts and any Local Acts ; (3) the general district rate for sanitary purposes ; (4) the education rate (where the urban district is a separate area for elementary education); and (5) Government grants for education and towards the salaries of medical officers and sanitary inspectors. The chief officers of the council are the clerk, treasurer, surveyor, medical officer, and inspectors, and (where necessary) education secretary.

SECTION 4

The Government of London. The present municipal organisation of the capital of England is based mainly upon the Local Government Act of 1888, and the London

Government Act of 1899. With its area of 121
square miles and its population of four and a
half millions, London presents a series of administrative problems greater and more complex than
those of any other city in the world. It is not
that the problems are different in kind, for the
needs of the vast urban populations are everywhere
the same, but that their larger extent renders it
practically impossible for all the administrative
details to be dealt with adequately by a single
authority. Consequently in London there are two
sets of authorities—central and local—and although
the arrangements of each group are open to much
criticism, the division of labour is in itself an
absolute necessity.

The principal "central" authority is the London The London
County Council, consisting of one hundred and County
eighteen councillors elected (two for each parlia- Council.
mentary division) for three years, and nineteen
aldermen chosen by the council for six years;
it selects a chairman, vice-chairman, and deputy-
chairman from its own ranks, and they hold office
for one year (re-elections were common in the
early years of the council's history, but have now
been abandoned). The elections of councillors are
always contested on party lines, but the attempts
made to identify political with municipal parties
have not been very successful; only at the general
parliamentary election of 1906 did the municipal
and parliamentary representation of London become at all identical. In its general form and

powers the London County Council resembles the other county councils; but it has the special powers and duties needed for the administration of a great urban area, and is therefore a combination of the councils of a county and of a large municipality. It meets once a week during the greater part of the year, and has about a score of chief committees, with a great number of sub-

Powers. committees. It deals with main drainage, river embankments, street improvements, bridges (except those within the area of the City of London), tramways, housing, lunatic asylums, parks and open spaces, licensing of music halls and some theatres, protection against fire, and a vast number of miscellaneous services; it is the education authority (with co-opted persons on its committee for that purpose), and as such (in addition to the elementary schools which it maintains) it has built up a great system of technical and secondary education, and contributes largely to university education. It has some public health powers of its own (infant life protection, inspection of common lodging-houses, licensing of slaughter-houses, regulation of obnoxious trades, etc.), and exercises a general supervision over the sanitary administration of the metropolitan boroughs; it also controls the raising of loans by them.[1]

The Metropolitan Police.
The Metropolitan Police have charge of an

---

[1] The estimated ordinary expenditure of the County Council for 1905-6 (not including working expenses of "trading" enterprises) was £9,494,355, including £4,086,094 for education.

area very much larger than the administrative county — it includes all the territory (except the 1 square mile of the City) included in a circle with a radius of 15 miles from Charing Cross, and embracing about 688 square miles. The force is under the control of a Commissioner, appointed by and dependent solely upon the Home Secretary; and although the local authorities of its area bear practically the whole of the cost (apart from the grant which the Government makes to all police forces, and a small additional contribution for the services of the force as a "state" police) they have no voice in the management.[1] Another authority for an area larger than the administrative county is the Metropolitan Water Board, established in 1903 to take over the undertakings of the eight private companies which had hitherto supplied London and surrounding districts; "water London" has an extent of some 620 square miles, and the Board is composed of representatives of the London County Council, the City Corporation, the metropolitan borough councils, and the councils of counties, municipal boroughs, and urban districts in the area of supply. The Metropolitan Asylums Board, founded in 1867, is the authority for the provision of isolation hospitals, asylums for

The Metropolitan Water Board.

The Metropolitan Asylums Board.

---

[1] Practically all European capitals have a special police organisation dependent solely upon the Government. This is due upon the Continent to political reasons, but in England to (1) the absence of any central local authority when the Metropolitan Police were established in 1829; (2) the largeness of the area; (3) the work done by the force as a "state" police (extradition, supervision of foreign criminals or suspects, protection of Government buildings, etc.).

imbeciles (as distinct from lunatics), and hospitals for Poor Law children for the Poor Law Unions of London; it consists of representatives of the Metropolitan Boards of Guardians and persons nominated by the Local Government Board.

The City Corporation.

The Corporation of the City of London occupies a peculiar position. It consists of a Lord Mayor, aldermen, and common councillors elected (the aldermen for life and the councillors annually) by the members of the "livery companies," which are the descendants of the mediæval guilds. The constitution of the city has not been changed in essentials for about four and a half centuries: the aldermen form a second chamber, are *ex-officio* Justices of the Peace, and serve the office of Lord Mayor for one year in order of seniority (though nominally elected). The Corporation is a "central" authority, since it has (apart from its historical position) special duties and privileges; it possesses its own police force for its one square mile of territory, is the port sanitary authority, maintains several bridges and central markets, and has a number of powers connected with the administration of justice, including the appointment of two sheriffs.[1]

The Metropolitan boroughs.

The "local" areas are the Metropolitan boroughs, formed under the London Government

---

[1] Two other "central" bodies are the conservancies of the Thames and Lea rivers. They have general charge of the navigation of those streams, and contain representatives of the various local authorities and other bodies interested.

Act of 1899. They are twenty-eight in number,
with populations ranging from 341,000 in Islington
to 53,000 in Stoke Newington. Each has a council
of not more than sixty members elected triennially,
and aldermen (to one-sixth of the number of
councillors) chosen by the council for six years.
The Mayor holds office for one year, and need not
be selected from the council itself. The borough
councils (like the Corporation of the City) are the
sanitary and highway authorities; they are
responsible for the assessment and collection of
local rates; and have the ordinary powers of
urban authorities in regard to the use of the various
Adoptive Acts, and the promotion of Private
Bills. The London boroughs do not enjoy the
same freedom from control as the true municipal
boroughs; they are subject to the audit of the
Local Government Board, to the approval of the
London County Council in regard to loans, and to
its supervision of sanitary administration. The
borough councils took the place of a very much
larger number of local bodies; the Act of 1899
was an important step in the direction of consolidation and simplification; and on the whole
the effect of the change has been a distinct
improvement alike in the composition and work
of the authorities.[1]

These various authorities naturally all have Finance.

[1] It should be added that for Poor Law purposes London is
divided into thirty Poor Law Unions, which do not necessarily
coincide with the boroughs.

power to levy the necessary rates, but as there are great differences in rateable value between the districts, and as on the whole the poorer the district the greater the amount and cost of administration, two attempts have been made at the equalisation of the financial burdens (apart from the rates levied by the County Council, which are uniform throughout the Metropolis). The Metropolitan Common Poor Fund is raised by a uniform rate in the thirty unions, and from it there is provided the cost of district asylums for imbeciles, dispensaries, vaccination, and 5d. a day for each indoor pauper. The equalisation of Rates Act, 1894, directed that a rate of 6d. in the pound on rateable value should be levied all over London, and the proceeds divided between the boroughs according to population.[1]

SECTION 5

The Poor Law
Union.

There remains one set of areas and authorities[2] established for one particular purpose—the relief

---

[1] An extension of this arrangement is now (1906) under the consideration of the Government. The fullest account of the administration of the Metropolis is given in the *London Manual* (annual volume).

[2] There are a number of other authorities scattered about the country—Port Sanitary Authorities (sometimes identical with town or urban district councils), Harbour and Dock authorities (often also identical with town councils), Commissioners of Sewers, Drainage Boards, Conservators of Commons and various Joint Boards (*e.g.*, for Asylums, Burial, Drainage, etc),—but they are comparatively few in number and need not be described here.

of the poor. Since the Poor Law of 1601 the parish has been the unit of Poor Law administration; but the ordinary parish is far too small to be satisfactory for that purpose. In the eighteenth century combinations of parishes were permitted and became fairly frequent, and the Poor Law Amendment Act, 1834, made the arrangement general by the formation of Poor Law Unions, consisting sometimes of a single parish, but generally (as the name implies) of a combination of parishes; "the general idea on which the union was formed was that of taking a market town as a centre, and uniting the surrounding parishes, the inhabitants of which resorted to its market, such a centre being supposed to be convenient for the attendance of guardians and parish officers. A limiting principle was that in the first instance the union should be small enough for the guardians to have a personal knowledge of all the details of its management, and it seems to have been intended that, as the business became simplified and understood, the area might be enlarged."[1] There are now six hundred and fifty-seven such unions: it must be remembered that the Poor Law organisation is the same for urban and rural areas alike, and that the boundaries of the unions have no necessary relations to the boundaries of any other local government areas except the parishes.[2]

[1] Wright and Hobhouse, *Local Government and Local Taxation* (2nd edition), p. 9.

[2] Thus the city of Birmingham includes one whole Poor Law Union, and parts of two others.

The Board of
Guardians.

The authority in each union is the Board of Guardians, holding office for three years;[1] women are eligible, and much valuable work is done by them. Actually separate elections of guardians take place only in urban unions or the rural portions of mixed unions; elsewhere the persons chosen as rural district councillors are *ipso facto* guardians for their electoral areas (parishes). Poor Law administration in England presents two peculiar features: first, it is the only general public service for which the *ad hoc* principle (*i.e.*, the election of a separate authority with a separate rating power) has been maintained;[2] and, secondly, it is of all branches of local administration the one most strictly controlled and directed by a central department. The retention of a separate authority, though undesirable on general grounds, may perhaps be justified in this case by the nature, extent, and complexity of the work; but the continuance of the very strict tutelage exercised by the Local Government Board over the guardians, necessary undoubtedly in the early years after 1834 in order to prevent a relapse into the former evils, now tends to become an obstacle alike to the activity

---

[1] The Board may elect a chairman and vice-chairman from outside, or co-opt two members.

[2] The Boards of Guardians have a few duties besides poor relief—the administration of the Vaccination Acts, the appointment of registrars of births, deaths, and marriages, and (outside the Metropolis) the supervision of the assessment and collection of most of the local rates based upon the poor rate. But the actual Poor Law administration is so much the largest part of their work that they are practically *ad hoc* authorities.

and enterprise of the guardians and to the efficiency of the central authority.

The guardians have nothing to do with the *Asylums.* provision or management of asylums for pauper lunatics, though the cost of the maintenance of each inmate is borne by the union upon which he is chargeable. But apart from this the guardians administer the whole of the poor relief system. The relief given falls into two great divisions— outdoor and indoor. The chief forms of out-relief are:—

(*a*) Weekly allowances in money or in kind. *Methods of relief.* The guardians may not pay rent, redeem tools, or buy clothes (except in rare cases), and they may not give this form of relief to ordinarily able-bodied adults outside the workhouse, except in cases of distress arising from such causes as " sickness, accident, bodily or mental infirmity in themselves and in their families." This means that out-relief cannot be given to the able-bodied who are out of employment; with the exception indeed that the guardians may by special permission provide for this class under the regulation that " every able-bodied person, if relieved out of the workhouses, shall be set to work by the guardians and be kept employed under their direction and superintendence so long as he continues to receive relief," but the difficulty experienced in finding satisfactory work has been so great that few boards now attempt to make use of this power, except in some towns.

(*b*) Apprenticeship ; boards of guardians may pay the premiums necessary for children to be bound apprentices.

(*c*) Medical assistance ; each board must appoint one or more medical officers to attend upon all poor persons requiring such assistance, and to supply the necessary medicines.

(*d*) Finally there is "burial by the parish."

The forms of in-relief are :—

(*a*) The casual ward, where a night's shelter is given to vagrants in return for a compulsory amount of work.

(*b*) The workhouse, which is the refuge chiefly for the disabled, either by age or infirmity, and for women and children.[1] A classification of inmates (aged and infirm, married persons, children, etc.), is in part required by law, and in part recommended by the Local Government Board ; but it is difficult in the small country workhouses to carry out this arrangement so far as is desirable. The best results attained so far have been in the provision of some extra comfort for the aged, and in the treatment of the children.

(*c*) The infirmary is practically a parish hospital.[2] The condition of the infirmaries was for long very

[1] The original idea of the workhouse was that willingness to enter it should be a test of the anxiety for help, and in it work was to be found for the able-bodied. Actually the name has come to be a misnomer : on 1st July 1905 there were only 7,615 able-bodied men in health in the workhouses, out of a total indoor workhouse population of 214,884.

[2] Hospitals for infectious diseases are provided in London by the Metropolitan Asylum Board, and elsewhere by county or sanitary district authorities.

unsatisfactory, but there has been a marked improvement in recent years.

(*d*) The schools. The provision for the
children, which is the most hopeful part of the
Poor Law administration, takes various forms.
There is the school in the workhouse itself, or the
arrangement whereby the children, whilst living
in the workhouse, attend the ordinary public
elementary schools; but both these plans are
undesirable, since they keep the children for all or
much of the time in the atmosphere of pauperism.
There are "scattered homes" for small groups of
children, who attend the ordinary school; there
are the large "barrack schools," maintained sometimes by a combination of unions; there is the
"boarding out" system, which works well if great
care is taken in the selection of the homes, and
constant inspection maintained; and, finally, there
are "cottage homes," where a small village is built
round a school and workshops, and a number of
children are placed in each cottage under the
charge of a workman and his wife.

It is the duty of the guardians to determine Finance.
in the case of each applicant the nature and
extent of the relief to be given, and in the work
of enquiry, and the distribution of relief, they
are assisted by professional relieving officers; the
definite decision rests with the guardians themselves, or the "relief committee" appointed by
them. This is one of the weakest parts of the
Poor Law machinery; the relieving officers are

generally few and overworked, whilst their enquiries (being merely professional,) are apt to become of a routine character, and there is no provision for that constant and detailed attention to individual cases which alone can make relief of permanent use. The cost of the relief of the poor and of the other duties of the guardians is borne in each union by a common fund, to which the constituent parishes contribute in proportion to their rateable value, the only items chargeable to the separate parishes being the salaries of assistant overseers and rate collectors. Asylums are provided by county or borough authorities, but the maintenance of the inmates is a charge upon the unions from which they come. The central government contributes (through the Exchequer Contribution Account) an amount equal to the fees of pauper children attending elementary schools, salaries of teachers in Poor Law schools, the salaries and superannuation (in 1887-88) of union officers outside London, salaries of Poor Law medical officers in London, some other small payments, and four shillings per head per week for pauper lunatics. Guardians may recover (if they can) the whole or part of the expenditure on relief from the responsible relatives of the person relieved.

Central control.

The whole of the work of the Boards of Guardians is under the strict control and surveillance of the Local Government Board, which can issue orders and regulations of all kinds, prescribing the duties of the guardians and the methods of work in great detail.[1] Its inspectors, each in charge of a district, can attend the meetings of the guardians, and visit and inspect thoroughly any Poor Law institution at any time; this arrangement not only enables the central department to maintain a constant watch, but also puts much expert advice at the disposal of the guardians. Further, the appointment of local officials (clerk, Poor Law medical officer, relieving officers and workhouse officers) must be approved by the Local Government Board, which on the other hand can dismiss any official without the consent of the guardians.[2]

It has already been remarked that the English Poor Law system is not adapted, and scarcely professes, to deal with distress arising from temporary lack of employment amongst the able-bodied workmen. This defect led to the Unemployed Workmen Act of 1905, which applies to London and towns or urban districts with not less than 50,000 inhabitants. In each London borough there is to be a "distress committee," consisting partly of councillors and partly of guardians and other experienced persons; and there is also a "central committee" of representatives of the London County Council

The distress committees.

[1] It has been estimated that the Poor Law statutes and departmental orders in force would cover 2,500 printed octavo pages; there is urgent need for consolidation.

[2] For the poor law administration see Fowle, *Poor Law*; Chance, *Our Treatment of the Poor*; the Annual Reports of the Local Government Board; and the Annual Reports of the Proceedings of the Poor Law Conferences.

and of the distress committees, with co-opted persons. The local committees are to make themselves acquainted with labour conditions in their boroughs, receive applications from unemployed workmen, and endeavour to find work (by opening employment bureaus, or inducing the borough councils to undertake public works, etc.), or they may hand over the cases to the central committee. The local committees may not themselves provide work; the central committee may do so [1] (by establishing farm colonies or in any other way), and may aid emigration or help the removal of the workman to another part of the country where there is a demand for labour. The expenses are to be defrayed out of a central fund formed from voluntary gifts and the proceeds of a limited rate, and aided by a government grant. The large urban areas outside London may have similar committees of councillors, guardians, and other persons, with powers like those exercised by the London central committee. The Act, which is to be in force for three years, is so recent that it is scarcely possible to express any opinion as to its working; but it inaugurates an attempt to deal seriously and on fresh lines with a problem which hitherto has been left mainly to the spasmodic and often ill-directed efforts of private charity.

[1] Subject to the restriction that the work so provided "shall have for its object a purpose of actual and substantial utility."

SECTION 6

The creation of a national system of Education Education. in England is entirely the work of the nineteenth century.[1] Up to 1833 the country depended for elementary education entirely upon private (mainly philanthropic or religious) enterprise, and when in that year the first small grant of £20,000 was made by Parliament, the money was distributed by the Treasury for school buildings according to the advice of the two great societies to whose activity such organised elementary schools as existed were chiefly due.[2]

Then after various enquiries by Parliamentary Development of central committees the decisive step in the direction of action. state action was taken in 1839, when the grant was increased, a contribution made to the two societies for the erection of training colleges, a special committee of the Privy Council appointed to administer the grants, and the principle asserted of the inspection of all schools in receipt of public monies. In the next decade progress was made chiefly in regard to the supply of teachers—the foundation of more training colleges was encouraged and scholarships to them were established by

[1] The purpose of this section is to sketch briefly the development of English state action in regard to education, and then to describe the existing machinery, without discussing the difficult problem of "religious education."

[2] The British and Foreign Schools Society, a nonconformist society giving in addition to secular instruction only "Bible teaching"; and the National Society, an Anglican organisation.

the Government, the pupil-teacher system was inaugurated, the state certification of teachers was established, and regulations were imposed as to the proportion of certificated teachers in the public elementary schools. Various attempts followed in subsequent years to organise local action and to lay the duty of providing elementary education upon the local authorities,[1] but nothing was done until 1870. The Elementary Education Act of that year laid down three principles, but modified them all in application. There was to be in each school district an elected authority for elementary education, but only where the supply of each education by voluntary effort was inedequate. A local rate was to be levied, but only where there was a School Board; and attendance was to be compulsory, but only where any School Boards chose to make bye-laws to that effect. Legislation in 1876 and 1880 made compulsory attendance general, and eleven years later elementary education became practically free.

Meanwhile there had been a slow development of state encouragement of secondary education, chiefly by the establishment of science and art schools at South Kensington, and by grants to institutions giving science and art teaching approved by the central department. A great

[1] It is noteworthy that the Royal Commission of 1858-61 recommended the formation of *county* and borough Boards of Education, with power to levy a rate. It was at first intended in 1870 to give elementary education in the boroughs into the hands of the town councils, but the advocates of the *ad hoc* system ultimately prevailed.

advance was made when in 1889 and 1890 the councils of counties, boroughs, and urban districts were authorised to supply or aid the supply of technical or manual instruction, to use for that purpose (if they thought fit) the proceeds of certain taxes on beer and spirits levied by the central government but handed over to the local authorities, and to supplement this by a small local rate.   For Wales special arrangements were made by the Intermediate Education Act, 1889, which enabled county and county borough councils to contribute to secondary (as distinct from technical) education.   In the same year small grants were made for the first time from the central Exchequer to a number of institutions recognised as giving education of a university type.

The Education Department was formed in 1856 by the combination of the "Educational Establishment of the Privy Council Office," and the "Establishment for the Encouragement of Science and Art," which had hitherto been under the Board of Trade.   The office of Vice-President was created, but the position of its holder was never quite clearly defined; always a politician, he was sometimes entirely subordinate to the Lord President of the Council (the official head of the department), and sometimes practically an independent minister.   In 1900 the office was reorganised as the Board of Education, under an independent President,

The central department.

assisted by a Parliamentary Secretary. It now directs and controls the whole of elementary education and science and art teaching, in schools which are supported out of public funds; it inspects those schools, and distributes the Exchequer grants; it also inspects training colleges. Its powers in regard to secondary (as distinct from science and art) education are confined to the inspection of such schools as desire it.

The conditions in 1902. By the year 1902 the need for a general reorganisation had become painfully apparent. The elementary schools fell into two groups— (a) "board schools," maintained by local school boards entirely out of Exchequer grants and local rates, and with simple biblical teaching; (b) the "voluntary schools," maintained by private subscriptions and Exchequer grants, and with denominational (usually Anglican or Roman Catholic) religious teaching.[1] But gradually subscriptions had fallen off, and the voluntary schools had sought more and more for state assistance, until nearly 80 per cent., of their revenue was derived from Government grants, though the schools were managed solely by foundation trustees. Rather more than half the children receiving elementary education were in voluntary schools, but, though some of these attained a very high standard of

[1] The "religious grievance," resulting from this was that there were 7,478 districts with only one school (generally Anglican) and in that school denominational religious instruction was given. The "conscience clause" permits the withdrawal of the children from the lesson, but such a step is not always possible or desirable.

efficiency, yet on the whole the financial limitations made the general level of the voluntary schools lower than that of the board schools. These latter, aided by the rates, had extended their sphere of action greatly; in "higher grade" day schools they were giving education practically of a secondary type, in evening continuation schools they provided elementary and more advanced teaching for both adults and young people, and they maintained centres for the training of pupil teachers. Some of this over-lapped the work of the technical education committees of the local authorities; and legal decisions determined in 1900 and 1902 that all the instruction given to adults, and the subjects taught in the higher grade schools, were illegal, since they were outside the meaning of the term "elementary."

For secondary education the technical committees were doing much valuable work, and in Wales the county and county borough authorities contributed largely to the maintenance of ordinary secondary schools; the central government aided only science and art teaching. For the training of teachers for the elementary schools neither the state-aided private institutions nor the school boards made anything approaching to an adequate provision. Finally, apart from the small central contributions to "university colleges," the public authorities did nothing for university education.

E

The Act of 1902 (a) abandoned the *ad hoc* system, and made the county and municipality the basis of educational organisation; and (b) put an end to all restriction upon the action of the new authorities. For elementary education the authorities now are the councils of all counties and county boroughs, of municipalities with at least 10,000 inhabitants, and urban districts with at least 20,000 inhabitants; [1] and they take over the whole of the elementary schools (whether board or voluntary schools) within their areas, and control entirely the secular teaching given in them. Every local education authority is required to appoint one or more committees, composed partly of councillors and partly of co-opted persons (including women); to the committees so appointed all the powers of the authorities may be delegated with the usual exceptions as to finance. In the case of a " council " (formerly " board ") school, there are managers, of whom two-thirds are appointed by the local education authority, and one-third by the local authority (if distinct from the education authority). For " voluntary " schools two-thirds of the managers are appointed by the old trustee managers, one - sixth by the local education authority, and one-sixth by the local authority,

---

[1] Municipalities and urban districts may surrender their powers to the local county councils, if the latter are willing to accept the transfer. This is in many ways desirable, but the extent of it will depend chiefly upon the financial effects.

if distinct (*e.g.*, in rural areas the parish council). In the council schools undenominational Bible teaching is to be given, in voluntary schools the religious instruction is to be in accordance with the trust deeds. The Government grants for elementary education (apart from office expenses) amounted in 1903-4 to £9,799,412.

For "higher education" (which is defined (ii.) **Higher** simply as "education other than elementary," education. and can therefore include secondary, technical, and university education, and the training of teachers) the authorities are the councils of all counties and county boroughs, and of all munici-palities and urban districts.[1] For this purpose they may expend the "whisky money," and supplement it by a small rate. The nature and extent of their action in this respect are left entirely to the discretion of the local authorities themselves, in consultation with the Board of Education, and with due regard to local conditions.

The increase of the Exchequer grants towards the university colleges, the proposed reorganisa-tion and extension of the state scientific institu-tions at South Kensington, the commencement of state contributions towards secondary educa-tion, the growth of the new universities and their close connection with the local education

---

[1] The inclusion of all the municipalities and urban districts as areas for "higher education" is somewhat unfortunate, since many of them are too small to be effective. But they can surrender their powers to, or act jointly with, the county councils.

authorities[1] are all evidences of a revived interest in national education, and the recognition of the need for a co-ordinated system embracing all three grades. The expenditure upon education by the central government is now more than £12,000,000 per annum, but more is necessary; and the working of the new Act will involve a considerable increase of taxation throughout large districts where hitherto there has been no education rate at all. This may act as a check upon the county councils, and probably secondary education (in regard to which there is no compulsion upon the authorities) will suffer to some extent. But, nevertheless, if only some compromise on the question of religious teaching can be obtained, and the controversy removed which has been so long a stumbling block in the path of educational reform, there is abundant opportunity and reasonable prospect for the construction of a really complete system of national education.

[1] *E.g.*, some of the universities are undertaking the training of teachers for the local authorities, and are represented upon the local education committees; whilst authorities are contributing to the universities and are represented upon their governing bodies.

CHAPTER II

SECTION 1

THE work of the central administration in France Ministries. is divided between the following eleven ministries, of which the last five alone are important from our present standpoint :—

(1) Ministry of Foreign Affairs.
(2) Ministry of War.
(3) Ministry of Marine.
(4) Ministry of the Colonies.
(5) Ministry of Justice.
(6) Ministry of Finance.
(7) Ministry of the Interior, which is concerned chiefly with police, local government and the control of local authorities, public assistance and public health, prisons, and the administration of Algeria. Under the Minister of the Interior is the Prefect of Police, who in many respects resembles our own Commissioner of the Metropolitan Police (entirely dependent upon the Home Secretary). He is the head at once of the local police of the

capital and the surrounding district, and of the "state" police (protection of the President of the Republic, extradition, etc.).

(8) Ministry of Public Works—administration of the national roads, state railways, supervision of other railways, provision and maintenance of lighthouses, harbour works, navigation of rivers and canals, and many other matters.

(9) Ministry of Commerce and Industry—technical education, patents, preparation of commercial treaties, administration of factory legislation, commercial and industrial statistics and information. Attached only nominally to this Ministry is the Department of Posts and Telegraphs, in charge of an under-secretary who is almost an independent minister.

(10) Ministry of Public Instruction—all three grades of national education, central educational institutions, and (through the Direction des Beaux Arts) instruction in Art, the national theatres and museums, and historical monuments.

(11) Ministry of Agriculture — agricultural legislation, education, information and statistics, irrigation and drainage, national woods and forests, etc.

The Ministry of Public Worship (Ministère des Cultes) has never of recent years (if at all) been possessed of an independent head; it is usually attached either to the Ministry of the Interior or the Ministry of Public Instruction. It deals with the subventions to the clergy and places of worship of the denominations recognised by the state.

In regard to these central departments there are a few points worthy of consideration. The first is the very small number of offices open to politicians; each department has only one parliamentary representative—the minister; except in the case of the Post Office there are no political under - secretaries or other officials as in Great Britain. A British Prime Minister has at his disposal nearly fifty administrative offices [1] of one kind or another, to which he can (and in fact must) appoint members of one or other House of Parliament; a French Premier has at most only about a dozen such offices. One reason for this is certainly the fact that a French minister can speak in explanation and defence of his policy in both the Senate and the Chamber of Deputies, even when he is a member of neither body (as is sometimes the case with the Ministers of War and Marine); and so the chief reason for the existence of parliamentary under-secretaries in Great Britain is lacking in France. Secondly, the peculiar conditions of political life in France have tended to give the permanent Civil Service still

[1] Exclusive of offices in the Royal Household.

more power there than in Great Britain, large as is its authority here. For the absence of definitely organised political parties, and the consequent dependence of ministries upon combinations of groups, have resulted in rapid changes of Government, so that the average life of a French ministry (until recent years) has been considerably less than twelve months. It is true that in a few cases a minister might stay in office under a succession of Prime Ministers, and that a change of ministry in France does not necessarily mean a change of policy, since it is often due chiefly to personal causes; but these facts do not affect the general result. When ministers come and go with such rapidity it is certain that each newcomer—anticipating but a short stay—will be disinclined (unless he be a man of exceptional force) to attempt to inaugurate any considerable changes, that he will be ready to let matters go on in the old departmental way, and that the permanent officials, who alone have any real acquaintance with the work and machinery of administration, will be in reality the directing force. In the last few years French Ministries have shown an unwonted stability, owing to the formation of something like ministerial and opposition parties; but it is as yet too early to estimate either the permanence of this or its effect upon the administrative system. Thirdly, much more use has been made in France than in Great

Britain of the method of consultative committees of experts attached to the various Government departments; most of the offices of internal administration have several such committees.

The executive chief of the French Republic is the President, but he acts by and with the advice of the ministers, given either individually or collectively (for the Council of Ministers, unlike the British Cabinet, has a legal status); and under M. Loubet the position of the President came to resemble closely that of a strictly constitutional monarch, in the English sense of the term. The presidential acts are thus classified by French legists:—[1]

The President.

A. Constitutional Acts — convocation and prorogation of the legislature, issue in some cases of decrees in matters of colonial government, conduct of foreign affairs (negotiation of treaties, declaration of war). In these the decision rests solely with the whole body of the President's responsible ministers.

B. Administrative Acts—issue of decrees and regulations (both general and applicable to particular cases only) in the exercise either (1) of the President's general powers as chief of the executive; or (2) of the authority conferred on him by particular laws. Ordinarily

[1] Cf. Bœuf, *Droit Administratif* (17th edition), pp. 14 *seq.*, and Berthélemy, *Droit Administratif*, pp. 87 *seq.*

the former class of Acts need only
the counter-signature of a responsible
minister; whilst for the latter the
Council of State must be consulted
(*le Conseil d'Etat entendu*).

This Council of State is the centre of the
whole administrative system of France. It owes
its present form to a law of 1872, amended at
various times and particularly in 1879, but the
institution itself is much older; it was founded
at the same time as the Consulate of 1799. Its
function is threefold: it is a *consultative* body,
giving advice upon legislative proposals submitted
to it by the ministry, or referred to it by the
legislature; it is an *administrative* body, since
all questions arising in the conduct of the national
administration may be submitted to it by the
President and his advisers, and some decrees
and regulations would be invalid unless the
advice of the council had first been taken,
though not necessarily followed; and it is a
judicial body, acting as the supreme administrative court. It is under the presidency of the
Minister of Justice (as Keeper of the Seals), and
consists (exclusive of the ministers) of thirty-
two ordinary paid councillors, appointed and
dismissed by the President of the Republic by
decree adopted in the Council of Ministers, and
nineteen extraordinary unpaid councillors, who
must be persons actively engaged in the ordinary
administration, and are appointed and dismissed

by simple presidential decrees. There are also subordinate members—*maîtres des requêtes* and *auditeurs*, whose business it is to prepare reports on the various problems under consideration.

The council does its work in five sections, of which four are concerned with administrative questions,[1] and consist each of a president, five ordinary, and a varying number of extraordinary, councillors. The fifth section deals with matters of administrative law, and consists only of a president and six ordinary councillors; no extraordinary members may be attached to it, since they are engaged in actual executive work, and the same disability extends to the Keeper of the Seals (who may take part in the work of the other sections), as he is a member of the Council of Ministers. The working of the Council of State as a supreme administrative tribunal will be considered in another place;[2] here we have to do with its action only in respect to general administration. On some matters referred to it the particular section concerned alone decides; in others, after a preliminary discussion by the section, a resolution of the whole council is required (and this applies to all really important matters). Ordinary councillors may vote on all questions, both in sectional and general meetings;

[1] The sections are for—(1) legislation, justice, and foreign affairs; (2) home affairs and education; (3) finance, army, navy, and colonies (4) public works, trade and commerce, post and telegraphs, and agriculture.

[2] *Vide infra*, pp. 309-10, 371-6.

extraordinary councillors may also vote in both, but only on matters relating to the particular government department of which they are members; the *maîtres des requêtes* may vote in both, but only on the particular matters on which they have reported; and, finally, the *auditeurs* may vote only in the sections, and there only on the subjects of their reports. Ministers may vote in the general meetings, and the Keeper of the Seals (as President) in all sections except the fifth.

The organisation thus briefly sketched is very elaborate, and the rules which determine its working are very complex. It is of the utmost importance, for it is not easy for a ministry to run counter to its advice, or to ignore its recommendations; and although the power of appointment and dismissal possessed by the ministry of the day may seem a peril to the independence of the council, it is not so in practice, partly because of the brevity of ministerial careers hitherto. Further, the council is undoubtedly a conservative force, but it has knowledge; and the most reforming ministry feels itself bound to give the council a patient hearing, even when it strongly disagrees. On the other side, whilst it is true that the judicial authority of the Council of State in administrative matters is liable to abuse, yet the legal tradition is strong enough, in its adherence to the strict methods of judicial interpretation, to prevent any serious wresting of the law to the advantage of the executive.

Lastly, in connection with the central govern- Cour des Comptes. ment of France it should be noticed that the Court of Accounts (*Cour des Comptes*) examines the whole of the accounts of national revenue and expenditure; it may call for all the evidence it requires; it may impose penalties on accounting officers who delay presenting their accounts; it may surcharge officials and authorise prosecutions. It reports annually to the President and the Chamber on the results of its work, and makes any suggestions for reform which occur to it. Its members are appointed by the President for life. It thus resembles (so far as the general character of its work is concerned) the office of the Auditor-General in Great Britain.

SECTION 2

The local administrative areas of France are four in number:—Department, Arrondissement, Canton and Commune; but only the first and last of these are of real importance. For one matter—education—there is a larger area, which will be described later. It will be observed that in the two important areas of general local government the plan has been adopted of setting up a single responsible, and more or less independent, executive official, controlled by an advisory body of councillors who take no part in the work of actual administration.

The
Department

The departments are the arbitrary geographical areas, eighty-six in number, into which France was divided by the reforming zeal of the Constituent Assembly.[1] They have undergone a number of changes since then, and their present constitution is due chiefly to a law of 1871.

(a) The
Prefect.

The department is an area at once of " deconcentrated " central administration, and of local self-government. At its head is the Prefect, who is its sole responsible executive official;[2] he is appointed by the Minister of the Interior, and is a professional administrator in receipt of a salary of 18,000, 24,000, or 35,000 francs according to the class of prefecture. The Prefect is first and foremost the local agent of the central government, and as such he is the head of practically the whole of the national administration within his area — he represents the Ministries of the Interior, Finance, Commerce, Public Instruction, Agriculture, Public Works, and even War. His activity is multifarious; it includes sanitary administration, the factory laws, education, encouragement of agriculture, highways, registration, state taxes, public lands, elections, conscription, billeting of troops, and all the other miscellaneous matters with which

---

[1] *Vide infra*, p. 247.

[2] " Le préfet sera seul chargé de l'administration du departement."
—Loi du 28 Pluviôse, l'an VIII.

the central government is in any way concerned. He controls the "police" — a term
which includes many things such as the surveillance of the Press, public meetings, aliens,
hunting and fishing, theatres, and a good deal
of sanitary law. His police authority extends
over the whole department, and he may make
regulations for the whole or any part of it, but
in each separate commune the mayor manages
the local police, and the Prefect may intervene
only if he deems the mayor's action inadequate.
Finally, he has very considerable powers of control
over the communes and their financial operations,
and over public institutions generally; he may
annul the decisions of a communal council, or
refer them to the Minister; he may suspend for
a month a mayor or any executive official of a
commune; he may even suspend a whole council,
or dissolve it with ministerial approval. In some
cases he must take the advice of the Prefectoral
Council, but he is not bound to follow it. He
appoints a large number of the lesser officials,
such as the smaller post-masters, letter carriers,
highway inspectors, and others, besides his considerable clerical staff. His chief assistant is
the Secretary-General, appointed by the central
authority.

On the other side, the Prefect is the executive
agent of the department, considered as a self-
governing corporation; he is therefore bound in
law to carry out the instructions which he

receives from its representatives. But it must be remembered that he is appointed by, and dependent upon, the Ministry, and not the Departmental Council; that he is the representative of the central control, and can appeal to the Ministry against any decision of the council; that he commonly has no particular interest in the Department, where he normally does not expect to make a long stay. The effect of this is that he is not so much the agent as the master of the local self-governing authorities.

In some matters the Prefect is given a fairly free hand, and can act on his own responsibility and initiative; in other cases (and these are the majority) he simply carries out the orders and instructions received from the centre. His dependence on the Ministry of the Interior is almost absolute; when he is not allowed to decide for himself in such small matters as the appointment of prison warders, the grant of leave of absence to inspectors of weights and measures, and the naming of streets by town councils, it is scarcely likely that, whatever the law may allow, he will make much use of his independence in other things. A recent critic has remarked that the Prefect does not administer: " he gives information to the administration; he supplies the information; with it the government bureaux do as they please; sometimes they act on it, often they ignore it."[1] The same writer

---

[1] Faguet, *Questions Politiques*, p. 48.

adds that a Prefect of the Third Republic is more closely bound than even his predecessor under the First Empire. His position is complicated by the fact that he is expected to act as the political and electoral agent of the government of the day;[1] and as ministers change rapidly, his task is not always easy.[2] The best appreciation of the position of the Prefect has been recently given by a distinguished French statesman and historian :—

"He hopes that his stay in that silent and peaceful city[3] will be short; he thinks that he is in a kind of purgatory, from which his merits and his prayers will enable him to escape to other scenes, and a pleasanter abode. Besides his claims to promotion, he has good reason to hope that his sojourn will be brief, for, since the fall of the Second Empire, fifteen prefects have succeeded each other under the cloisters of the secularised monastery (become the prefecture). Meanwhile, he does his work as well as he can. In our present political and administrative conditions that work requires tact, talent, skill, patience, and resignation — qualities which are derived only from an original gift of statesmanship, and the experience gained in a long series of sub-prefectures.

The Prefect was originally the chief and

[1] For an account of the electoral activity of the prefects, see Bodley, *France*, II., pp. 114 *seq.* (edition 1898).

[2] "Les fonctions des préfets ont un caractère politique trés accentué. . . . Quand la majorité ne se déplace dans les chambres que pour osciller entres les modérés et les avancés du même parti, les fonctions de préfêt sont relativement établies. Quand les partis qui se succédent sont de principes opposés, les changements de préfets sont fréquents." Berthélemy, *Droit Administratif*, p. 123, n.

[3] Laon, regarded as a typical departmental capital.

F

governor of the department. Agent of a strong power, he obeyed and commanded. To-day, placed between universal suffrage which really rules, and the central power which wishes to govern, he is between the anvil and the hammer. Since he is concerned in everything, he concentrates in his own person the perpetual conflict of authority and freedom. He reports to the authorities the demands of the crowds, and to the crowds the needs of the authorities. There is no question now of the old high-handed prefects, who led the mayors as a colonel leads his regiment. The Prefect no longer commands; he simply requests. More than any other official, he must dictate by persuasion. He is at once the agent of the Government, the tool of a party, and the representative of the area which he administers. Yet he must remain impartial, foresee difficulties and disputes, and remove or mitigate them; conduct affairs easily and quickly, avoid giving offence, show the greatest discretion, prudence, and reserve, and yet be always cheerful, open, "a good fellow"; he must be always accessible, speak freely, and in his official position be neither affected nor churlish. His marriage is a matter of great importance; for Madame la Préfète spends her whole time in "Society," that is to say, she is subject constantly to a most exacting and thorough scrutiny.

All this, however, counts for nothing in comparison with the Prefect's other anxieties. He is in daily contact with the elected representatives of the department, senators, deputies,[1] councillors

---

[1] One of the great difficulties of the Prefect is the pressure which senators and deputies can and do exercise upon the central government offices on behalf of their departments, an influence which is one of the evils of French political life. Thus the Prefect may constantly find his representations and proposals overruled by this political influence at Paris.

of the department and arrondissement, mayors,
and communal councillors; he is assailed by all
the various ambitions, claims, demands, frauds;
he is bombarded at short range by the local
Press, much more daring and less indulgent
(under the sway of local interests) than the Press
of Paris; and he is obliged to pay attention to
and conciliate all the opinions, interests, and
jealousies, which rage around him or which turn
towards or upon him." [1]

The Prefectoral Council exists solely for the
purposes of the central government, and its task
is threefold. (1) It is an administrative court of
first instance, dealing with disputes between
private citizens and the administration, especially
in regard to such matters as direct taxes (which
supply the great majority of cases), public works,
roads, public health, and national lands; appeal
lies from its decisions to the Council of State. [2]
(2) It is a board of control, examining the
accounts of the receivers of taxes, collectors of
octroi duties, the various institutions for the
relief of the poor, and some others; and it
authorises communes and departmental institutions of various kinds to commence legal proceedings. (3) It is an advisory board; the
Prefect is bound to consult it in many matters
(such as taxes, public works, control of the
communes), but he is not bound to take its
advice. There are a number of cases, however,

(b) The Prefectoral Council.

[1] Hanotaux, *L'Energie Française*, pp. 129-131.
[2] *Vide infra*, pp. 374-5.

where he would generally do so, particularly in
the annulling of the decisions of municipal
councils, or the enforcement of adequate
expenditure by the communes upon obligatory
public services.

The prefectoral councillors are either three
or four in number; they are appointed by the
central government, and must be lawyers, or
have received an administrative training.
Membership is incompatible with the exercise
of any other public office, or of any profession;
yet the salaries are very small, even for
France, as they range only from 2,000
to 4,000 francs. The Prefect may preside, even when the council sits as an administrative court (and may thus be reviewing some
of the Prefect's actions), but commonly then the
vice-president takes his place. In some cases the
councillors may be required to act as deputies
for the Prefect. When the Prefectoral Council
sits as an administrative tribunal, its sittings are
public.

The whole institution is unsatisfactory. The
smallness of the salaries, and the absence of any
prospect of advancement deter able men from
accepting the office; the result of this is that
the Prefectoral Councils are said not to be very
competent; and the combination of administrative and judicial work of this particular kind
is a hindrance to confidence in their impartiality.
Various proposals for reform have been made

from time to time, but so far nothing has been done.[1]

We pass now to the representative authorities of the department regarded as a self - governing community. The chief of these is the Council-General, elected by universal suffrage at the rate of one member for each canton, whatever its population. The members hold office for six years, one-half retiring every third year; the number varies from seventeen to sixty-seven. A large number of officials of various kinds are ineligible. There are two ordinary sessions a year; the first must begin on the second Monday after Easter, and may not extend over more than fifteen days — which of course does not mean that the Council - General sits for the whole of that period, but simply that all the meetings must be held within it. The second session — which is much the more important, since it is devoted to the consideration of the departmental budget, and the questions connected therewith — commences on the first Monday after the 15th August, and may last for a month. Extraordinary sessions may be summoned, either by direction of the central government, or at the request of two-thirds of the councillors. Each council elects its own president, and makes its own rules of procedure; its sessions are public. The Prefect can be present, except at the meetings at which his accounts are examined.

(c) The Council-General.

[1] Berthélemy, *Droit Administratif*, pp. 870-872.

The Councils-General were made elective in 1833; their powers were extended in the liberal period of the Second Empire in 1866, and considerably increased in the first year of the Third Republic. The law of 1871 provided that in a larger number of cases the Councils - General could give a final decision, and for all other matters it established a distinction between decisions which require the formal approval of a higher authority, and those for which approval is assumed, unless the controlling authority takes action within three months of the close of the session. The legislation as to the Councils-General differs from that in regard to most other French authorities in that it is not in general terms, but specifies the powers entrusted to them.

The Council - General of a department has one political function—its members form part of the electoral college which elects the senators for the department. Its powers in local administration are varied and extensive; it is the legal representative of its area, and as such administers all departmental property; it is entrusted with the assessment upon the various arrondissements of the departmental share of the direct taxes; it is responsible for the upkeep of certain highways; it maintains training colleges for elementary and secondary teachers, but is not concerned with the schools, for which there is a special organisation; it makes provision for destitute, orphaned, and abandoned children; it may provide lunatic asylums; it may establish *depôts de mendicité*, which are roughly equivalent to the English casual wards. For some of these services it may combine with neighbouring Councils-General. The Council has also certain powers of control over the action of the communal authorities; thus its approval is required for the establishment or suppression of fairs and markets, for changes of boundaries, and for increases in various local taxes, such as the octroi. It has a voice in the distribution of state grants to charitable institutions, to the communes for school-houses, and to the agricultural and other societies which the state desires to encourage. It obtains the necessary funds partly by additions (fixed by itself within the limits imposed by the annual Budget Law) to the state direct taxes, partly from state subventions for various purposes, and partly from the proceeds of any departmental property; and it may raise loans repayable in thirty years (for longer periods a special law is required). The Prefect is the sole executive agent, and the directions of the Council-General are addressed to him; he prepares and submits the annual departmental budget; he may attend at the meetings, and speak wherever he pleases.

The decisions of the Council-General fall into four groups. Some need no approval—such are resolutions relating to assessment, departmental taxes within the legal limits, loans for thirty years, additional taxation in the communes, the management of departmental property and institutions for poor relief, and the local roads. Other resolutions are valid unless annulled within three months by a decree, giving the reasons for the action of the central government—this applies to most resolutions not included by law in the previous class. A third group need the express approval of a ministry; these relate chiefly to financial affairs, and to a few administrative matters such as light railways and tramways. It illustrates the dual character of the Prefect, that whilst he is the official who has to carry out the will of the Council-General, he is also the agent of the central government, responsible for the prevention of any illegal or unauthorised action by the Council. This fact, and the strength of the bureaucratic influence and tradition in France, result in keeping the Councils-General under a tutelage much stricter even than that established by law. Finally, there are resolutions which are simply expressions of opinion, issued by a Council-General on its own initiative, or at the wish of the central government when in quest of information or advice; instances of the latter are the resolutions passed some years ago on the proposals for an income tax, and the occasional resolutions on educational questions. Committees may be appointed for special matters.

(d) The Departmental Commission. But the Council-General is in session only for a small part of the year, and there is need

for a more constant supervision of the departmental administration. For that purpose the
law of 1871 directed that there should be elected
each year, in the August session, a commission
of from four to seven members; it elects a
president and secretary, and must meet at least
once a month; the Prefect or a representative
may attend and speak at the meetings, which
are private. It may discharge any duties
specifically entrusted to it by the Council-
General, but powers in regard to the levying
of taxes and the raising of loans may not be
delegated.[1] It watches the administration of
departmental affairs by the Prefect, receives
monthly financial statements from him, examines
his budget estimates and reports on them to
the Council-General, and it has some other
powers in regard to finance. It has also special
duties laid upon it by law as an independent
body,[2] as for example the classification of the
smaller local roads. In the event of a conflict
between the Prefect and the Commission in
regard to departmental matters, the decision
rests with the Council-General; and otherwise
the Commission is subject to the ordinary control.

The Councils-General represent in the main
the middle class, the *bourgeoisie*; M. Hanotaux
describes the Council-General of the Department

[1] Berthélemy, *Droit Administratif*, p. 164.
[2] In this respect perhaps the only English authority with which
it can be compared is the Standing Joint Committee of a County
Council Quarter Sessions for Police.

of the Aisne as consisting of ten manufacturers, eight farmers, seven men of independent means, three doctors, six lawyers (three retired from practice), a publicist, a contractor, and an architect.   He adds:—

"The men who form the Council-General, whatever the political party to which they belong, are certainly by intelligence, education, and merit, at the head of the small area which has elected them. The majority of them keep their seats for years, and so acquire valuable experience. These assemblies, if I may judge by the one with whose work I am acquainted, are really excellent in every way, except that a slight oligarchical tendency and a somewhat excessive regard for the interests of the bourgeois class cause them sometimes to close their eyes to the needs and reasonable aspirations of the democracy. However that may be, I do not think that in all our constitutional system there is any assembly in which one can acquire a better or more exact knowledge of public affairs. There the aptitude of the race for self-government really appears. The praises which we often bestow on certain foreign institutions might be given, at least in part, to these local, reasonable, and unobtrusive assemblies, which in their quiet way are truly an ornament to our politics and constitution." [1]

The office of President is one of distinction, and is frequently held by men prominent in national life. Thus at the August meetings in 1905 amongst the presidents elected were a

[1] *L'Energie Française*, p. 139.

former Prime Minister, some other present and past ministers, about thirty senators, and nearly a score of deputies. The elections to the Councils - General are fought generally on political grounds, and at the commencement of the session political resolutions are frequently passed,[1] but after that the councils settle down to their work, and national politics pass into the background.

SECTION 3

The second administrative division is of little importance. Each department is divided into two or more arrondissements, which are divisions in which the Prefect, as the agent of the central government, is represented by a sub - prefect, who may exercise within the area any powers delegated to him by his official superior; he is of use chiefly in the surveillance of the numerous small communes, and is very valuable as an electoral aide-de-camp. He has just so much initiative as is allowed to him by the Prefect, and no more.

The Arrondissement.

In each arrondissement there is a council of at least nine members, elected by the cantons by universal suffrage : its members form part of the college for the election of senators. As the

---

[1] Thus, at the commencement of the August session of 1905 many resolutions were passed on the proposed separation of Church and State.

arrondissement does not constitute a corporation, and is not an area of local self-government, the powers of the council are very limited; it divides between the various communes the share of the direct state taxes imposed upon the arrondissement by the Council - General. It meets just before the August (financial) session of the latter body to make any representations on the subject which it may think desirable; and just after the session to learn the result of its representations, and to make the necessary assessments. It may also pass whatever other resolutions it chooses in regard to departmental affairs.

The arrondissement is then administratively unimportant and uninteresting. There have been many proposals for the abolition of the sub-prefects,[1] and in 1886 the Chamber of Deputies passed a resolution to that effect; the Budget Committee made the same recommendation in 1899. But so far nothing has been done, mainly it seems because the sub - prefects are useful electorally.[2]

The Canton.   The next administrative area, the Canton, is

[1] "Une réforme profonde devrait être faite a l'égard des sous-préfets. Il faudrait les supprimer.   On pourrait les remplacer par un modeste et actif fonctionnaire qu'on appellerait sergent d'élections: il y aurait une certaine franchise dans cette réform et aussi dans cette désignation." Faguet, *Questions Politiques*, p. 55.

[2] Berthélemy, *Droit Administratif*, p. 135.   Cf. Bellangé, *Gouvernement locale en France*, p. 58: "Simple agent de transmission entre le préfêt, qui lui addresse ses instructions pour les municipalités, et les municipalités, qui lui adressent, pour le préfêt, leurs déliberations, il fait l'office, comme l'on dit, de 'boîte aux lettres', et ne se connait pas d'autre destination."

of even less importance.   It consists of a group of
communes; it does not form a corporate body,
and is merely an area for some judicial purposes—
the jurisdiction of a *juge de paix* — and for
elections.   It is of interest chiefly because in any
real reform of French local government its importance must be increased;[1] it would be the natural
means of grouping for many local government
purposes those communes, extremely numerous
in France, which are really much too small to
have a satisfactory independent existence.[2]   What
is wanted in France is some local area resembling
the English rural district; and this seems to have
been the original intention of the organisers of
the canton under the First Republic, but the
idea was speedily abandoned.   It has constantly
been put forward again, in one form or another;
but hitherto without avail.

SECTION 4

The unit of French local government is the The Commune.
Commune, a term applied equally to towns with
nearly half a million inhabitants, and villages with
a few hundred.   French law does not distinguish
between communes of various sizes; all those
areas which in England would form county

---

[1] Cf. Bellangé, *Gouvernement locale en France*—an elaborate argument
for the cantonal organisation of local government.

[2] "Ce qui existe donc en France réellement, c'est la département
et le canton, rien autre." Faguet, *Questions Politiques*, p. 62.   Cf. De
Lanessan, *La République Democratique*, c. vii.

boroughs, boroughs, urban districts, rural parishes, are classed together in France, and have the same organisation, so far at least as the legal form is concerned; the only exceptions are Paris (which has a special constitution which will be described later) and Lyons, which differs in some details. There are in all about 36,000 communes in France, and of these 18,000 have populations of 500 or less, nearly 10,000 others do not exceed 1,000 inhabitants, and over 7,000 of the remainder have not more than 3,000.   It has already been remarked that most of the communes are in fact too small to have any administrative usefulness; in this they resemble the greater number of the English rural parishes.

(a) The Mayor.

The municipal law at present in force dates from 1884.   At the head of the commune is the Mayor, elected by the municipal council from its own ranks for four years, and unpaid: in the rural communes re-election is very frequent, and often the same person holds office for several consecutive periods.   His duties are twofold [1]— he represents the central government for the publication and enforcement of laws and central regulations, state police, registration of births, deaths, and marriages, recruiting, the preparation

[1] "Le maire exerce ses attributions, tantôt comme chef de l'association communale, en vertu des pouvoirs qu'il tient directe-ment de la loi, tantôt comme délégué de l'administration supérieure. Dans le premier cas, il agit, soit sous le contrôle du conseil municipale et la surveillance de l'administration supérieure, soit seulement sous cette surveillance.   Dans le second cas, il agit sous l'autorité de l'administration supérieure."   Ministerial Circular of May 1884.

of electoral lists, and some other matters; and in
the discharge of these duties he is subject to the
control and direction of the Prefect as his superior
officer.　But he is also the sole responsible executive officer of the commune; he is assisted by
adjoints, who vary in number from one (in (b) The
adjoints.
communes with populations not exceeding 2,500)
and two (in communes with between 2,500 and
10,000 inhabitants) up to twelve, or seventeen in
the special case of Lyons.　These adjoints are
elected by the Municipal Council at the same time
as the Mayor; they are merely his lieutenants,
possessing only so much independence and initiative as he chooses to grant them by decree, though
he cannot divest himself of responsibility for their
acts.　The Mayor is the representative of the
commune in all legal matters; he conducts the
whole communal administration, including the
local police.　In these two capacities he is heavily
burdened, and it is obvious that a small village
cannot always produce men capable of discharging
not merely the work of the local self-governing
authorities, but also the multitude of detailed
duties cast upon them by the central government.
M. Paul Deschanel (a recent President of the
Chamber of Deputies) writes:—

　" To-day the Mayor is, for those whom he rules,
an almost omnipotent master; his adjoints have
no other share in the administration than that
which he condescends to give them; and yet how
he is loaded down with responsibilities, with

innumerable and absorbing duties. He has not only to administer alone all the affairs of the commune, but the State makes him act on its behalf in the execution of a crowd of general laws. . . . Now the law has placed all that heavy burden upon the shoulders of a petty citizen in a village, often a man of little education and busy with his own affairs. The actual result is that the majority of the communes are administered by the prefectoral or sub-prefectoral bureaux." [1]

There is one other interesting result — the schoolmaster is often the only man in the village able to find his way through the mass of official documents which the central government showers on the Mayor; consequently he frequently becomes the Mayor's secretary, and really manages the local administration. [2] In his character as agent of the central government the Mayor may be suspended for a month by the Prefect, and for three months by the Minister of the Interior; or he may be dismissed by Presidential Decree.

(c) The Municipal Council. The Municipal Council consists of not less than ten or more than thirty-six members, except at Lyons, where there are fifty-four. In communes with not more than 10,000 inhabitants there are no divisions into wards, and in the others there need not be; where there are wards, each must return at least four members. The suffrage is

---

[1] *La Décentralisation,* p. 7.

[2] In the arrondissement of Bayeux recently out of ninety-five male teachers ninety-two held such posts; it is stated that in some cases the office is held even by female teachers. Brereton, in *Board of Education Special Reports,* vol. vii., p. 40.

universal, *i.e.*, it is possessed by every man over twenty-one years of age, resident in the commune for six months or paying local taxes there, and not disqualified by any law; second ballots are frequent. The elections in the large towns are fought generally on political party lines, except where there are combinations against the Socialists —though in recent years the Socialists have presented themselves as supporters of the Ministry. The council must have at least four ordinary sessions a year; three of these may last for fifteen days, whilst the other (the budget session) may extend over six weeks; extraordinary meetings may also be held. The Mayor presides at all meetings. A council may be dissolved by a Government Decree; but its successor must be elected immediately. The composition of the councils varies considerably; in the greater number of the communes, which are of a rural character, they consist naturally almost solely of small farmers and peasant proprietors; in the small towns the middle class, trading and professional, is predominant; whilst in the large towns the rise of socialism, aided by universal suffrage, has brought in a great number of working men or of the young professional men who are drawn so much into the socialist movement in France.

The combination of executive and deliberate functions in the council, which is so pronounced in England, is unknown in France, where the law draws a sharp distinction between the two.

G

The council is the controlling and advisory body; it determines policy, but the detailed and daily application of its decisions rests with the Mayor and his assistants.[1]   The English committee system does not exist; the council may appoint committees to consider particular questions, or to watch any part of the administration, but not to participate in it.   Harmony is secured partly by the financial control of the council, and still more by the fact that the Mayor and his adjoints are the nominees, and generally the leaders, of the predominant party in the council.   Where this is the case, and the Mayor is a strong man, like M. Augagneur[2] at Lyons, he is almost a municipal dictator.   The deliberations of the councils are subject to a stringent control by the central government, acting through the Prefect.   All its decisions must be reported to this official; so far as the majority of these are concerned he has merely to see that they are within the law; for others —finance, highways and streets, markets and fairs, communal property, legal proceedings, his expressed or implied approval is required.   A French student of English local government remarks that the concentration of departmental and communal administration in the hands of the Prefect and Mayor produces a feebleness of civic life and public spirit, an inexperience of the

[1] It is noteworthy that to a French lawyer, the term *municipalité* means only the Mayor and his assistants, *i.e.*, the executive of the communes.

[2] Now (1905) appointed Governor of Madagascar.

councillors in the conduct of business, and a strict tutelage ("perhaps necessary") by the central government. He adds that electoral and political interests have far too much influence in French local government.[1]

Coming now to the functions of the communes, it will be convenient to begin with the police authority of the Mayor. He organises the municipal police in communes with less than 40,000 inhabitants; elsewhere the organisation is determined by the central government.[2] Under the "municipal police" powers of the Mayor are included the regulation of the streets and buildings, the lighting and cleaning of all streets, protection against fire, and sanitary administration generally. The Mayor also presides over the school commission, which corresponds in some respects to the old English school attendance committees, but has a much wider range of action: the commune provides and maintains school buildings and equipment, makes grants for scholarships and prizes, provides dinners for the children at low rates in Paris and some of the socialist towns, and contributes to the salaries of teachers;[3] it also assists technical and art training. The communes may establish art galleries

Powers of communes

---

[1] Arminjon, *Le Gouvernement locale en Angleterre.* Cf. Taudière, *Restrictions apportées aux libertés locales depuis un quart de siècle,* in *La Reforme Sociale,* November 1904.

[2] Lyons has a special police organisation, controlled by the Prefect of the Department of the Rhone.

[3] *Vide infra,* sec. 6.

(which are common), libraries (less frequent), and parks and gardens.

The Municipal Council may establish *bureaux de bienfaisance*[1] for the relief of the poor; but such establishment is not compulsory, and in the greater number of the communes of France there is no provision for poor relief except what is done by the departments. Where a bureau is set up, it obtains its funds from municipal grants, gifts, legacies, and the proceeds of a small tax on tickets for theatres and concerts. Its operations are limited only by its financial resources; it may give outdoor relief and free medical attendance, provide or contribute to hospitals and almshouses, establish night shelters, and in fact do anything for which it has sufficient means, and can obtain administrative approval. One widely-spread institution in France is the municipal pawn-shop.

Municipal ownership has not gone very far, except in the case of water; for other services the policy generally adopted has been to grant "franchises" for a term of years in return for annual payments or on other prescribed conditions, such as hours of labour and cheap fares. The rise of the socialists to power in recent years has been accompanied by the appearance of advanced programmes of municipalisation — the

---

[1] The Mayor presides, two other members are elected by the Municipal Council, and four nominated by the Prefect. Paris has a special organisation.

socialists of Dijon proposed to apply it to lighting, means of transit, water, meat supply, bakeries, pharmacies, etc., but although the socialists have captured the government of many towns they have so far been able to do little, largely because of the strength of the adminstrative control. As to French municipal administration as a whole, the explorer of French provincial towns finds himself compelled regretfully to agree with the judgment of an American observer :—

"The chief French provincial towns, if one may generalise sweepingly, have indeed much more to show the visitor who is attracted by imposing boulevards, by elegance in public architecture, by well kept parks and squares, by interesting and artistic monuments, and by the other externals of municipal aggrandisement, than they can reveal to the enquirer who cares most for the achievements of sanitary science and for kindred social services. In this regard they have much to learn from the large British towns, which, while less attractive in many of their external appointments, have, as a rule, accomplished far better results in the provision of pure water and wholesome drainage, in housing reforms, and in aggressive sanitary and social administration along various lines."[1]

That was written in 1895, but in spite of some improvements it remains true, and applies still more to the small towns of 15,000 to 25,000 inhabitants, where one commonly finds art galleries, museums, boulevards, and pleasant

[1] Shaw, *Municipal Government in Continental Europe*, p. 191.

open spaces, but bad water and insanitary conditions. It should be added that as many of the communes are too small to do much alone, a law of 1890 permitted combinations for the purposes of poor relief, schools, local roads, museums, and some other matters.

The revenues of the communes are derived from (i.) local additions within the limits prescribed by law to the state direct taxes; (ii.) proceeds of municipal property, licences of various kinds, and rents from companies enjoying municipal concessions; (iii.) state grants for education, and for other purposes to necessitous communes; and (iv.) the octroi.[1] The latter calls for some special notice, since the system of duties levied upon various commodities (chiefly food and drink) at entrance into the commune produces on the average rather more than one-third of the total communal income of France; but as it applies only to communes with more than 4,000 inhabitants (1,504 in number in 1903), it is in any particular case much larger than this average—thus it provided recently about two-thirds of the whole municipal revenue of Lyons, and considerably more than half at Dijon. It is open to many grave objections; not only does it strike the food supply brought into the commune[2] and

[1] For a detailed discussion of French communal finances, see Acollas, Les Finances Communales.

[2] The octroi duties are levied upon wine, beer, cider, alcohol, vinegar, meat, poultry, game, fish, cheese, hay, straw, firewood, faggots, charcoal, coal, coke, and building materials.

thereby tend to increase slightly the cost of
living, but from the administrative standpoint
it is cumbersome and costly. It requires that
every commune shall be surrounded by a chain
of officials; and the consequent cost of collection
is high, especially in the small towns. In Paris
in a recent year it was 6·8 per cent., but in the
same year at Orleans (61,000 inhabitants) it was
16·5 per cent., and at Montluçon (about 30,000)
23·6 per cent.; and instances of 33 per cent. are
not uncommon. In rather more than one-fifth
of the communes where it exists the octroi is
" farmed " to a contractor. The abolition of the
system has been constantly advocated, and communes may prepare schemes, needing legislative
approval, for replacing it by increased or new
direct or indirect taxes; and Lyons has recently
even abolished all the duties except those upon
alcohol. But the great difficulty is to find fresh
sources of revenue to replace the proceeds of the
octroi. Government legislative proposals have
constantly been promised; but so far nothing has
been done except, in 1897, to authorise communes to remove the duties on " hygienic
beverages " and impose instead higher duties
on alcohol or certain fresh taxes.[1]　In this
respect the octroi is like most other matters
of French local administration during the last
thirty years; reforms are constantly proposed,

[1] The best work on the octroi system is Tardit and Ripert, *Traité
des Octrois Municipaux*, 1904.

constantly demanded with energy, but scarcely ever realised.

SECTION 5

Paris and the Department of the Seine. The city of Paris and the Department of the Seine, in which it is geographically situate, have an organisation distinct in important respects from that of the other departments and towns of France. The reasons for this are well known: the French Government has always considered itself bound to pay special attention to the capital city, and to spend money lavishly upon it; and, further, the history of the revolutions of Paris has made every Government (including that of the Third Republic) anxious to keep it under the closest possible control.[1] And although there is a party which demands greater autonomy, there can be no doubt that the large majority of the inhabitants of Paris favour the continuance of this strict supervision.

Paris: (a) The Prefects. Paris dominates the Department so completely, that it will be convenient to take its municipal system first. At its head are two prefects—the Prefect of the Department of the Seine, who

---

[1] Paris has generally been in opposition to the Government of the day, and the municipality has been the centre of the opposition. Until 1870 all the revolutions of France were Paris-made; but the rise of the large manufacturing towns and the growth of rapid means of communication has somewhat diminished its influence. Paris took up the Boulangist and Nationalist movements, but could not induce the rest of the country to follow its lead.

is practically Mayor of Paris, and the Prefect of Police, who deals with what in England would be called "state" police (extradition, protection of state authorities, supervision of political offenders and alien suspects), unhealthy and dangerous industries, *police des mœurs*, highways, sanitary administration, etc. Both are appointed by the central government. The Prefect of the Seine, so long as he has the support of the Minister of the Interior, is practically supreme in the city government, since the law requires that for the validity of almost all decisions of the Municipal Council there must be agreement between the latter and the Prefect.[1] Actually conflicts are not very frequent, except when, as occasionally happens, a violently anti-ministerial party gets control of the council and proceeds to harass the Government as much as possible. The great municipal staff of Paris is, however, unaffected by these struggles, and is altogether uninfluenced by party considerations. For subordinate administrative purposes Paris is divided into twenty arrondissements: in each there is a Mayor and three adjoints (or five for any arrondissement with more than 120,000 inhabitants). They are appointed by the President of the Republic, and are merely the agents of the Prefect of the Seine; they register births, deaths and marriages, prepare electoral lists, collect taxes, conduct the poor relief administration, and are concerned with

[1] Law of 1867.

elementary education, recruiting, and a number of other matters.

(b) The
Municipal
Council.
The Municipal Council consists of eighty members, elected four by each arrondissement in single-member districts; they hold office for three years and are unpaid, but receive a substantial sum for expenses. They choose their own president; the Prefects may attend the meetings and speak whenever they please. The Council's ordinary sessions are four a year, each lasting ten days; but it has so many extraordinary meetings as to be really permanent. It may appoint committees for the consideration of special subjects, or to watch particular branches of the city administration. Its power lies in its authority over the finances—taxation and loans—which enables it to keep some check upon the Prefect; but since this official has what is almost a veto upon all administrative proposals of the council, it is evident that the latter does not possess anything like the authority and power of the London County Council or the Town Council of Berlin.

The
Department
of the Seine.
Paris and some suburban districts constitute the Department of the Seine. At the head of the administration of this area are the two Prefects, and the authority of the Prefect of Police extends over part of the next department also. The Prefectoral Council exercises the ordinary functions of such a body, but as its work is naturally much heavier and more important than in any other department, it is larger—containing

nine members — and far better paid. The Council-General consists of the eighty municipal councillors of Paris, and twenty-one members elected by the surrounding districts: as with the Municipal Council, almost all its decisions require Government approval. There is no departmental commission; there are Arrondissement Councils for the extra-municipal areas, but not for Paris.[1]

Much use has been made in the French capital of Advisory Boards. There is the great *Conseil d'Hygiène et de Salubrité,* under the presidency of the Prefect of Police, and composed of persons nominated by the central government, two members of the Municipal Council, and such *ex - officio* members as professors of the faculty of medicine at Paris, the director of municipal public works, the president of the Army Sanitary Board, the chief architect, two engineers holding official posts, and others; it meets regularly, and is consulted upon all branches of public hygiene. It is supplemented in each arrondissement by a small committee, which meets every month, under the chairmanship of the Mayor; among its nine members there must be two physicians, one veterinary surgeon, one architect, one engineer, and one pharmacist; its duty is to report on local conditions to the central council. There is also a *Commission des Logements Insalubres,* which

Commissions: (a) Sanitation.

[1] Berthélemy, *Droit Administratif,* pp. 211-4.

receives complaints, and reports to the proper
authority upon insanitary dwellings : it consists
of unofficial persons interested in the subject.

(b) Public assistance.

The great system of " Public Assistance" in
Paris is supervised by a Board, consisting of the
two Prefects and eighteen other persons. Five
of these are appointed by the President of the
Republic, and the remaining thirteen "must
include two members of the Municipal Council,
two mayors or adjoints of arrondissements, two
representatives of the local *bureaux de bienfaisance*, one representative of the Council of
State, one of the Court of Cassation, a hospital
physician, a hospital surgeon, a professor of the
faculty of medicine, a member of the Chamber
of Commerce, and a member of one of the
councils of *prud'hommes*" : they hold office for six
years, one-third retiring every second year. The
Board administers the hospitals, asylums, homes
for the aged poor and for children, lodging-
houses and shelters, out-door relief (including
medical attendance), and the vast municipal
pawnshop. The chief executive official is the
Director.

In each arrondissement there is a *bureau de
bienfaisance*, composed of the Mayor and twelve
administrators appointed for two years, half by
the Prefect of the Seine, and half by the
Municipal Council. This Board reports on the
needs of its district to the central authority; it
distributes the grants which it receives, and any

special contributions from private sources which may come to it; and it has an attached medical staff. The arrondissement in its turn is divided into twelve districts; each is under a member of the local *bureaux*, whose duty it is to know all relief cases in his district, and to distribute relief, with the assistance of a large number of voluntary workers: the purpose of the whole arrangement being "to render it reasonably certain that in the actual relief of the poor the unpaid services of trustworthy neighbours may be secured, rather than those of perfunctory officials. It is also intended that the small districts may insure complete supervision and intimate knowledge of conditions."[1]

SECTION 6

The organisation of two public services in France deserves special description. The first of these is National Education.[2] Education in France.

The modern French educational organisation began with the foundation of the "University"[3] by Napoleon I. in 1808; but that was intended (a) History.

---

[1] Shaw, *Municipal Government in Continental Europe*, p. 107. See the whole description of Paris, pp. 1-145. Cf. Strauss, *L' Œuvre du Conseil Municipal de Paris* in *La Grande Revue*, April 1900.

[2] This sketch is concerned solely with the organisation, and not with the educational problems presented by France. For those *see* Marion, *L' Education dans l' Université;* Ribot, *La Réforme de l' Enseignement Secondaire*, and Vol. VII. of the Board of Education's *Special Reports*.

[3] "University" in this case meant a teaching body for the whole of France.

only to give an education, which suited the
purposes of Napoleon — that is, to produce
"officers and functionaries, a middle - class
characterised chiefly by its discipline, an obedient
nation."[1] The faculties of law, theology, medicine, science and letters were for the most part
ill-equipped; secondary education was organised
as a combination of "the convent and the
barrack"; and for primary education nothing was
done by the central government — it was left
entirely to local action. Though a Ministry of
Public Instruction was created under the Restoration, it remained for the Monarchy of July to take
the first real steps forward, when Guizot was
minister between 1832 and 1834. Every commune was bound (either alone or in conjunction
with others) to maintain one elementary school;
in large communes higher grade schools were
required; the children were to pay fees, except
in the case of the very poor; the departments,
and even the central government, were to
contribute where necessary; an inspectorate of
elementary schools was created, and minimum
salaries for teachers were established.[2] The next
important enactment was the famous "Loi
Falloux" of 1850, which recognised two classes of
schools — public, maintained by local authorities
and absolutely controlled by the Government;

[1] Marion, p. 4.
[2] This legislation was in 1833, the same year as the first Government
grant in England.

and private, founded and maintained chiefly by
the religious associations of various kinds, and
inspected only in regard to sanitary conditions
and the regulation that nothing should be taught
"contrary to the laws, the constitution, and
morals." Provision was made for separate girls
schools (compulsory in communes with more
than 800 inhabitants), and adult and technical
classes. Later, France was divided into academies,
whose rectors controlled education throughout
their areas; and departmental councils for
primary education were created. Under the
ministry of Duruy (1865-69), the range of
elementary education was increased, teachers'
salaries raised, and the schools rendered free to
all the poorer classes (and to all classes in any
communes which chose to make them so);
and substantial improvements were made in
secondary education. In the early days of the
Third Republic university education was made partially "free,"[1] *i.e.*, universities independent of the
state (and chiefly avowedly Catholic) were allowed
to give degrees recognised under certain conditions.
Then, finally, chiefly under the ministry of Jules
Ferry, the central government gave large grants
(1878) for school buildings, the departments were
directed to provide for the training of elementary
teachers (1879), and minimum qualifications were
imposed (1881), primary education was made

---

[1] "Libre" in relation to education always means "independent of
state control."

obligatory and free (1881-82), public secondary schools for girls were authorised, and the general schemes of secondary education re-arranged. The state votes for education [1] amounted to a little under 10,000,000 francs, in 1870, and had risen to over 223,000,000 in 1902-3.

(b) Organisation.

(i) Ministry.

The French national system of education includes all three grades — called primary, secondary, and superior (*i.e.*, education of a university type); and the Ministry of Public Instruction has for each grade a division in charge of a director. The authority of the Ministry over private schools extends only to staffing (no one may teach in France unless possessed of qualifications recognised by the state) and sanitary conditions. At the side of the Minister there is a *Conseil Supérieur de l'Instruction Publique*, consisting of fifty-seven members including the Minister, who presides; it contains thirteen persons nominated by the Ministry, and forty-three members elected by the Institute of France, the faculties and various educational institutions such as the École Nationale des Chartes, the École Normale Supérieure, the École des Beaux-Arts, and others, or representative of the teaching staffs of the secondary and primary schools. There are also representatives of the *enseignement libre*. The Council, whose members hold office for four years, is an advisory body on a great

[1] Including salaries of the Ministry of Public Instruction.

number of questions—establishment of faculties, normal schools and *lycées*, courses of study, general regulations — concerned chiefly with secondary education; and also a court of discipline (mainly on appeal). Attached to the Ministry are the Inspectors - General, some thirteen in number, who travel about the country to inspect the normal schools and to report on the condition and problems of education generally,[1] and form a valuable medium of communication between the central and local authorities. It should be added that the agricultural education is directed by the Ministry of Agriculture, and technical and commercial schools are controlled mainly by the Ministry of Commerce.

France is divided for educational purposes (ii) University. into seventeen university "regions," or groups of departments.[2] In each there is a Rector of the University, who presides over the general administration of education in all three grades. He is the head of the University, which is a state institution in part, receiving large contributions from the central government, and conferring degrees which are required by the state as a necessary condition of entrance upon various

---

[1] There are four women inspectors for infant schools.

[2] Of recent years there has been a vigorous movement in France towards the recognition of the regions (corresponding roughly to the old provinces) as the proper areas of local self-government. Except for education, little has been done in this way; but many voluntary "regional" societies of various kinds have been formed. See *La Revue Universelle* for 1st September 1905.

H

1) Rector. official and professional careers.[1] The Rector
also directs all public secondary schools within
the region; these are of two kinds—*lycées* both
for boys and girls, founded and maintained by
the state with the assistance of the departments
or towns, and *collèges* for both sexes, founded
and maintained by the large communes, and
frequently subsidised by the central authorities;
there are about one hundred and ten of the
former, and about twice as many of the latter
class. The Rector also supervises the private
secondary schools,[2] and controls the training
colleges for teachers. This last he does through
(2) Academy Inspectors. the Academy Inspectors, of whom there is one
for each department, and through them he
superintends also the primary schools; generally
they are responsible to the Rector in all matters
that relate to teaching, but in respect to *personnel*
and administration they are left independent
except of the prefects. The Rector is assisted
(3) Academic Council. by a council[3] composed of the deans of faculties,
the Academy Inspectors, representative professors
of the University and of the *lycées* and colleges,
and delegates of the departments and municipal councils which contribute to university or
secondary education; membership is for four years,

[1] The "free" universities (Catholic) have the same privilege, so
long as they do not fall below the standard of the state universities.

[2] These are both for boys and girls; but the "free" secondary
schools for girls, usually attached to a religious sisterhood, are much
the more numerous.

[3] This body is distinct from the University Council.

and the council is an advisory body for secondary education (and to some extent for the highest grade) and a disciplinary court of first instance.

The department is the administrative unit *Primary education.* for primary education, and the real heads of the organisation there are the Prefect and the Academy Inspector.[1] The former is the chairman, and the latter the vice-chairman of a *Conseil Départmental de l'enseignement primaire*, which is formed of two heads of training colleges, two inspectors of primary schools, four councillors - general, and two male and two female teachers elected by their colleagues.[2] It meets every month, and is an advisory and administrative body for all matters connected with primary schools—code of instruction and management, provision of new schools, etc.— and a disciplinary court for primary teachers. The Prefect appoints all the teachers in the public primary schools, usually on the nomination of the Academy Inspector;[3] there was a

[1] "The Academy Inspector strikes one as being the real pivot between the central authority and the schools. He is not too far removed from the latter to have a thorough acquaintance with their working and their wants. His intercourse with the central authority is sufficiently close, and his rank sufficiently elevated, to make his voice listened to and respected. As quasi-independent, for much is necessarily left to his judgment and discretion, he has the opportunity of giving an active and steady support to any ideas which he wishes to encourage." Brereton, in *Board of Education Special Reports*, Vol. VII., p. 20.

[2] Berthélemy, *Droit Administratif*, p. 724.

[3] "Pour des raisons de politique générale, la République jusqu'ici a cru devoir laisser les instituteurs dans la main des préfets, ou les regimes précédents les avaient mis. Il s'ensuit que par l'immense

time when political reasons greatly influenced the appointments, but cases of this kind seem now to be very uncommon. Under the Academy Inspector there are the Inspectors of primary schools, usually one to each arrondissement; they are selected by competitive examination, whereas the Academy Inspectors are appointed by the Ministry chiefly from the ranks of secondary education. Then in each canton there are delegates, appointed by the Departmental Council, to visit the various schools in their canton, and to report on local needs and conditions. Finally, in each commune the Mayor has the right to visit all schools, public and private, and to have them medically inspected, and he presides over a school commission, which answers roughly to our old "School Attendance Committee."

Primary education is compulsory for all children from six to thirteen years of age; and in the public schools it is free. Every commune must have at least one school, either for itself alone or in combination with others; and any commune which cares to do so may establish a higher grade school. Much interest is taken in

majorité de son personnel, l'enseignement primaire semble ne pas faire partie de l'université, dont un caractère essentiel est d'avoir ses chefs propres et d'echapper en grand partie aux fluctuations politiques . . . à cet état des choses (necessaire ou non) il faut attribuer pour une grande part un certain manque d'unite entré les parties du corps universitaire . . . Une et cohérente par en haut, l'Université ne l'est point pas en bas." Marion, *L'Education dans l'Université*, pp. 8, 9.

these schools, and the annual presentation of prizes is in many of the small communes almost the chief event of the year.

There remain two other matters relating to education which require notice. The first of these is the training of teachers and their position in the state. The central government maintains the great École Normale Supérieure at Paris, but its pupils (who are training for professorships at the *lycées*) "form in their own eyes, and in fact, only a privileged group of students," many of whom take a secondary mastership only as a step towards some higher academic post. Wherever possible the various university faculties make arrangements to secure for their students some practical experience in teaching. The central government also maintains two large colleges to provide instructors for the training institutions for elementary teachers. Each department must establish one of these, under the supervision of the Rector of the University; but the central government pays the salaries of the teaching staff and the keep of the pupils. The state lays down minimum qualifications for all elementary and secondary teachers, both in public and private schools: it fixes and pays a minimum salary to all teachers in public schools, which is supplemented according to the inclination of local authorities and to the varying local conditions, and the teachers have a secure pension.[1]

Training and position of teachers.

[1] It has been pointed out previously that in the small communes

The other matter is the finance of education. It has already been remarked that the central authority pays the teachers salaries, and maintains certain training institutions and the *lycées*; it also makes special grants for such things as technical and agricultural education, and gives subventions for other purposes. The departments maintain the training institutions for elementary teachers, and colleges, and may aid *lycées*; they bear the office expenses of Academy Inspectors and the Inspectors of primary schools, and contribute to necessitous communes for building purposes. The communes provide and maintain elementary school buildings and equipments; they may vote money for school prizes, libraries, and special classes; and they may establish colleges and classes for adults.

Briefly, then, in France the co-ordinating and controlling authority of the state dominates all three grades of education, which are largely maintained by grants from the central Exchequer. The areas for the administration of education are large, and in each the whole system gathers round the University, which can make its

the schoolmaster often acts as Mayor's secretary. This adds a trifling amount to his salary; it tends to make the communal government more dependent upon the Prefect, since he can dismiss the schoolmaster at any time, and the latter will therefore carefully avoid any cause of dispute; and it keeps the schoolmaster in contact with his old pupils, since he meets with them in all those numerous matters in which the French citizen is brought within the reach of the administration. To the extreme clerical party in France this influence of the schoolmaster, who usually represents anti-clerical tendencies, upon local administration is a great grievance.

influence felt throughout the whole. The state, either directly or through the local authorities, provides a training for *all* teachers; it can therefore impose a minimum qualification (as high as it cares to make it) for all. The communes provide the school buildings, but the central government by its agents appoints the teachers and pays them a minimum salary, and this, combined with the influence of the officials, effectually prevents any lowering of its standard owing to local indifference or dislike to expenditure. The French system of education undoubtedly has defects—the various grades of education too frequently coincide with social divisions, the administrative system is sometimes too methodical and exacting, the *régime* of the *lycées* produces results (in education as distinct from instruction) which are far from satisfactory, and the whole question is still complicated by the struggle between the state schools (absolutely secular) and the denominational schools, with all the connected problems. But this last difficulty is small in France as compared with England; the general plan of the educational organisation is coherent and intelligible, and it does provide a way of bringing all three grades into their proper relations one with another.

SECTION 7

Highways.

There is one other public service in France which deserves a brief examination, if only for the sake of the contrast which it presents with England; and that is the organisation of the highways. Probably no state in the world has developed so highly as France its plan of internal communication by road, and it is certain that in no country has the actual technical work of road-making reached a higher point of excellence.[1] Legislation on the subject commenced in the seventeenth century, under the influence of Sully, and the roads were constructed either by private individuals or companies authorised to levy tolls, or by the state authorities making use of the *corvée* (a system of compulsory labour). The First Republic abolished the toll system, but the *corvée*, in a modernised form, still continues in part. The nineteenth century witnessed much activity, both legislative and administrative, in the matter of highways of all kinds; a carefully organised system has been established, closely controlled by the central government, and with a large part of the cost borne directly by the state Exchequer.

National roads.

The fundamental principle of French high-way administration is a distinction between *la*

[1] See the special consular reports on "Streets and Highways in Foreign Countries" issued by the United States Bureau of Foreign Commerce, 1897.

grande voirie and *la petite voirie*. The first includes the national and departmental roads, together with the streets of any town or village which form a continuation of the main routes. The national roads consist of those which connect Paris with the frontier or with great army or navy stations (the chief military roads), similar roads of less importance and therefore less width, and roads which connect Paris and some of the cities of the interior, or the most important towns with one another. The departmental roads are those which unite the chief town of a department with the arrondissements, or which form a main line of communication between two departments. All these roads are under the general control and supervision of the Minister of Public Works, represented in the department by the Prefect. All national roads must be, and departmental roads may be (and commonly are) constructed and maintained by a special office of the central government, *le service des ponts et chaussées*, and the expenses are borne by the central authority [1] and the department respectively. The police of both groups of roads (*i.e.*, the regulation of traffic) is in the hands of the Prefect. The classification of the roads is made by a ministerial order or a vote of a Council-General, but the construction of a new national highway requires a special law. The finances of the departments are limited, and

Departmental roads.

[1] The state spends about £1,500,000 per annum on the maintenance of roads. Berthélemy, p. 416.

there has been a strong tendency for the Councils-General to rid themselves of all responsibility in the matter by simply transferring all departmental roads to the charge of the inferior local authorities;[1] but a movement to denationalise the main roads has met with little encouragement.

Local roads.   The *petite voirie* includes urban and rural roads. The urban system embraces simply the streets within any city or town which do not form continuations of main roads (national or departmental); they are controlled by the town councils, subject to the approval of the Prefect, and are maintained out of the municipal revenues.[2] The rural system is much more complicated; there are two classes of roads, *chemins vicinaux* and *chemins ruraux*. The first consists of (*a*) *chemins vicinaux de grande communication*, which unite several communes and commonly connect with main roads; (*b*) *chemins vicinaux d'intérêt commun*, smaller roads of the same nature as the last; (*c*) *chemins vicinaux ordinaires*, which join two communes but do not traverse a town or village.[3] All these are under the control of the Minister of the Interior, represented locally by the Mayor, and in some cases by the Prefect; they are constructed by the communes, and the expenses are met in various ways. The maintenance of

[1] Fifty-seven Councils-General had done this up to the year 1900.

[2] The streets of Paris (owing to the extensive Government grants) are included in the *grande voirie*.

[3] Bœuf, *Droit Administratif* (17th edition), p. 357.

the first two classes of the *chemins vicinaux* is compulsory, and towards the expenditure the communes generally receive grants-in-aid from the departments. For the *petite voirie* as a whole they often receive grants, and more frequently loans, from the central government; but the difficulties of national finances in recent years have diminished the inclination of the legislature to vote subventions for the local roads. Finally, the *chemins ruraux* include simply what in England would be called foot-paths, and would be entrusted to the parish councils. The classification of the roads is made by resolution of the local authorities (for the more important groups by the Councils-General subject to the approval of the Prefect).[1]

Mention has already been made of one interesting survival. Should the ordinary resources of a commune not suffice for the work which it has to do in the maintenance of roads, it may either impose an additional (temporary) rate, or it may make use of "presta-tions," which are simply the survival of the old *corvée*, with the difference that they fall upon all classes of the community alike. Every head of a household can be called on to furnish three days' work by himself and every male between eighteen and sixty years of age resident with him, and the same for every beast

[1] The names proposed to be given to any street in a town must be approved by the Prefect.

of burden, waggon, or plough; or he can pay a sum of money in lieu of service.[1] Apparently it is common for the peasants to give labour, and for the other classes of the community to compound for the service due from them.[2]

The most striking features of the French system are the control exercised by the central government over highway administration, and the network of national roads with which the country has been covered. The tendency seems to be for the department to cease to be a highway authority, and for the work to be divided between only the central power and the small local authorities. The same result would be attained in England if the main roads at present controlled and maintained by the county councils were transferred to the charge of a special Government department, and the whole cost thrown on the National Exchequer. We may not be ready for such a change, and it might be inadvisable; but it would be well for us to imitate the French example in establishing a strong central control which should give us a satisfactory and intelligible system of internal communication by road, especially now that the development of the motor car and the electric tramways are once again bringing the highways into use for long-distance travelling.

[1] The Prefect must see that the demand is not made at a time when it would interfere seriously with agricultural operations.

[2] In 1898 a proposal for the abolition of the prestations found approval in only nine out of eighty-six departments.

CHAPTER III

LOCAL ADMINISTRATION IN PRUSSIA

SECTION 1

THE central administration of the Kingdom of Ministries. Prussia is conducted by the following nine ministerial departments :—[1]

- (1) Ministry of Foreign Affairs, which is at the same time the Foreign Office of the German Empire: the occupant of the office is at once Minister President of Prussia and Chancellor (that is, sole responsible Minister) of the Empire.
- (2) Ministry of War.
- (3) Ministry of Justice.
- (4) Ministry of Finance.
- (5) Ministry of the Interior, which is concerned with the supervision and control of the various local authorities, the relief of the poor, and many "police" matters. Dependent directly upon the Ministry are the statistical offices of Prussia, and the police authorities of Berlin.

[1] The Navy and Post Office are Imperial, and administered by departments of the Imperial Government.

(6) Ministry of Ecclesiastical, Educational, and Medical Affairs. This is divided into four sections, dealing respectively with (*a*) ecclesiastical matters and the relations of the state to the religious denominations, especially the Evangelical and Catholic Churches; (*b*) higher, technical and art education; (*c*) elementary education; (*d*) medical questions. Directly dependent upon it are the universities, technical high schools, national museums, and other educational institutions; and attached to it are Advisory Medical Boards for matters of public health.

(7) Ministry of Trade and Industry, dealing with general questions of trade and commerce, the state control of banks, labour legislation and conditions, mines and quarries, and commercial and trade schools.

(8) Ministry of Public Works, which amongst other duties has charge of the national railways, and supervises private undertakings.

(9) Ministry of Agriculture, Public Domains, and Forests. It is assisted by several Advisory Boards, and has charge of some agricultural institutions.

The ministers at the head of these departments

are appointed by the King of Prussia alone, and the Prussian Parliament exercises no influence upon his choice. They are selected not from among the prominent politicians, but from the civil servants of the Crown; so that whilst in Great Britain and France the Civil Service is headed by the permanent under-secretaries or directors of departments, in Prussia the ministers themselves are included in its ranks. There is nothing in Prussia resembling the close and constant control of the administration which is exercised by the British and French Parliaments; the ministers are not members of either House, though they may appear and speak as often as they please, either in person or by deputy; the Houses may appoint committees of enquiry, but ministers may refuse information; and an adverse vote does not affect them, as long as they retain the support of their royal master and he does not think it necessary, for political reasons, to sacrifice them. This practical independence of the Ministry from the legislature, and the consequent power of the highly trained and organised Prussian bureaucracy are characteristic of the administration of Prussia in all its grades; the historical development of the kingdom, in combination (it may be) with the military system, seems to have made the representative assemblies, both central and local, ready to acquiesce in the system of bureaucratic rule. The control of the finances does, it is true, give the representative bodies the deciding voice; but they seldom run counter, for any length of time, to the official policy.[1]

The Ministry of State.

As there is no necessary harmony between the legislature and the executive, so also there is no necessary agreement between the ministers themselves. The Minister - President does not choose his colleagues, though he may influence the choice of the King; and he cannot control them. It is true that the whole number constitute the Ministry of State, over which he presides; and that in some respects this body is much more definitely organised than the British Cabinet, and corresponds rather to the French Council of Ministers. It meets once a week; it has its own secretary and staff; there are some state institutions which depend upon it alone, and not upon an individual ministry; it is a court of appeal in disciplinary cases affecting the higher officials; all matters of importance must be laid before it; it decides questions which concern a number of departments, and it may issue decrees in a few special cases. But there is no necessary cohesion; there is no joint responsibility; in most cases it only gives advice, the majority does not bind the

---

[1] This is aided by the fact that the Prussian Parliament is much less democratic than the Reichstag. In the latter, elected by universal suffrage, the Socialists are a large and powerful body, polling more electoral votes than any other party: in the Prussian Parliament, elected by the "three-class system" which apportions voting power according to the amount of taxation paid, they are hardly represented at all.

minority and the decision rests with the monarch alone.[1]

There is a Council of State, which dates originally from 1604, and was revived in 1817 to be an advisory body, and to exercise some control over the executive. It is composed of princes, great officers of state, ministers, judges, and nominated persons; thus resembling in form the British Privy Council. It may be consulted on legislative proposals, disputes as to the respective spheres of the various ministries, and other matters referred to it for consideration either under any law or by the monarch. But practically it is no more important than the British Privy Council. There is one other advisory body which deserves notice—the Economic Council—composed partly of members nominated by the Crown, and partly of representatives of the Chambers of Commerce; it gives advice on all commercial and industrial questions referred to it, such as treaties, tariffs, and trade and labour legislation.

The Council of State.

The Economic Council.

Reference has been made to state institutions dependent upon the Ministry as a whole. The most important of these is the Supreme Administrative Court, composed of a President, a number of presidents of sections or "senates," and about forty councillors: it is the final court of appeal in all cases of "administrative law," but it is also a court of first and final instance in a small number

The Supreme Administrative Court.

[1] For the position of ministers see Von Seydel, *Preussiches Staatsrecht*, pp. 91-104.

I

of cases.[1]   Half of its members must be qualified
for high judicial office, and half for the superior
administrative posts; and they are far more independent than the French councillors of state,
since they are appointed for life.

The Supreme Court of Account.

There is one other central institution of great
importance — the Supreme Court of Account—
which resembles closely the French Cour des
Comptes.   Its members are in the same position
as the judges: the President is appointed by the
Crown on the nomination of the Ministry of
State, and the other members by the Crown on
the nomination of the President.   It examines all
the accounts of state revenue and expenditure,
and of the national debt; it is the guardian and
interpreter of all financial legislation.   For these
purposes, it is armed with extensive powers, and
it reports to the Crown the results of its investi-
gations, and the reforms which it deems
advisable.

Some principles of Prussian administration.

Before we proceed to examinine the local
administration of Prussia, it will be convenient
to notice some of the general principles upon
which it is based, since to do so may simplify
the examination.   The first of these is the
careful distinction drawn between those internal
affairs in which the central government is thought
to be directly concerned, and those which are
held to be primarily of only local interest.   The

---

[1] For a detailed account of the working of the Supreme Administrative Court, *vide infra*, pp. 376-381.

former group includes, besides the army, the state taxes and domains, ecclesiastical affairs, police (in the wide Prussian meaning of the term),[1] and the supervision of local authorities; whilst roads, poor relief, and a number of miscellaneous matters are left to the localities. These two groups are kept carefully separate, even when they are entrusted to the same authority. Secondly, the work of the central government is "deconcentrated," that is, the country is divided into districts (which may or may not be coincident with the areas of local self - government), in each of which there is a delegation of the central authority, doing its work, and thereby lessening the pressure upon the departmental offices in Berlin. Something like this deconcentration is found in the educational organisation of France, and also in the office of the Prefect, but it is far more elaborate, and the machinery much more complex, in Prussia. Thirdly, the comparative independence of the executive from the deliberative authority, and the predominance of the officials, which characterise the central government of Prussia, repeat themselves throughout the whole of local government; the Prussian ideal is administration by the professional expert, checked by lay criticism and the power of the purse. And, finally, in all except the largest of the Prussian

[1] "Die nöthigen Anstalten zur Erhaltung der öffentlichen Ruhe, Sicherheit und Ordnung, und zur Abwendung der dem Publiko, oder einzelnen Mitgliedern desselben, bevorstehenden Gefahr zu treffen, ist das Amt der Polizei." *Landrecht*, II., 17, sec. 10.

areas of local self-government, the executive
agents of the locality, elected by it, are also the
representatives of the central government; as
such they are members of the bureaucracy and
controlled by it, and in consequence they naturally
look to the centre for guidance and direction in
regard to local affairs. Therefore, whilst it
would be inaccurate to say that local self-government, as understood in England, does not exist
in Prussia, it is true that self-government there
is weak, that it is not so much the exercise of
the will of the locality within limits prescribed
(for the protection of the whole community) by
the central power, as the exercise of the will of
the latter by the locality.[1] In fact, the bureaucracy rules; and it is fortunate for Prussia that
hitherto the bureaucracy has remained intelligent
and respective of new ideas.

SECTION 2

The areas of local administration.

As the classes of administrative areas in
Prussia are somewhat numerous, it will be
convenient first to set out the general scheme.
The following are the areas:—[2]

[1] The Prussian term for local government—"Lokal Selbst-ver-
waltung"—suggests this idea of the execution of the policy of the
central government by the locality rather than the determination of
its own policy by the latter. Cf. *supra*, pp. 3-8.

[2] The most convenient summary of Prussian administration is
H. de Grais, *Handbuch der Verfassung und Verwaltung* (12th edition). The
text of the chief laws is in Anschütz, *Organisations-Gesetze der inneren
Verwaltung.*

(1) The Province.

(2) The Government District (*Regierung-Bezirk*).

(3) The Rural Circle (*Landkreis*) and Town Circle (*Stadtkreis*), the latter being a town which, because of the size of its population, has been made an independent Circle.

(4) The Official District (*Amtsbezirk*), a subdivision of the Rural Circle for administrative purposes.

(5) The Town Commune (*Stadtgemeinde*) and Rural Commune (*Landgemeinde*).

The Provinces, Circles, and Communes are areas for the purposes of both central administration and local self-government, and they form bodies corporate: the Government and Official Districts are areas for central purposes only, and are normally not incorporated. The present territory of the Prussian state was formed only very gradually: the social and economic conditions vary greatly, from the mainly industrial provinces of the west to the agricultural and almost feudal provinces of East and West Prussia: many parts of it had, when acquired for Prussia, their own peculiar institutions. These variations still exist; there is nothing like absolute uniformity in detail; but the general plan is almost everywhere [1] the same, and it will be best to concentrate our attention upon that.

[1] The fact that after more than a century Prussia has failed to

The Province.   The largest areas are the Provinces, of which there are twelve, ranging from the Rhineland with 5,760,000 inhabitants in 1900, and Silesia with 4,669,000, to Schleswig - Holstein with 1,388,000. Many of these were once independent areas — Hanover is the old kingdom once united with the Crown of Great Britain, Schleswig - Holstein represents the duchies in personal union with Denmark until 1864, Prussian Saxony is the territory taken from the kingdom of that name at the close of the Napoleonic wars, and Prussian Poland (Posen) represents Prussia's share in the partition of the kingdom at the end of the eighteenth century. The Provinces are organised under the law of 1875, which, passed originally for the eastern provinces (except Poland), has been subsequently extended to the others.

(1) The Chief President.   The authorities of the Province are four. At its head is the Chief President, a professional official of high rank, whose authority is based on a Royal Decree of 1815. He is appointed by the Crown, and is mainly the representative in the Province of the central government; in this respect he resembles the French Prefect, though he is a far more important and dignified official. As the agent of the Crown he controls the administration of state affairs, so far as they concern the whole of his Province, or extend

reconcile Prussian Poland to its rule causes a special form of government to be retained for that Province.

beyond the sphere of one Government District; he watches, but does not control the administration of the Government Districts, and reports thereon to the respective ministries; he presides over the provincial boards for education, ecclesiastical matters, public health, and inland revenue; in conjunction with the commanding general he deals with military affairs (recruiting, billeting, supplies, etc.); and he represents the Crown over against the Provincial Assembly, at whose meetings he is entitled to be present. In the event of any great emergency, such as war or civil disturbance, he becomes almost autocratic in his Province; and at all times he represents and advocates the Government policy; though he is not, like the French Prefect, an electoral agent.

The Chief President is assisted in his work (2) The Provincial Council. by a Provincial Council (*Provinzialrath*) composed of one high professional official, appointed by the Minister of the Interior practically for life, and five lay members chosen by the Provincial Committee[1] usually for six years. The Chief President, or a representative, is chairman of the Council, whose approval is necessary for all ordinances issued by him, except in emergencies. It also hears and decides appeals from some subordinate administrative bodies, especially town councils, in regard to orders issued to them.

For the purposes of local self-government (3) The Provincial Assembly.

[1] Except in Hesse-Nassau, where they are appointed by the Provincial Assembly.

the representative authority is the Provincial
Assembly (*Provinziallandtag*) which is not
directly elected, but consists of representatives
appointed for six years by the Circle Assemblies
in proportion to population.[1]   It must be
summoned by the Crown, through the Chief
President, at least once every two years, but
may meet oftener; and the session lasts as long
as is necessary for the discharge of business.
There is little or no "popular" representation
even from the towns; the members are local
administrative officials of the Circles, large
landowners and other well-to-do persons; and
the Provincial Assemblies are naturally conservative in character. They choose their own
presidents, make their own standing orders, and
determine electoral disputes; they appoint the
administrative staff for local affairs; they
maintain and control the provincial roads (the
Prussian plan thus being midway between the
national highway system of France and the
small areas of England); they may make light
railways, they are bound[2] to establish institutions
for lunatics, imbeciles, epileptics, and for blind,
deaf and dumb persons, and may create labour
colonies and houses of correction for vagrants;
they may promote agricultural improvements
and agricultural education; they may establish

[1] Except in Posen, where the old representation of the three
estates (landowners, towns, and country communes) has continued.

[2] Where (as is usually the case) the Province is identical with a
Landarmenverband. *Vide infra*, p. 179.

or assist fire insurance institutions, and land banks; and they may make bye-laws. They control the provincial finances, and obtain the necessary funds partly from contributions from the central Exchequer, and partly from contributions levied by them upon the Circles. For the consideration of these various undertakings they usually appoint committees, and the full meetings of the Assemblies are concerned chiefly with the discussion of the recommendations and reports, and the necessary resolutions. The Chief-President may suspend any resolution which he believes to be *ultra vires*; all loans, taxes above a certain amount, bye-laws, and some resolutions require the approval of the Crown or its ministries; and the Crown may dissolve an assembly at any time.

The actual conduct of local matters is entrusted to a Provincial Committee (*Provinzialausschuss*), consisting of a chairman and not less than seven or more than thirteen persons elected for six years by the Provincial Assembly not necessarily (though practically always) from its own members; one-half retires every third year. This standing committee meets as often as it finds necessary; it prepares the business for the meetings of the Assembly, carries out its resolutions, and directs the various provincial institutions; as the sessions of the Assembly are infrequent, it naturally has a fairly free hand in regard to details. Its chief official is the *Landes-*

(4) The Provincial Committee.

direktor or *Landeshauptmann*, a salaried official elected by the Assembly with royal approval for six or twelve years; he is the head of the staff, both administrative and clerical, and represents the Province in all legal matters and in its relations with other authorities and with private persons; but he is more than the mere servant of the committee, since he is *ex-officio* a member of it. The Provincial Assembly may entrust particular branches of the administration to special commissions.

The communal life of a Prussian province is comparatively very small; little interest is taken in the work of the local provincial authorities, partly because the area is so large, and partly because the method of election is so very indirect.[1] The great advantage of the provincial system is that it provides large areas for some branches of administration, such as education, poor relief, and roads; and also renders possible a real deconcentration of the work of the central government, and regard for local conditions, without the consequent variations becoming unduly numerous.

SECTION 3

The next area is the Government District,
which exists solely for central purposes, and does

The
Government
District.

[1] The Assembly is elected by the Assemblies of the Circles, which in the country districts are elected by a complicated and far from democratic method, and in the towns by the "three class system." It is therefore indirect election at the second stage.

not form a corporation.[1] Each province is divided
into two or more Government Districts (there are
thirty-five in all), with the exception of Schleswig-
Holstein, which forms only one; the largest
number in any one province is six, in Hanover.
The organisation dates originally from 1723, and
in its present form from 1808 ; and its working
is determined by the *Landesverwaltungsgesetz* of
1883.

The arrangement is somewhat complicated. (1) The
At the head is the District President (*Regierungs-* President.
Präsident), a professional official appointed by
the Crown. He presides over the Government
Board and the District Committee, and in addition there are a large number of matters in which
he acts alone, and on his own responsibility.
Amongst these are all branches of police—which
includes public safety and order, the maintenance
of prisons, preventive measures against epidemics
and the adulteration of foods and drugs, the
enforcement of sanitary and building laws, and
a multitude of other things. He exercises
general supervision over the subordinate local
government officials, in so far as they are
agents of the central government. To assist him
in his work he has his own personal staff of
officials.

The second authority is the Government (2) The
Government
Board.

---

[1] Except in Hesse-Nassau and Hohenzollern. The latter—the
small enclave of Prussian territory in the midst of Wurttemberg—
forms a Government District of a special kind. H. de Grais,
Handbuch, p. 63.

Board (*Regierung*) formed by a number of professional officials appointed by the Crown.   Normally this Board is divided into two sections, one for church and elementary school matters, and the other for direct state taxes, domains, and forests, etc., but there are local variations.[1]   Each consists of a number of councillors, presided over by a Director (*Abtheilungsdirigent*): care is taken to include appropriate technical experts in each. Each section divides its work between its members, but all decisions (except where merely of a routine character) are determined by vote; if the head of the section is dissatisfied he may appeal to the Government President, who may either decide the matter himself, or call the whole Board together to consider and vote upon the question. All important matters must be so decided in full meeting, but the Government President may suspend the action of any resolution and appeal against it to the higher authorities.

(3) The District Committee.
The third body is in some ways far more important and interesting.   The District Committee (*Bezirksausschuss*) has seven members; three of these are officials—the Government President, and one judicial and one official member appointed by the Crown for life, and four are unofficial members (who must be resident in the district) chosen for six years by the Provincial Committee.   This committee controls the police administration of the Government President to some extent, since

[1] H. de Grais, *Handbuch*, p. 66.

all ordinances made by him in that department require its approval; and under his presidency it exercises a certain supervision over subordinate authorities. But its most important task is to act as an administrative court of first instance in some cases, and of appeal from the decisions of the Circle Committees; when it acts in this character the judicial member presides, and the Government President takes no part in the proceedings.[1]

As regards the Government District as a whole, a recent American observer remarks:—

" The organisation of the *Regierungsbezirk* seems to a foreigner needlessly complex, and the division of its functions between the two bodies somewhat unnecessary, especially when we consider that both of them act as agents of the central government and deal only with those matters that are supposed to affect the whole state. But the system is in fact only the result of a careful and logical application of the modern Prussian theories of administration. In the first place, it was thought . . . that the matters of state taxes, schools, etc., ought to be managed entirely by professional officials, but that the police, in its wider sense, and the supervision of the organs of local self-government, ought to be largely under the control of laymen. Hence the separation between the *Regierung* and the *Bezirksausschauss*. In the second place, it was felt that a sharp line ought to be drawn between executive action and judicial decisions, that the *Regierungs-Präsident*, who might be concerned with the issuing of police

[1] For the working of the administrative courts, *vide infra*, pp. 376-381.

ordinances by the subordinate local authorities, ought not to sit in the tribunal that passed upon their legality. From 1873 to 1875 the same body had exercised both classes of functions, but experience showed the evil of this arrangement, and in the latter year two separate bodies were created. In 1882 they were again united, for the sake of simplicity, and the lay members were suffered to act in both capacities; but it was provided that the professional members should be changed according to the nature of the business to be transacted." [1]

It will be seen that the authorities of the Government District constitute a deputation of the central government, exercising within their area very wide powers and bearing a heavy responsibility; particularly the office of Government President is one of very great importance. That the arrangement is most convenient and useful from the point of view of the central departments there can be no doubt; the officials of the Government District are highly trained, and their work is thoroughly well done. The only criticisms which can be made upon it are two—but they are by no means unimportant. First, it renders possible and promotes that minute and detailed regulation of all departments of national life which the ordinary Prussian citizen endures, if not willingly, at least without active opposition, but which would be intolerable to Englishmen. And, secondly, the administrative

[1] Lowell, *Parties and Governments in Continental Europe*, I., p. 320.

work is practically all done by officials, and there
is little opportunity for the non - professional
citizen, however active and able, to exercise any
influence upon policy or to acquire experience
in the conduct of large public affairs.

SECTION 4

The third area—the Circle (*Kreis*)—exists, like The Circle.
the Province, for the conduct of affairs both of
the central authorities and of local self-government. The Circle organisation in its present
form was determined by the *Kreisordnung* of
1872, issued originally for the six eastern
provinces (excluding Poland) and gradually
extended to the remainder of the monarchy.
Towns of at least 25,000 inhabitants may be
formed into separate Circles by ministerial
order;[1] in that case the powers and duties of
Circle authorities are exercised within the
municipal area by the civic government.[2] So
that in the present sketch of the organisation
we are concerned solely with the Country Circles
(*Landkreise*).

They are about 490 in number, with populations varying from 20,000 to 80,000. The
authorities are three in number — the Circle
Assembly (*Kreistag*), which represents the district

---

[1] Smaller towns may be given the same rank by royal decree.
[2] Cf. the English counties and county boroughs.

as a self-governing corporation; the Landrath, and the Circle Committee (*Kreisausschuss*), both of which are the executive agents of the locality and also representatives of the central government.[1]

(1) The Circle Assembly.

The Circle Assembly contains at least twenty-five members. Where the Circle has more than 25,000 inhabitants there is an additional member for every further 5,000 up to 100,000, and beyond that number (which is hardly ever surpassed) one for every 10,000. The method of election is complicated. Three "electoral colleges" are formed: the first is composed of the large landowners (*i.e.*, those who pay land and building taxes varying from 150 to 300 marks according to the Province[2]) and those large manufacturers in the rural parts of the Circle who pay a trade tax of 300 marks; the second consists of the rural communes, and those landowners and rural manufacturers who are not included in the previous group; and the third is composed of the towns. The landowners are formed into groups; so are the rural communes, which appoint electors; the towns act singly or in groups—in the former case the elections to the Circle Assembly are made by the magistracy and town council, in the latter representative electors are chosen by each town. The numerical representation of each of the three

[1] This combination resembles that found in the French Prefect, and the result is much the same.

[2] *Kreis-ordnung*, sec. 86. The variations within these limits may be made by the Provincial Assemblies.

divisions is determined thus—the total number of members of the Assembly is divided between town and country in proportion to the population at the last census, and then the number of members allotted to the country districts is divided equally between the great landowners and the rural communes. But the representatives of the towns may not exceed one-half, or where there is only one town one-third, of the complete membership of the Assembly. The elections are for six years, one-half of the members from each electoral group retiring every third year. In the elections politics play a very small part — the system gives scarcely any opportunity for them; and the plan tends generally to give the predominance to the landowners, or in the industrial provinces to the manufacturers, and to the officials, since both towns and rural communes generally choose their representatives from this last class.

The Circle Assembly meets usually only three or four times a year, and often only twice. It controls the finances of the Circle, and raises money for its own purposes, and for the Circle share of the provincial expenditure, by means of additions to the direct state taxes;[1] it is the highway authority for the smaller roads; it may establish hospitals and other institutions for poor relief, and contribute to charitable associations;

---

[1] These surtaxes may not exceed 50 per cent. except with the approval of superior authorities.

it must provide two - thirds of the cost of maintenance of persons in the institutions for defectives established by the provinces; and it may undertake anything else for which it can obtain approval from the superior authorities. But its functions in all these things are purely deliberative; the executive work is done by the Landrath and the Circle Committee. It also elects the representatives of the Circle in the Provincial Assembly.

(2) The Landrath.

The Landrath is appointed for life by the Crown, usually on the nomination of the Circle Assembly. The office is an ancient one, dating back, in the Mark of Brandenburg, to the six-teenth century : " he was at first appointed by the ' States,' and was necessarily a leading person among the *Ritterschaft* or holders of knights' fees in the Circle; but, little by little, he became an officer of the Crown, pure and simple, and by the Constitution of 1850 he was changed into the direct nominee of the Crown."[1] He is a professional official, who must have received a suitable semi - legal training, have had at least four years' administrative experience, and resided in the Circle for one year. His chief duty[2] is to represent the central government; as its agent he has charge of the police, and may make bye-

[1] Morier, in *Cobden Club Essays on Local Government* (1875), p. 422.

[2] " Der Landrath führt als Organ der Staatregierung die Geschäfte der allgemeinen Landesverwaltung im Kreise und leitet als Vorsit-zender des Kreistages und des Kreisausschusses die Kommunalver-waltung des Kreises." *Kreis-ordnung*, sec. 76.

laws; he superintends education, controls subordinate officials, and presides in the administrative court of first instance (the Circle Committee.) He is assisted by one or more assessors, and has a staff of medical officers, inspectors of foods, analysts, school inspectors, and other necessary officials. He is under the control of the Government President as regards police, and of the Government Board for other matters. Like the French Prefect he is expected to represent always the views of the Government — so much so that some years ago a number of Landräthe, who were members of the Prussian Parliament, were suspended or dismissed because, in accordance with the wishes of their constituents, they voted against certain ministerial proposals.[1] The Landrath is also the chief executive official of the Circle as a self-governing corporation; but this function is only secondary with him, for he is entirely dependent upon the central government, represents its views in all things, and is its agent to watch the proceedings of the Circle Assembly and to see that it does not exceed the law, and that its resolutions are submitted, whenever necessary, for the approval of the superior authorities. The net result of this, and of the fact that he presides in the Circle Assembly and Committee, is that the Landrath is the real ruler of the Circle, limited only by the supervision and financial control of the Assembly. That body

[1] The first definite proposals for a Middle-German Canal.

may entrust duties to special commissions, but the Landrath is a member, and practically director, of them all.

3) The Circle Committee.

The Circle Committee (*Kreisausschuss*) consists of the Landrath and six unofficial members elected by the Circle Assembly (not necessarily from its own ranks) for six years.[1] Its functions are three in number : (*a*) it is the executive committee of the Circle, meeting as often as is necessary for the conduct of business, but leaving all the routine work to the Landrath ; (*b*) it exercises supervision over the acts of all lesser local authorities, and is a court of discipline for agents of the central government ; (*c*) it is an administrative court of first instance. When it acts in this last character, its sittings are open to the public ; otherwise they are private. As a judicial court, its members enjoy the ordinary privileges and immunities of judges ; as a supervisory body they are agents of the central government and subject to bureaucratic control ; and as the executive committee of the self-governing circle they are more or less independent. To the outsider the arrangement thus described seems very involved, but apparently the members of the Committee do not find it so, perhaps because (like all Prussians placed in any office) they become imbued very quickly with the bureaucratic

---

[1] In some cases an attempt is made to represent all three classes of the Assembly upon the Committee. Thus the committee of the Teltow Circle (on the outskirts of Berlin) used to consist (and perhaps still does so) of two landowners, two burgomasters of small towns, and two headmen of rural communes.

tradition, and adopt and represent the official views.

In the eastern provinces the rural communes are grouped into Official Districts (*Amtsbezirke*), each containing about 1,500 inhabitants, for police purposes. A single commune, if large enough, may form an *Amtsbezirk* by itself. For each there is an *Amtsvorsteher* (a term for which there is hardly an English equivalent) who administers the police under the direction and control of the Landrath:[1] he is often the headman of a commune. He is assisted by a Committee (*Amts-ausschuss*) nominated by the councils of the various communes, which also contribute (in proportion to population) towards the cost of the work, so far as it is not covered by the proceeds of fines and by state grants-in-aid. Its approval is required for various regulations which the *Amtsvorstehr* may issue.[2] Similar police areas, under different names and forms, exist in Prussian Poland, Westphalia, and Rhineland.[3]

The Official District.

SECTION 5

It will be convenient to take the Rural Commune (*Landgemeinde*) next: and it must

The Rural Commune.

---

[1] He is appointed by the Chief President of the Province on the nomination of the Circle Assembly.

[2] For the detailed rules as to the *Amtsbezirk*, see the *Kreis-ordnung*, sec. 47-73.

[3] H. de Grais, *Handbuch*, p. 298.

again be repeated that we are dealing only with the normal type, whose organisation is based on the *Landgemeinde-ordnung* of 1891.[1] Where a commune does not contain more than forty voters, there is an assembly which is equivalent to an English parish meeting; for a larger commune there is a council (*Gemeinde-vertretung*) with not

(a) Communal Council. more than twenty-four members.[2] The electors are all persons resident in the commune, or owning property in it, who pay a certain minimum amount of taxes; and the election is by the "three-class system," which will be described later.[3] For the executive work there is in all communes a Headman (*Gemeindevorsteher*), elected by the assembly or council for six years, and unpaid; but communes with more than 3,000 inhabitants may (subject to approval) appoint a paid headman, for

(b) Headman. twelve years. The headman has from two to six assistants (*Schöffen*), and in large communes he and they may be formed into an executive committee (*Gemeinde - vorstand*); elsewhere the assistants act simply under his directions. There are over 36,000 rural communes in Prussia, and the great majority of them are very small, and do little. They may spend money upon poor relief, small roads, protection against fire, drainage, street cleaning, etc., control whatever communal property there may be, and where the local government

---

[1] Text and notes in Keil, *Die Landgemeinde-ordnung* (1896).

[2] A commune with less than forty electors may have a council. if it so desires and can obtain permission from the Circle Committee.

[3] *Vide infra*, pp. 154-5.

communes are coincident with school communes (*Schulgemeinden*) they have duties in regard to elementary education.   Money is obtained from the proceeds of any village property ; from taxes on dogs, entertainments and public spectacles, and in some cases (where they existed prior to the Communal Finances Act of 1893)[1] upon the consumption of food stuffs of various kinds ; and from additions to the taxes levied by the state. Unions of communes for specific purposes are permitted, and communes may be amalgamated by royal decree.

The headman is the chief of the local police, and acts under the direction of the *Amtsvorsteher* ; he is to that extent a member of the bureaucracy.

In Rhineland and Westphalia the old arrangements still exist, whereby the communes are grouped into districts (*Burgermeisterei, Amt*) ; each commune has its own headman and assembly, but all matters which affect several communes are controlled by the Burgomaster or Amtmann, acting with the advice and direction of an assembly of representatives of the communes.   There are other variation in Hesse-Nassau and Hanover.[2]

There still remain throughout Prussia, and The Manors. particularly in the eastern provinces — the region of great estates — a very large number

[1] *Das Kommunalabgabengesetz*, sec. 14.
[2] H. de Grais, *Handbuch*, p. 103-105.

of Manors (*Gutsbezirke*), that is, communes entirely contained within the estate of a single landowner. The internal organisation of these estates is of course not uniform, but so far as the administration is concerned, the Lord of the Manor (*Gutsbesitzer*) has all the rights and responsibilities of a commune: he is either himself the headman, or appoints a representative to the office.[1]

It is almost unnecessary to add that the greater number of the rural communes are so small that they have neither the administrative ability nor the financial resources to enable them to do much; in this respect they resemble most of the French communes and English parishes. And so, as in France, they are guided and directed, as far as they do anything at all, by the authorities of the Circle, and hardly move without obtaining the Landrath's advice and approval. Moreover in the east the economic dependence upon the landowner is very great, he is the chief taxpayer, and disinclined to do more than the necessary minimum imposed by the superior authorities. Communal self-government can prosper only in the provinces where the system of small holdings prevails, or where the population is engaged wholly or partially in industry—and is consequently more or less independent; but the commune is generally too small for much effective work to be done

[1] H. de Grais, *Handbuch*, p. 103.

even there, and, as in England and France, the plan of grouping these small areas would be much more satisfactory.

SECTION 6

We come now to the towns *(Städte)*, whose The Towns. organisation varies somewhat; the seven eastern provinces have a uniform system which will be described here, whilst in the remaining provinces there are differences of some importance. There are in all about 1,270 towns in Prussia, and of these somewhere about ninety (mainly those with populations of 25,000 and upwards) form as already mentioned independent Circles. But this affects the actual form of the municipal government only very slightly.

The rank of a municipality is conferred by (1) Town Council. royal decree; there is no necessary limit of population, and there are a very large number of small municipalities in existence; but the status is conferred now infrequently and only upon populous areas. The centre of the civic government is in the Town Council, whose membership ranges from twelve in towns with less than 2,500 inhabitants to sixty in towns with 120,000, and then increases by six members for every additional 50,000 of population. This council is elected by the remarkable "three class - system," which is so characteristic of Prussia that it must be described somewhat fully.

The voters for each electoral district are arranged in the list in the order of the amount of direct taxes which they pay for all purposes. The total so paid is divided into three equal parts; those taxpayers at the head of the list who together pay one-third of the total amount constitute the first class of voters. The next in the list who pay another third form the second class; whilst all the others, who together pay the remaining third, make up the third class. To this scheme some modifications have lately been made. The general rule now is that a person who in any class pays more than the average for that class is to be placed in the next higher group; but to this two limitations may locally be made—the required amount may be one and a half times the average, or the division of the amount of taxes may be not into thirds, but into five-twelfths, four-twelfths, and three-twelfths for the three classes. The result of these changes is to increase the number of voters in the first and second classes, and to reduce those in the third.[1] Each class returns one-third of the members to the Town Council, and clearly the effect is to give the large taxpayers the predominance, in spite of the fact that they are generally only a very small proportion of the population. In Halle in 1899

[1] It was estimated that in Berlin out of every 1,000 inhabitants there were 180·29 voters, divided thus:—Cl. I., 0·39; Cl. II., 4·40; Cl. III., 175·50; under the new plan the numbers would be 0·78, 16·6, 162·6.

(before the above modifications had been made) there were 140 voters in the first class, 914 in the second, and 16,645 in the third; and each group returned eighteen members to the Town Council.[1] Of course in the small communes the disproportions are not so great; but in the large towns the number of electors in the first class appears rarely to exceed 5 per cent.[2] In Essen, a town created by the great Krupp works, there were, in 1895, 4 persons in the first class, 353 in the second, and 12,197 in the third.[3]

The councillors are elected for six years—one-third retiring every second year. The councils are filled with much the same class as the English town councils, though perhaps there is a larger proportion in Prussia of professional men.[4] Party politics play a very small part in the elections, and the voting system effectually prevents the socialists, who are very strong in the great towns, from getting control of the town councils, though they are represented there; the re-election of good councillors is as frequent in Germany as in England. The council elects its own president.

The municipal executive consists of a Burgo- (2) The Burgomaster. master and a Board of Magistrates (*Magistrat, Stadtrath*). The burgomaster is a salaried pro-

---

[1] James, *Municipal Administration in Germany*, pp. 25-26.

[2] For a discussion of the whole question, see Jastrow, *Das Dreiklassen-system*.

[3] Shaw, *Municipal Government in Continental Europe*, p. 308.

[4] There are some curious limitations: a father and son, or two brothers, may not be members of the Council at the same time—*Stadte-ordnung*, 1853, sec. 17.

fessional official, appointed by the council (subject to approval) and holding office for twelve years.[1] He presides over the Administrative Board, and distributes the work amongst its members: he is the co-ordinating power in the civic administration; he discharges many duties analogous to those of an English town clerk. Commencing his career in a subordinate post, he looks for promotion by being called to preside over a larger town, with Berlin as the summit of his ambition. When the office falls vacant, applications for it are usually invited by advertisement. The burgomaster has the social precedence enjoyed by an English mayor, combined with the real direction of the whole city government.

(3) The Administrative Board. The Magistracy or Administrative Board may best be described as a combination of the salaried heads of departments and the aldermen of an English town council. It consists of a number of unprofessional members appointed by the Town Council for six years, generally from among old and experienced members; and a number of technical experts who are appointed for twelve years and paid by the Council.[2] The number of members of the Board is fixed according to population, with a minimum of two, and

[1] Large cities may have two burgomasters, one being the chief.
[2] There are further curious regulations as to membership. A father and son, father-in-law and son-in-law, brother and brother-in-law, may not be members of the Executive Board, nor may one be in the Board and the other in the Town Council at the same time. A more important limitation is that keepers of hotels, inns, and public houses may not be members of the Executive Board.

rising to nearly forty in the case of Berlin: the proportion of paid members varies according to local requirements—in the small towns the unprofessional magistrates form the large majority, but where a city has many technical enterprises (gas, water, electric lighting, tramways, etc.) it naturally has more professional members, though they never exceed one-half of the total. The function of this Administrative Board, under the presidency of the burgomaster, is threefold :—

(1) It is the agent within the municipal area of the central government, and in this capacity it is independent of the control of the Town Council. The burgomaster manages the police, in the wide meaning already explained, but the regulations which he issues require in most cases the assent of the Administrative Board. The Board, where the Town is also a Circle, appoints the Town Committee, consisting of the burgomaster (4) Town Committee. and four members of its own body, which discharges the same duties as the Circle Committee.[1] In towns of more than 10,000 inhabitants a special Chief of Police may be appointed by the Crown, with the title of Police - President or Director, and this is commonly done in the large cities. In such a case the cost of the police is divided between the central government and the municipality.

(2) It is the administrative authority for municipal affairs. As such it conducts the whole executive work of city government, it appoints the municipal civil service, and it may take

[1] Including the issue of licences for the sale of intoxicants, pawnshops, and public amusements: and the very important work of an administrative court.

definite decisions in all matters which do not involve expenditure, or are simply the carrying into effect of resolutions of the Town Council. Each member of the Board has a particular department entrusted to him, but except in matters of mere routine resolutions are taken by vote of the whole Board.

(3) It is on an equality with the Council in the consideration of all questions of policy : " all resolutions of the city council, with comparatively few exceptions (relating to its own constitution, the passing upon the election of its own members, etc.) must receive the approval of the Administrative Board before they can have the effect of local ordinances. The Administrative Board is authorised to make recommendations to the city council upon all subjects relating to city legislation and administration. . . . While the city council has also the right to initiate legislation, as a matter of fact nearly all legislation is initiated in the Administrative Board, and even when the city council desires to pass an ordinance upon any given subject, the form of action usually consists in a request to the Board to submit an ordinance to the city council." [1]

The members of the Administrative Board attend the meetings of the council; they may be called upon to answer questions, and to explain their actions; and they may intervene in the discussions as often as they choose. But it must be remembered that the responsibility rests with the whole Board, and not with individual members.

Though the members are appointed by the

[1] James, *Municipal Administration in Germany*, p. 14.

Council, it is evident that the Administrative
Board is practically independent. The long tenure
of office, the position which it holds as an agent of
the central government, its exercise of some un-
controlled executive powers, its co-equal authority
and practical initiative in municipal legislation,
and its expert knowledge, all combine to make
it the real guiding and determining force in
city government ; the Town Council is rather
a controlling and checking body, and the Administrative Board cannot do anything which
involves expenditure without its approval. But
conflicts between the two bodies are very
infrequent.

But members of the Town Council are not (5) Town
entirely excluded from participation in the admini- Commissions.
strative work. Many branches of the town
administration are entrusted to commissions composed, generally, in part of councillors and in
part of other persons interested in a particular
subject—education, poor relief, sanitation, tramways, waterworks, museums, etc. This arrangement has the very great advantage that, whilst
retaining the concentration of authority and
financial responsibility in the Administrative Board
and Town Council, it enables the municipality
to make use of the services of large numbers of
citizens, and to obtain the benefits which used to
be claimed in England for what is known as
the *ad hoc* system. Over each commission a
member of the Administrative Board usually

presides; and the commission reports to that body, and not directly to the Town Council.

The powers of a Prussian municipality are very extensive. The law in fact does not confer any specific powers, except in so far as this is done by general enactments for special matters (as education), but simply authorises the local authorities to do whatever they think necessary or advisable in the interests of their localities—subject to the requirement that their proposals shall be submitted for the approval of the central authorities, usually the Circle or District Committee. This plan of general grants of power removes the necessity for that constant recourse to Parliament for legislative approval, which is so striking a feature of English local government. It is the duty of the Administrative Board to see that the necessary approval is obtained, and also to reserve and submit to the competent authority any resolution of which it may doubt the legality.

The Prussian municipalities are bound to make provision for elementary education by the establishment and maintenance of schools; they may supply or aid secondary and higher education, and are especially active in regard to technical instruction of all grades.[1] They are the poor law authorities, and have built up an elaborate system of relief which will be described later.[2] They usually own the water supply;

[1] *Vide infra*, pp. 169-171.   [2] *Vide infra*, pp. 179-185.

many have their own gasworks and electric lighting stations; and the municipalisation of the tramways is gradually taking place. Where these services are not owned by the municipalities, it is customary for stringent conditions as to the supply and prices to be imposed, and a charge to be made in return for the use of the streets. As the public health authority, a town council carries out sewage and drainage works and sewage farms,[1] it provides slaughter-houses (of which it may compel the use), and markets, and it may maintain parks and open spaces; it also maintains hospitals for infectious diseases. It can encourage thrift by the establishment of savings banks (which are municipal or local in Prussia, and not national); it may provide municipal pawnshops and other loan institutions; and it may open employment bureaux. Municipal housing has so far made little progress, since the authorities have confined themselves to providing for municipal employés, and to advancing money at low rates of interest to private persons or companies who undertake to build working class dwellings at moderate rentals.[2] Fire insurance institutions are frequently municipal. Finally, a town council may make provision for recreation by establishing libraries and museums,

[1] Berlin has turned many hundreds of acres of waste land in the plain round the capital into arable land (market gardens and orchards) by its sewage farms.

[2] Sinzheimer, *Die Arbeiterwohnungsfrage*, c. iv.

L

art galleries, municipal concerts, and even a municipal theatre.[1]

Municipal revenues. The revenues of the municipality are derived from (a) proceeds of municipal enterprises and property; (b) fees; (c) state grants towards education, etc.; (d) local licences; and (e) additions to the direct state taxes, chiefly to the income-tax, which commences at £45 a year. Most of a town's financial operations, including taxation beyond certain limits, loans, and dealings in municipal property, require administrative approval.

It will be seen that the activity of the Prussian cities is as great and varied as that of the British municipalities, and in some directions it is even wider.[2] But it is important to remember that all this work has been done at the instigation and under the leadership of the Administrative Boards, that is, of bodies which are in no sense democratic in constitution or feeling, and have not been influenced by the socialist propaganda; and further, that it has been encouraged and aided by the central departments, that is, by the bureaucracy. Of the work itself it is almost impossible to speak too highly; vast progress has been made in the last generation; and Prussian city administration is, as a whole, probably the most

[1] E.g., At Breslau, Cologne, Barmen, and Düsseldorf.
[2] Vide Shaw, Municipal Government in Continental Europe, cc. v.-vi.; and James, Municipal Administration in Germany (a description of Halle a/S).

highly organised and technically skilled in the world.[1]

There is one other type of municipal organisation which must be noticed. It is the so-called *Burgermeistereiver-fassung* for towns which have no more than 2,500 inhabitants, but yet possess municipal rank. In these, on the proposal of the Town Council approved by the District Committee, the number of councillors may be reduced to six, and the burgomaster takes the place of the Administrative Board. The whole administration is concentrated in his hands, and he also presides in the council; two or three assistants are appointed by the council, but act entirely under his directions.[2]

The "Burgermeistereiver-fassung."

Like most European capitals the City of Berlin occupies a special position—the object being to keep it under an even closer control by the central ministry than the other cities. It is isolated from the other areas of local government, and is assimilated to a Province, a Government District, and a Town Circle. It has its municipal government, but (1) police affairs are in the hands of a special Police-Presidency, which may be compared to the Prefect of Police in Paris; (2) the administrative supervision is exercised by the Chief President of the Province of Brandenburg, as Chief

Berlin.

[1] There is an association of German cities, corresponding to our Association of Municipal Corporations.

[2] *Stadte-Ordnung*, 1853, Part VIII. Cf. Schön, *Das Recht der Kommunalverbande in Preussen*, pp. 336-339.

President of the City of Berlin; (3) some of the provincial Boards—for school matters, taxes, medical affairs, and others—exercise authority over Berlin, without the interposition of the officials of a Government District; and (4) there is a special District Committee for Berlin, consisting of a President appointed by the Crown and four persons elected by the Executive Board and Town Council in common session.

SECTION 7

National education.

In no other large state of Europe[1] has the Government paid so much attention to education, and for so long a period, as in Prussia.[2]   As early as the year 1717 an edict issued by Frederick William I. directed parents to send their children to school daily in winter, and at least twice a week in summer; if they could not afford to pay the fee they were to be helped out of the funds for the relief of the poor.   In 1736 the *Principia Regulativa* made the upkeep of the school building a duty of the communes, and allowed them to take timber from the royal forests for that purpose.   It also made provision for the support

(a) History.

---

[1] Some of the Swiss cantons had taken action earlier. In 1675 the Canton of Berne directed that schools should be provided for every commune out of public funds; the attendance of children was to be compulsory.

[2] The best critical history is Paulsen, *Geschichte des gelehrten Unterrichts in Deutschland.*

of the schoolmaster, partly from church funds (in return for which he acted as verger), partly from an allotment worked for him by the commune, and partly from contributions in money and in kind from the parents of the school children. These elementary schools were all under church control, and so were the secondary schools (which were rather the only good elementary schools); the sole change in the latter (which existed only in towns) under Frederick William I. was that candidates for teaching posts in them had to be examined before the Consistory.[1]

There was much legislation under Frederick the Great; and it is characteristic of Prussian educational history that the chief edicts (for the Lutheran and Catholic schools) were issued in 1763 and 1764, immediately at the close of the Seven Years' War, when Frederick was setting to work to repair the ravages inflicted upon his kingdom by that long struggle. The principle of compulsory attendance was re-affirmed; plans of studies, lists of school books, methods of discipline, were all prescribed; and a system of inspection established. By 1778 there were nine seminaries for teachers in the country. The schools formed part of the ecclesiastical organisation which subjected all denominations — Lutheran, Reformed, and Catholic — to state control. Just after Frederick's death the *Allgemeines Landrecht* laid

---

[1] For the history of the Prussian secondary schools, and their present condition, see Russell, *German Higher Schools* (1899).

the duty of providing and maintaining school buildings upon the "house fathers" of each school commune, which will be described later; and the *Oberschulkollegium* was established to supervise and improve the whole of national education. Thus a full decade before the close of the eighteenth century Prussia had a central organisation and definite plans for compulsory national education, at least of an elementary kind; doubtless the realisation was often very far from complete, but the ideal was higher than that of any other European state.

Then came the French Revolution and its wars, leading to the crowning disaster of Tilsit. But the task of re-organisation was taken up vigorously by Stein and his colleagues, and agreeing fully with the declaration of Fichte, that "nothing but education can rescue us from all the miseries that overwhelm us," they began at once the reform of national education. The *Oberschulkollegium* was abolished as being too clerical; a Bureau of Education was made a department of the Ministry of the Interior, and Wilhelm von Humboldt was placed at its head. The University of Berlin was created in 1807; school programmes were reformed; the state certification of teachers was made compulsory; and Prussian students were sent to Switzerland to study under Pestalozzi, and to prepare for teaching in the training colleges. In the following years the training institutions were much extended and improved, and the secondary schools were strengthened by the establishment of the " leaving certificate " system.

Since then the chief developments have been, first, the growth of the " modern " schools, and, secondly, the extension of state authority and control.　In 1817 an independent ministry for ecclesiastical and educational matters was established ; in 1825 provincial School Boards (*Provinzial-Schulkollegien*) were formed ; in the same year the laws regarding compulsory attendance were re-enacted and made really effective ; and in 1850 public school teachers were declared to be civil servants.　In 1872, during the long Kulturkampf, all private schools were brought under state inspection.

At the foot of the ladder of educational institutions [1] in Prussia are the elementary schools (*Volkschulen*), supplemented by the *Bürgerschulen* (which correspond roughly to our higher grade schools) and evening continuation schools. Attendance at the elementary schools is free and compulsory between the ages of six and fourteen, and there is no " half-time " system ; whilst attendance at the evening continuation schools (trade and other) can be made compulsory up to eighteen years of age.[2]　The secondary schools are the *Gymnasien* (classical schools) and *Progymnasien*

(b) The present organisation.

---

[1] A useful short account of the institutions will be found in Stötzner, *Das öffentliche Unterrichtswesen Deutschlands.*

[2] H. de Grais, *Handbuch*, p. 506.

(classical schools of a lower standing), the *Real-gymnasien* (in which Latin is taught), and the *Realschulen* of various grades, which are entirely "modern." Generally the *Gymnasia* and *Real-gymnasia* prepare their students for the universities, and the *Realschulen* for the technical institutions.[1] Tertiary education is divided between the universities and the technical high schools, which are now on the same footing and may grant degrees. The secondary schools and higher institutions are greatly strengthened by the fact that education in them, and the leaving certificate which they give, are necessary preliminaries to admission to the universities and technical high schools, and to state employment in any branch of the civil service.

(1) Ministry.   Coming now to the machinery of administration, there is at its head the department of the Ministry for Ecclesiastical, Educational, and Medical Affairs, with an under-secretary, two directors, and an advisory council; it controls the universities and technical high schools directly, and supervises education generally. In each of the twelve provinces there is a provincial School Board (*Provinzial - Schulkollegium*), consisting of four or five educational experts (often ex-directors of training colleges) under the chairmanship of the Chief President. This Board manages the state secondary schools, holds the certificate examinations for teachers, issues general regulations for

---

[1] But the *Oberrealschulen* prepare also for the universities.

the province, supervises training colleges, and inspects all secondary schools not established and maintained by the state. In each Government District there is a church and school section of the Government Board, which is entrusted with the control of the elementary schools; it actually inspects them through the Landrath, for buildings and accommodation, and through Circle School Inspectors (usually clergymen in the district), for educational matters. Finally, in every school area there is an inspector, generally the local clergyman of the predominant religious denomination.

The unit for the provision of elementary schools is the School Commune (*Schulgemeinde*). In four of the provinces this is usually identical with the local government commune: elsewhere it may be (1) a group of communes; (2) part of a commune; or (3) an association of inhabitants who desire to have a denominational school. In any case a rate is levied on the "House Fathers," that is, the group of householders who make use of the particular school or set of schools. Religious instruction is given in all schools, but parents who have to make use of schools where the teaching is not according to their creed, may withdraw their children from it on condition that they undertake to provide proper teaching elsewhere.

In the towns there is a *School Deputa-* *tion*, composed of town councillors and other persons interested in education — all appointed by the Town Council; usually this is under the presidency of a member of the Executive Board (the *Stadtschulrath*), who may be compared to the superintendent of education often found in American cities, and is the chief administrative official. The denominational schools of minorities are generally under small separate commissions. In the rural communes there is a School Committee (*Schulvorstand*) elected by the communal council or by the school commune. The duties of both the school deputation and school committee, which deal only with elementary schools, are to see to the adequate supply of school accommodation, to pay the teachers, to provide prizes and generally to do everything to promote the efficiency of the schools. But where these bodies are appointed by the local councils they cannot impose a rate or raise a loan; all they can do is to submit estimates to the council, which grants so much as it finds possible. It must be admitted that in some instances the schools are alleged to have been cramped as a result of this, but such cases are not numerous, for in the towns there is a real enthusiasm for education, and in the rural districts official pressure is usually strong enough to secure an adequate provision. The central government gives large contributions, allocated chiefly to teachers' salaries.

Secondary schools.

The secondary schools are maintained in various ways. Some are state schools, established and

directed wholly by the Ministry; these are chiefly
in the rural districts. Others are municipal or
guild schools, founded and administered by some
local authority or association, and often subsidised
from state funds: they are subject to the state
regulations as to organisation and curricula. In
the provision of such schools, and especially those
of a "modern" character, the great municipalities
of Prussia have displayed much activity and
enthusiasm. Others are private institutions, which
are allowed only when the supply is otherwise
inadequate: "they must comply with all the
regulations of the state in regard to equipment
and the conduct of the work. The course of
study, the methods employed, and the teachers
must all be approved."[1] Usually the municipal
institutions are controlled by Boards of Trustees,
appointed by the Town Council and containing
representatives of that body and of the Executive
Board.

The universities (of which there are nine) and The
the technical high schools (five in number) are universities.
financed largely by the central government, which
appoints the professors.

The state lays down a minimum qualification The teachers.
for secondary and elementary teachers,[2] and fixes
a minimum salary towards which it contributes:
it provides the training colleges (administered by

[1] Russell, *German Higher Schools*, p. 78.
[2] No one is permitted to teach in Prussia (even as a private tutor
or governess) who does not possess the qualifications required by
the state.

the provincial school boards) for elementary teachers. The course of training required for secondary teachers is long and elaborate, and there are many complaints as to its excessive length, and the stringent manner in which the state controls the whole career and activity of the secondary (and for that matter also the elementary) teacher. Teachers are appointed by the higher authorities always (provincial school board or government board), sometimes on the recommendation of the locality.

Summarising the system, we find that an attempt has been made to co-ordinate the three grades of education, and bring them all under central supervision. To them all the state contributes largely, and in return the elementary schools are free, and in the higher institutions the fees are very low. The state also imposes a minimum qualification for all teachers, and a minimum salary towards which it contributes: in all schools which it recognises it controls the curriculum, but allows local variations and extensions. Finally, by its requirements for entry into various professions and into the civil service it influences the whole educational system. There are many defects in Prussian education, but they do not arise from indifference on the part of either the central government or the localities.

SECTION 8

The problem of poor relief in Prussia is greatly simplified by the existence of the system of compulsory insurance against sickness, accident, infirmity, and old age, which was established (for the whole of the German Empire) by Prince Bismarck between 1883 and 1890; and a very brief account of the institution is desirable in this place.[1] *Poor relief.*

Insurance against sickness is compulsory for all work-people engaged in the building trade, mines, quarries, factories, foundries, railways, shipyards, etc., for all such persons as foremen and clerks in these occupations whose salaries do not exceed 2,000 marks a year, and for employés in any other occupation which may be included by order of the Federal Council. The policy adopted has been to encourage the formation of trade, factory, or voluntary societies; but if these should not be formed, or should be insufficient, then the necessary societies are organised by the local authorities; all the societies are carefully supervised by the central government. The employer pays one-third of the contributions, and the workmen two-thirds; the benefits are: (1) free medical treatment and sick pay (one-half of the *Sickness insurance.*

[1] The fullest information as to the laws and regulations of German compulsory insurance, and the most recent statistics are contained in Gotze-Schindler, *Jahrbuch der Arbeiterversicherung,* 2 vols.

average earnings) for twenty-six weeks; or (2) hospital maintenance and one-quarter of the average earnings (the money being paid to the dependents); and funeral money. The societies are managed by committees consisting of representatives of employers and employed in proportion to their respective shares of the contributions. In 1901 the adult working-class population of Germany was estimated at 16,500,000, and of these 10,320,000 (or 62·5 per cent.) were insured in 22,770 societies.

Accident insurance. Insurance against accident is obligatory for all persons employed in the factories, mines, and metallurgical works, railways and shipping, building trades, agriculture and forestry, and other occupations; it includes all employés whose annual salaries do not exceed 3,000 marks. The responsibility for the insurance rests with the employers, who pay the whole of the contributions, and are organised in "professional associations" of mutual liability, which are controlled by the Imperial Insurance Office. For state or municipal industrial undertakings there are special institutions. For the first thirteen weeks after an accident the injured worker is a charge upon his sickness insurance society (if a member of one); if the incapacity for work still continues the burden is transferred to the accident insurance society, and the worker is entitled to (1) free medical aid and a pension amounting to not more than two-thirds of the average salary or wage; or (2) free main-

tenance in an institution, and a smaller pension
paid to dependents. In the case of a fatal accident
there is funeral money, and a pension to the
dependent survivors (including children up to
fifteen years of age); the maximum total pension
is three-fifths of the yearly wage of the deceased.
As the employers provide all the funds, they
naturally alone administer them; but the workers
appoint representatives to take part in the enquiries
into accidents, and to the courts of arbitration
which deal with disputes as to pensions. In 1902
over 19,000,000 persons were covered by this
system.

The present law as to pensions in cases of Infirmity and
old age
infirmity and old age came into force in 1899 pensions.
(ten years after the first legislation on the matter),
and applies to all workmen and apprentices,
ships' crews, and domestic servants, whatever
their salaries; all others engaged in industrial
occupations, and all commercial clerks, teachers,
and tutors, whose salaries do not exceed 2,000
marks;[1] and it may be extended by order of
the Federal Council to other classes. The
obligation to insure begins at sixteen years of
age. Voluntary insurance in the same institutions is allowed to all industrial employés, clerks,
teachers, etc., with salaries of not more than
3,000 marks a year, and to small tradesmen,

---

[1] In any consideration of the figures as to German insurance
the lower standard of wages and salaries (as compared with England)
must be borne constantly in mind.

farmers, and others, who have not exceeded forty years of age at the time of entry. The pension institutions are either " general " or " special "; the former (thirty-one in number) are coincident with the great administrative areas, and include all persons bound to insure, with the exceptions of those dealt with by the nineteen special institutions formed for such large undertakings as railways and mines. Both classes are under the stringent control of the central government. The contributions (where insurance is compulsory) are paid in equal parts by employers and employed; they vary according to average earnings and range from about 1½d. to 3½d. a week, in five grades, and forty contributory weeks are required in each year. A pension for permanent incapacity (defined as inability to earn one-third of the current local rate of wages) resulting from ill-health may be claimed at the end of two hundred weeks; it consists of a state contribution of £2, 10s., together with a fixed minimum sum for each of the five grades, and of from 3 to 12 pfennigs for each contributory week; the minimum is about £5, 16s. 5d. per annum, and the maximum about £20, 15s. 5d. The old age pension can be claimed first at seventy years of age, and consists of a Government grant of £2, 10s., and a fixed additional sum of from £3 to £9 according to grade—the minimum pension being thus £5, 10s. and the maximum £11, 10s. At the beginning of 1902 there were 675,000 persons in receipt of pensions, and about 180,000 of these were for old age.

The great importance of this system, in relation to the general question of poor relief, hardly needs emphasis. The sickness and accident insurance clearly provides a safeguard against one of the most frequent causes of recourse to the poor law authorities; and the infirmity and old age pensions, though they are small, may yet be just large enough to enable the recipient to do without public aid, either because of his own additional resources or through the help of relatives who could not undertake his whole support. Certainly the German officials believe that in this way the burden of the poor law authorities has been, if not diminished, at least prevented from increasing in the same ratio as the population.[1] The insurance societies contribute largely to hospitals and convalescent homes, and maintain entirely a number of institutions of the latter kind; and they have been particularly active in their support of the sanatoria established for consumptives by a national society.[2] Some

[1] " The purpose I have in view is to relieve the communes of a large part of their poor law charges by the establishment of an institution having state support and extending to the entire Empire. . . . I believe that the parishes — especially those over-burdened with poor—and under certain circumstances the Circles also, would experience considerable relief . . . if all persons requiring aid, from such natural causes as incapacity or old age, were to be received into an insurance institution established by the state." Bismarck, 29th March 1889. Cf. Zahn, *Workmen's Insurance and National Economy* (prepared by the German Government for the St Louis Exposition, 1904), p. 26.

[2] Zahn, p. 24. Cf. Bielefeldt, *Workmen's Insurance and National*

M

of the sickness societies (*e.g.*, in Berlin and Magdeburg), inspect workman's dwellings; and many lend from their funds at low rates of interest for the erection of tenements.[1]

Undoubtedly the schemes thus briefly sketched are far from perfect, and in particular the limit of seventy years of age for pensions has been much criticised — though the invalidity pension arrangement removes many of the objections. But as a whole there can be no doubt that the Insurance Laws are working well, and their popularity is evinced by two facts—first, that the Socialists who opposed the original legislation now support it, and, secondly, that plans are being prepared to extend the insurance system by enabling provision to be made for widows and orphans.

Labour bureaux.

Before we pass now to the poor law proper, mention may be made of two pieces of work done by local authorities. One of these is the provision of labour bureaux, founded mainly by the municipalities; in 1902 there were 276 such offices in Prussia, and through their action places were found for 221,000 workmen.[2] And the other is the attempt made in many towns to provide work during the periods of acute economic

Health (prepared for the same purpose as Zahn). The Accident Insurance Societies have been very active also in the making of rules for dangerous trades.

[1] Zahn, p. 25.

[2] Zahn, p. 27.   Attached to the central registry office at Berlin is a "poor man's lawyer," who gives advice gratuitously.

distress, such as the winter of 1902-3. The employment was chiefly on public works, road-making, etc., but in some instances there were efforts to provide suitable occupation for skilled artisans.[1]

The local authorities for poor relief in Prussia are two — the *Landarmenverband* and the *Ortsarmenverband*; the former is usually identical with the province,[2] whilst the latter consists of a commune (town or country) or a manor. The *Landarmenverband* provides or assists institutions for lunatics, imbeciles, epileptics, and for deaf and dumb or blind persons; the cost of maintenance is borne by the *Ortsarmenverband* with contributions of at least two-thirds from the Circles.[3] The *Landarmenverbände* may also come to the aid of the smaller local authorities by grants of money, and by the provision of labour colonies, of which some sixteen have been formed by them. The *Landarmenverband* is administered by a provincial Board, and the cost of the work is divided between the Circles according to the proportion of their shares of state taxation; and the latter also render assistance often by the establishment of hospitals.[4]

The poor law authorities.

(1) Landarmen-verband.

[1] Zahn, p. 28.

[2] In the Province of East Prussia the Circles, and in Hesse Nassau the Government Districts, form the *Landarmenverbände*.

[3] H. de Grais, *Handbuch*, p. 359.

[4] This, as the provision of hospitals in towns, is done by the local authorities as part of the Public Health Administration (*Gesundheits-polizei*).

The *Ortsarmenverband* has the task of general relief, which is either indoor or outdoor, and is administered by a committee of the Communal Council, or in a manor by the lord or his representative. In the rural districts it appears that the arrangements are still far from satisfactory, and the absence of any groupment of the communes renders effective action almost impossible. The smaller ones have no institutions for indoor relief; the larger ones do possess them, but they often provide for the sick only by arrangement with the local doctors, and have no infirmaries. Hence the action of larger authorities already described becomes absolutely necessary. The funds of the *Ortsarmenverband* are derived from gifts and legacies, proceeds of some fines, and a local rate which in a small commune produces very little. For children, orphanages may be established, but it is more usual for the communes, both large and small, to adopt the "boarding out" plan. In many of the manors poor relief is apt to be neglected,[1] and there is no such strong central control or uniform administration as is found in England. It is in the large towns that the organisation for the relief of the poor has taken its most complete and instructive form. There is no limit to the activity of the Town Councils (beyond the occasional necessity for administrative approval); they can do all that they

Poor relief in large towns.

[1] Oertzen, *Armenpflege in Deutschland*, p. 37.

think desirable or necessary. They may provide
or assist hospitals as part of their public health
administration, and frequently do so, and they
may establish orphanages and other homes for
children; and they may adopt practically whatever methods they like both of organisation and
relief. For the purposes of the distribution of
relief the plan now commonly used is what is
known as the Elberfeldt system.

The work is controlled and the financial re- (1) Poor law
sponsibility borne by the Town Council, but the deputation.
administrative work is conducted by a deputation which varies in constitution, but includes
members of the Executive Board and of the
Town Council, and a number of co-opted persons
interested in the problems with which the
deputation has to deal; a member of the
Executive Board presides. It is the task of
this deputation (*e.g.*, in Halle[1]) to determine the
general principles and methods to be adopted,
to supervise hospitals and other institutions, to
guide and superintend the district committees, to
conduct the negotiations (as to the support of
paupers) with other poor law authorities, to
purchase all necessary supplies, and to prepare
an annual budget for presentation to the Town
Council, which votes the necessary funds — or
so much as it thinks proper.

The town is divided into a number of districts (2) The
(23 in Halle with a population of 155,000, and District
Committee.

[1] James, *Municipal Administration in Germany*, pp. 40-41.

over 250 in Berlin) and in each there is a
District Committee, composed of citizens
(now often including women) appointed by the
Town Council; the number of members varies
according to the size of the district. Any
citizen may be appointed by the Town Council;
and if appointed he is bound to serve (under
penalties); it is probably true that there are
cases in which the office is accepted very reluc-
tantly, but these do not appear to be very frequent.
Each committee has a chairman, who is often
(where the committees are not too numerous) a
member of the central deputation; it is his
duty to divide the committee work between the
various members, to supervise their action, and to
keep in constant communication with the central
authority. The committee receives applications for relief, makes the necessary enquiries,
and determines the amount of assistance to be
given; specially difficult cases it refers to the
deputation. The usual plan is for each member
to take charge of a group of streets;[1] and it is
then his duty to enquire into any case arising
there, to report on it to his committee, to act
as almoner, to keep the case under constant
supervision,[2] and to give all the advice and aid

---

[1] "Jede Armen-Kommission bestimmt selbst fur die einzelnen
Mitglieder deren Geschäftskreis, dergestalt, dass die sämmlichen
einzelnen Strassen-theile des Armen-Kommissions-Bezirks unter die
einzelnen Mitglieder, mit Ausnahme des Kommissions-Vorstehers,
geographisch vertheilt werden." *Geschäftsanweisung fur die Armen-
Kommissionen* of Charlottenburg, sec. 4.

[2] "Die Armenpfleger haben die ihnen übertragenen Untersuchung

in his power. The great objects aimed at are
the avoidance of hard and fast routine methods
of enquiry, security that the investigation shall
be made by persons who are not so overburdened
with cases as to be unable to give much time
and attention to each, and the use of the local
knowledge and services of persons who are
likely to be regarded by the poor as neighbours
rather than as officials. Of course this calls for
a great number of voluntary workers (or at
least unpaid workers), but these are in most
cases readily forthcoming.[1] In many towns the
local charitable associations combine to establish
a central information office, to which each sends
a list of its cases, so as to avoid over-lapping,
and to spread information as to imposters and
their methods; and this union is generally in
close communication with the town poor law
deputation.

The aim of the poor law administration is Institutions.
to deal with the cases of "deserving" poor, so
far as possible, by out-door relief, and to provide

vorzunehmen . . . die bewilligten monatlichen Unterstützungen
auszuzahlen, und sind verpflichtet, regelmässig einmal im Monat alle
laufend unterstützten Personen ihres Reviers aufzusuchen, und sich
über ihre Verhältnisse unterrichten. Sie haben den Armen mit Rath
und That zur Seite zu stehen." *Geschäftsanweisung fur die Armen-
Kommissionen* of Charlottenburg, sec. 7.

[1] There seems no obvious reason why, in any reform of the English
poor law administration, the services of the great number of philanthropic workers in the English large towns should not be placed at
the disposal of the Guardians far more than they are at present.
The widespread committees of the Charity Organisation Society, for
example, could render great service in this way.

almshouses and infirmaries for the aged and permanently infirm who could not receive proper care (for lack of relatives or other reasons) in their own homes. For the children there are, as already mentioned, orphanages either maintained or aided by the towns, or more usually the boarding-out system, and in some cases (*e.g.*, Dantzic, Berlin, Frankfurt) there are municipal deaf and dumb asylums. The towns may set up asylums for all the same classes of " defectives " as the provinces, if they choose to do so and have the means. Workhouses may be erected, but many of the great towns and provinces (for the rural districts) have established labour colonies,[1] and in some of these provision is made for two classes of workers, the genuine workman out of employment, and those who are in poverty clearly through their own misconduct. The latter are kept apart, so far as possible, from the deserving poor, and may be detained for periods usually of not less than six months or more than two years ; when discharged they are given clothing and a small sum of money to start them on their way again, and they are also brought into relations with private benevolent agencies, which undertake to

[1] The first labour colony in Prussia was founded near Bielefeld in 1882. Between that date and the end of 1897 the labour colonies had received 98,622 men, and discharged 95,615. The main object is to train what may be called the "shiftless and idle" class in habits of industry, but this end seems scarcely to have been attained—a very large proportion of those discharged come back again and again.

watch and assist them so far as practicable. The best known instance of an institution of this kind is the Berlin "House of Correction" at Rümmelsburg; persistent disorderly persons, beggars, etc., may be drafted there by order of the poor law authorities, and kept there for from six months to two years; the house is near to the lands gradually being reclaimed by the Berlin municipality in connection with its sewage disposal system, and the persons committed to it are employed partly on those lands and partly in gangs on other farms in the neighbourhood, or on the roads. They are kept under strict supervision; and receive a small wage of which they may spend a portion, the remainder being retained by the authorities until discharge. For the old or permanently infirm of this class there are special institutions.[1]

The towns also establish night shelters of both the municipal lodging-house and casual ward type; but in the former there is in some instances (as at Berlin) provision for homeless families. There is generally a restriction on the amount of use which may be made of these shelters, unless reasonable cause can be shown against it.

On the whole it must be said that the Prussian system of poor relief is admirable in

---

[1] For a recent and enthusiastic account of the poor law institutions of Berlin, see *The Brass Workers of Berlin and Birmingham; a Comparison* (1905), pp. 56-82.

the large towns, obtains excellent results, and might with advantage be copied in some respects by England; that the work of the provincial organisations is also satisfactory so far as it goes; but that in the small country districts it is by no means all that could be desired, and is in fact far inferior to the poor law administration in the rural parts of England.

It should be added that disputes between areas as to the responsibility for relief are decided by the District Committee sitting as an administrative court, with appeal to the *Bundesamt für Heimatwesen* in Berlin, which was established to settle disputes on this point between different states of the Empire, but was recognised by Prussia as a court of appeal for cases arising within that kingdom.

CHAPTER IV

THE GOVERNMENT OF AMERICAN CITIES

SECTION 1

THE municipalities of the United States present a remarkable diversity of organisation, due mainly to the fact that local government is a matter for each separate state, and therefore offers opportunities for the experiments of some fifty distinct legislatures. But in spite of considerable differences in detail, during recent years American city constitutions have tended towards a uniformity of type, and show some common characteristics. *Some characteristic features.*

The first of these is the municipal independence of all control except that exercised by the legislature, and enforced by the Courts of Justice. In the separate states of the Union the state executive is very weak, and possesses practically no authority whatever over the "cities" (a term applied to all municipalities in America, whatever their size); and the result of the absence of any strong central department is that the legislatures find or think it necessary to try to provide in the municipal law for all possible contingencies, and to work out the minutest details. So in the *(i) Legislative control.*

municipal codes of the United States there is
not only an elaborate and very detailed specifica-
tion of the powers to be exercised by the
municipal authorities, but generally the organisation of various branches of the civic administration is carefully determined and regulated.[1] As
the cities vary greatly in size, it may be
undesirable to grant the same powers to all, or
to impose an absolutely uniform system throughout a state, and so in most cases the plan has
been adopted of dividing the cities of each state
into a number of groups according to population,
and then legislating for each group separately.
But it is impossible to foresee all the possible
requirements of urban populations, and all the
powers which municipal authorities may find it
desirable to possess, and so (as in England,
where the same method of "specific grants of
power" is employed), the cities constantly have
recourse to the state parliaments for fresh legislation. There, however, they are encountered by
the frequent prohibition (in state constitutions)
of all "special legislation," i.e., legislation affecting any one local authority.[2] The usual method

[1] Many regulations as to city government, and restrictions upon
the powers of municipal authorities, are imposed not in ordinary
legislative enactments, but in the state constitutions; and the use
of this method of control has rapidly increased in recent years, as
the state constitutions are frequently revised.

[2] E.g., Constitution of Pennsylvania, III., sect. 7: "The general
assembly shall not pass any local or special law regulating the
affairs of counties, cities, townships, wards, boroughs, or school
districts, creating offices or prescribing the powers and duties of

of evading this is an adaptation of the classification system[1]—the law courts have shown themselves ready to accept as a general law (thus
coming within the constitution), a statute applying to a class of cities so defined as to include
in fact only a single city.[2] This constant legislation for particular cities far exceeds anything
with which we are acquainted in England, since it
applies not merely to powers, but to organisation,
and is often directed even against the cities. A
distinguished American student of civic administration writes:—

" Charters and charters amendments are passed
[by the state legislatures] not only without public
and local discussion, but also, in many cases, against
the wishes of the local officials and local members
of the legislature. Sometimes such legislation
has had, ostensibly at least, the immediate object
of remedying some municipal delinquency; but
in many cases the most effective motive has been
to secure some partisan advantage for those in
control of the state government, when the city
officers belong to another political organisation;
whilst in some instances such legislation has been
enacted through the worst kind of political
jobbery, to confer privileges which could not be
secured from the local authorities. By such
means acts have been passed substituting state

officers in counties, cities, or boroughs; . . . . nor indirectly enact
such law by the repeal of a general law." A similar clause appears
in the constitutions of about half the states.

[1] *Vide infra*, p. 332.
[2] In 1902, however, the Supreme Court of Ohio reversed its
previous decisions, and held that enactments applying nominally to
a class, but in reality to only a single city, are unconstitutional.

appointed officials for local officers, compelling
cities to carry out expensive and unnecessary
undertakings, and granting franchises in the
public streets with little or no compensation to
the city. The legislatures of New York,
Pennsylvania, Ohio, and Missouri, have been most
active in these methods of interference; but
instances are not lacking in Massachusetts,
Illinois, Michigan, and other states." [1]

Various attempts have been made to check
this kind of abuse, and two of the experiments
are of considerable interest. The first is the
provision in the constitution of the State of
New York, which divides the cities into three
classes, and provides that any legislation not
applying to all the cities in any class must be
submitted to the authorities of the cities concerned, and if disapproved by them, can come
into force only if passed by the legislature a
second time. More important is the plan known
as "municipal home rule," whereby cities are
allowed to frame their own charters within the
limits prescribed by the state constitutions. Thus
under the Missouri Constitution of 1875, in cities of
over 100,000 inhabitants a Board of thirteen persons
may be elected to draw up a charter, which must
then be submitted to popular vote, and receive
four-sevenths of the votes cast. [2] This method

---

[1] J. A. Fairlie, "Problems of City Government" in *Annals of the
American Academy*, xxvii. 1, p. 146. The most notorious recent instance
is the overthrow of the city government of Pittsburg by the Pennsylvania legislature in 1901, mainly in the interests of a political
party.

[2] Fairlie, *loc. cit.*, pp. 148-149.

has been adopted in several states for much
smaller cities, and is recommended by the
reforming National Municipal League for all
cities with not less than 25,000 inhabitants. The
arrangement checks legislative interference, but it
tends to make American municipal law still more
confused, and might be so used as seriously to
diminish state sovereignty.[1]

The next most striking feature in municipal (ii) "Separa-
organisation in the United States is the tendency tion of
to reproduce the principles and methods of the powers.
federal and state governments, and particularly
that separation of the legislative and executive
authorities which is so prominent a feature of
American constitutions. The general movement
of American civic government in recent years
has been to make the Mayor independent of the
council, and to entrust to him alone the conduct
of the city administration, just as the President
is the sole responsible executive officer of the
United States. There is another method, by
which not only the Mayor, but also the heads
of the various executive departments are elected
by popular vote; but this, which is an imitation
of the way in which the state executives are
commonly formed, produces the same evils of

[1] The "platform" of the Cleveland City Democratic Convention
in 1901 contained the demand "that in place of the present legislative interference in matters of purely local concern, we should have
municipal home rule, to the end that bond issues, local taxation, and
the granting of local franchises, may be submitted to a direct vote of
the people."

divided responsibility, and the municipal reformers of America are agreed in advocating the sole responsibility of the popularly elected Mayor, appointing his own subordinates.

The general line of development is perhaps best illustrated by the municipal history of Philadelphia.[1] Under the charter of 1789 (as amended in 1796), the Mayor was elected by the city councillors from the ranks of the " aldermen " (magistrates appointed by the governor of the state); then in 1826 the council's range of choice was extended to include the whole body of freemen; and, finally, in 1839, the right of election passed to the freemen themselves. From 1799 to 1839 the Mayor appointed to all salaried municipal offices, but in the latter year the power to make such appointments passed back to the councils; and in fact up to 1854 the councils were steadily extending their authority over the administration both by the appointment of officers and by the growth of " the committee system." The city councils of Philadelphia were approximating to the type with which we are familiar in England, but this was a violation of the principles of political science as understood in the United States.[2] The Consolida-

[1] Allinson and Penrose, *Municipal History of Philadelphia, passim.*

[2] "If there is one thing in the history of this period which stands out more clearly defined than any other, it is the trend of the policy exercised by councils of vesting more and more the executive duties in the hands of committees of their own body, thus confounding the true theory of republican policy, which should tend to keep the line between these two arms of government sharply defined. . . . All

tion Act of 1854 made the Mayor much more powerful, and weakened the councils; the Mayor, elected by general vote of the citizens, was empowered to veto any resolutions of the city councils; he had control of the police and of the general administration; the councils could appoint committees to supervise the work of the various departments, and to report on particular matters, but under express directions "to perform no executive acts." But the councils persisted in their efforts to secure complete control[1] until in 1887 the new constitution (for cities of the first class, which includes only Philadelphia) carefully confined the councils to deliberative functions, and placed the actual administration in the hands of the Mayor and officers partly appointed by him, and partly elected by popular vote.[2]

history teaches us that the constant tendency of all legislative bodies is to absorb, when unchecked, executive, and even judicial functions. We see this every day at Washington, and the integrity of our political system demands that it be jealously watched and sternly checked." Allinson and Penrose, pp. 124-125.

[1] "It had been already intended by the Act of 1854 that the councils of Philadelphia should confine themselves to their legislative duties; and they were specially prohibited by Section 50 of the Consolidation Act from performing any executive duties whatever, whether as committees or as councils. This injunction was disregarded in practice. Councils usurped all powers, legislative, executive, and visitorial. The executive arm of government was the system of "government by committees." . . . The system was thoroughly and inherently bad. As an attempt at organisation it was ill-fitted in principle and outgrown in practice. It was contrary to the theory of scientific government, against the weight of experience, and in bold defiance of common sense."—Allinson and Penrose, p. 169.

[2] Since 1887 there has been a growing tendency to transfer the appointment of some of the heads of departments from the Mayor to the councils.

N

Another illustration of this development is furnished by Chicago, where

"the election of the Mayor passed from the council to the people, and became the starting-point in the separation of executive and legislative functions. . . . With each succeeding charter, the position of the Mayor was strengthened by the addition of new powers taken from the council. Although the common council remains to-day as the central fact in the municipality of Chicago, the theory of executive concentration has been consistently followed out until the Mayor is possessed of the responsible powers of the direction and supervision of the administration, as well as of appointment and veto. He has been given many financial and legislative powers formerly exercised by the council, which places this body in a weakened position. . . . The chasm that separates the Mayor and council is partially bridged on the one hand by the executive veto of the ordinances of the municipal legislature, and on the other hand by legislative confirmation of the appointments of the executive. These checks, designed to create harmony in administration and to restrain hasty action in appointment and legislation, have reared two almost independent organs appealing for popular favour." [1]

The reasons for the adoption of this policy seem to be two in number. There is first the strong influence exercised upon American political thought by the federal constitution, which in spite of defects arising from the extreme application of the doctrine of "the separation of powers" does

[1] Sparling, *Municipal History of Chicago*, pp. 12-13.

on the whole work well. But it hardly seems
probable that it would have been so closely copied
in American municipal government but for the
unfortunate state into which that had fallen. Many
of the cities suffered, and continue to suffer, from
extremely corrupt and inefficient administration,[1]
due partly to the undisputed sway of national
political parties and the prevalence of the "spoils
system" in local affairs, and partly to the consequent disinclination of the best class of citizens
to enter municipal life. It was believed that the
only remedy for both corruption and mismanagement was to take the administration away from
the councils and entrust it to a single person
elected by popular vote, independent of the
councils and able to keep them in check, and
bearing the whole responsibility before the citizens.
It is difficult to say how far the plan has succeeded.
In some cases a good mayor has been elected, but
he has not always succeeded in carrying out many
reforms, and unfortunately the civic enthusiasm
which has carried the reformers to power has
hitherto been very intermittent, though there are
now signs of distinct improvement. When on the
other hand the administration of a city is concentrated in the hands of a representative of a party
which is not scrupulous in its methods, the last
state of that city is likely to be worse than the

---

[1] Corruption and inefficiency, however, do not always go together;
a corrupt administration is often astute enough to give a city at
least an appearance of good government.

first.[1] But it is noteworthy that the municipal reformers of the United States still support the policy, and that must be taken to mean that on the whole they are satisfied with the results so far obtained.

(iii) Influence of the Federal Constitution. The parallel between the Federal Constitution of United States and the Municipal Constitution of Philadelphia is so curious that it merits a brief summary. The President is elected by popular vote for four years ; so is the Mayor. There are two Houses of Congress—the Senate, consisting of two members for each state of the Union, and the House of Representatives, elected according to population ; the city council of Philadelphia has two chambers, the Select Council composed of an equal number of members for each ward, and the Common Council elected by the wards according to population. The President communicates with Congress by message, and the Mayor communicates with the councils in the same way ; the President may veto any law passed by Congress, and the Mayor has a similar veto upon ordinances passed by the councils—in each case the veto may be over-ridden by a two-thirds vote. The President's appointments to the chief executive offices must be approved by the Senate, and the Mayor's principal appointments (so far as he has that power) require confirmation by the Select Council. Finally, the President can be impeached by the

[1] Eaton, *Government of Municipalities*, pp. 257-285. This writer is a strong opponent of the theory of " autocratic mayors."

House of Representatives before the Senate, and the Mayor can be impeached by the Common Council before the Select Council; and in each case the only penalty seems to be dismissal from office.[1]

Reference has already been made to one other characteristic feature of American city government —the influences exercised in local affairs by the national political parties. Attempts have constantly been made in England to identify national and municipal parties, but they have not been very successful; in the United States the process has gone very much further, and the party machine rules almost undisputed.[2] This is largely due to the application to municipal government of the "spoils system," or rather the existence of a host of municipal services with which they could reward their faithful followers made the party leaders anxious to secure control of the city governments and to turn them into party possessions.[3] The

(iv) Influence of political parties.

[1] For an account of the organisation of the City of Philadelphia see James (ed.) *Municipal Government of Philadelphia*, which needs to be brought up to date by reference to subsequent legislation.

[2] The remark of Edmonds on "The Recent Reform Movement in Philadelphia" in the *Annals of the American Academy*, Vol. XXVII. 1, p. 183, is instructive. The city government was entirely in the hands of the Republican machine, and (speaking of the reformers) he observes that "equally strong was the element which had hitherto been deterred from political" (*i.e.*, municipal) "action by the fear that in so doing they would unsettle the system of protective tariffs, which has been a potent factor in the development of Pennsylvania's industrial resources. The re-election of Mr Roosevelt, however, convinced many honest Republicans that an attack could be made upon the local machine without in any way disturbing the economic policies of the nation."

[3] "The organisation is the term popularly applied to the

consequences of this have been, however, so disastrous as to call into existence the numerous non-
party organisations which call themselves "municipal
leagues" and aim at abolishing the influence of
national political parties in civic affairs, and destroying the "spoils system"; they have a very difficult
and uphill task, since they come into conflict with
both the highly - organised national parties, but
there is now evidence that their work is beginning
to bear fruit.[1]

SECTION 2

The City Executive. The head of the city executive is the Mayor,[2]
always elected by vote of the whole body of

irresponsible governing agency which, unknown to either law or
constitution, has absolutely controlled the political destinies of
Philadelphia during the past decade. Its backbone consisted of the
fifteen thousand office-holders—municipal, state, and federal—who
in one way or another draw salaries from the public purse in ex-
change for public services. With the election to the mayoralty of
the Hon. Samuel H. Ashbridge in 1899, every department was
made tributary to its influence; its representatives and agents
were to be found in every one of the eleven hundred wards of the
city. No one could hope to receive public employment unless his
application was *viséd* by his division leader and ward boss."
Edmonds, *loc. cit.*, p. 180. The similar organisation of "Tammany"
at New York is probably more familiar to English readers.

[1] On American city government see Bryce, *American Commonwealth*
cc. l.-lii. ; Goodnow, *Municipal Problems* and *Municipal Home Rule* ;
Eaton, *Government of Municipalities* ; Fairlie, *Municipal Administration* ;
and the Quarterly Review entitled *Municipal Affairs*, published by
the Reform Club of New York.

[2] The "Act for the government of cities of the second class"
(Pittsburg, Scranton and Alleghany), passed by the Pennsylvania
State Legislature in 1901, abolished the office of Mayor and replaced
that officer by a Recorder, who is only the Mayor under another
name and armed with larger powers.

citizens, and holding office for a term ranging
from one year (in many small cities) and two
years (in New York, Boston, Brooklyn, Chicago,
San Francisco, and numerous other cases) to four
years, as in Philadelphia, St Louis, and Baltimore;
where the Mayor has the responsibility of con-
ducting the whole administration it is obviously
desirable that there should be a fairly long tenure
of office, to enable him to carry out to completion
any policy which he may inaugurate. In most
large cities, and in many small ones, he receives
a salary which varies in amount up to $10,000,
or in a very few instances $15,000. In the
smaller municipalities it is customary for the
Mayor to preside over the meetings of the city
council; and he does so in a few large cities, such
as Chicago and Providence. Elsewhere the Mayor (a) The
Mayor.
has no such connection with the council, but only
communicates with it by message from time to
time, reporting on the condition of the administration and recommending the enactment of such
ordinances as he may deem necessary or desirable.
In numerous cases, both of large and small cities,
the Mayor may veto resolutions passed by the
council; to come into force despite this they
must be re-enacted by a two-thirds or even larger
vote (in New York a five-sixths vote is necessary).
It may be added that the municipal government
of the federal capital, Washington, is in the hands
of commissioners appointed by the President; the
inhabitants have no voice in it whatsoever.

(b) Other officials.

The mayoral powers of appointment to salaried municipal offices vary greatly. On the one hand, " in many small cities, and in some of considerable size (the latter mostly in New England and Ohio), the Mayor has even yet little or no appointing power, and no effective means of controlling the other officials," [1] who are often elected by general vote. On the other hand, in Baltimore the Mayor appoints the heads of all departments except the comptroller, who is elected by the citizens in order that he may be an independent check upon the financial administration ; the appointments must be approved by the Select Council (usually as a matter of course), and are for the same period as the Mayor's tenure of office ; the departmental heads themselves appoint their subordinates. In New York, Albany, Boston, Buffalo, Cleveland, and elsewhere the Mayor's appointments do not require even confirmation by the council. Between these two extremes there are many different arrangements ; in a large number of instances the Mayor makes some appointments, and others are filled by popular election ; [2] in a few cases some of the appointments are made by the city councils. The tendency on the whole seems to be towards the concentration in the Mayor of

[1] Fairlie, pp. 140-141.

[2] "In St Louis the following administrative officials are elective, and hold office for four years : the Comptroller, the Treasurer, the Auditor, the Register, the Collector of Revenues, the Marshal, the Inspector of Weights and Measures, the Board of Assessors (consisting of a President and ten District Assessors), and the Coroner." Fairlie, *Municipal Administration*, p. 402.

all responsibility, and therefore of all powers of appointment (except in the case of the comptroller, who is almost everywhere elected); the attempts at Philadelphia to transfer appointments from the Mayor to the councils in joint session are apparently exceptional. Where the Mayor has the almost sole power of appointing (and generally of dismissing) municipal officers his authority is very great, and if he is the representative, as is generally the case, of a party organisation, the effect is far from good. In approving a Bill, which in 1905 transferred certain appointments from the Mayor of Philadelphia to the councils, the Governor of the State of Pennsylvania wrote:—

The "mayoral autocracy."

"The most thoughtful observers, and those most familiar with the practical difficulties of the subject, would probably concede that it would be better for the administration of public affairs in Philadelphia if the power which is given by existing laws to the Mayor, could be, in certain directions at least, lessened. He has, in effect, absolute control over the contracts for all the public work, over an army of police and attendants, and over all the affairs of the municipality. He, in substance, has the appointment of officials, of greater or less importance, estimated to be in number from seven thousand to twelve thousand. If this great authority could be exercised intelligently, and only as a trust for the good of the people, it would undoubtedly be the best system of government; but if, unfortunately, it should fall into corrupt or even incapable hands it would prove to be the very worst."

202 GOVERNMENT OF AMERICAN CITIES [CHAP. IV.

The unfortunate condition of affairs suggested in this last sentence has not infrequently come about; but the National Municipal League is nevertheless convinced that the supremacy of the Mayor is the most desirable plan, partly for reasons already indicated, and partly because if, as sometimes happens, a reforming mayor is elected he can carry out his policy unhampered by the councils or by practically independent officials. It is defended also by reformers and anti-reformers alike, on the ground that where the Mayor is given so responsible a position, where he represents the executive over against the councils and the citizens, it is only right that he should have a very full measure of control over all the administrative departments.

The "Mayor's cabinet." In order to secure in any case some co-ordination of the various departments of the municipal administration there has grown up a system under which the various heads meet from time to time in consultation under the presidency of the Mayor. A typical example is furnished by the second-class cities of Pennsylvania, where the law directs that the " city recorder " (as the head of the executive is styled there)

" shall call together the heads of departments for consultation and advice upon the affairs of the city at least once a month, and at such meetings he may call on the heads of departments for such reports as to the subject matters under their control as he may deem proper, which it shall be their duty to prepare and submit at once to the city recorder. Records shall be kept of such meetings; and rules and regulations shall be adopted thereat for the administration of the affairs of the city departments not inconsistent with any law or ordinance."[1]

The same arrangement has been recently made general for the cities of Indiana and New York State, and seems likely to be widely adopted. It clearly has many advantages, and is in fact an absolute necessity where the Mayor is not given complete control; and it will be observed that under such conditions the municipal " cabinet," discussing policy and authorised to make rules and regulations, is approximating to the Administrative Board of the German cities. Even where the arrangement has not been carried so far, departments which are in any way connected are often grouped together, and the heads meet at intervals for consultative purposes.

In some cases the departments are under single directors, in others there are Boards. There is no uniform policy in this respect, but though in most cases the Board system is partially in force the other method has gradually become predominant. Thus in Chicago, education, fire-brigade, police, public health, water supply, and drainage, were all under elected Boards until 1867; in that year the appointment of the Boards was given to the Mayor; and then in 1876 they began to be replaced by single commissioners.[2]

[1] Act of 1901, Part I., sec. 1.   [2] Sparling, p. 96.

In most cases the Boards are small in number, and they seem now to exist chiefly for education, parks, water supply, and charities; sometimes they are chosen by the Mayor, sometimes by the council, or by popular vote.

Education authorities. The diversity which is so remarkable a feature of American city systems may be illustrated by an account of the various ways in which school authorities are constituted. There is generally a School Board, and in Boston, Cleveland, Detroit, St Louis, Denver, and other cities, it is directly elected. But in New York, Baltimore, Chicago, St Paul, and San Francisco it is nominated by the Mayor; in New Orleans eight members are appointed by the governor of the state, and twelve by the city council; at Milwaukee the Mayor appoints four commissioners, who then appoint the School Board; at Charleston six members are directly elected, and four appointed by the state governor; whilst at Philadelphia the Board is appointed by the Judges of the Court of Common Pleas of Pennsylvania, and is assisted by elected local committees. At Buffalo the schools are controlled directly by the City Council. Under the Board there is usually a superintendent of schools, who is the chief executive officer; he is commonly appointed by the Board, but at Buffalo and San Francisco he is elected by the citizens. In some instances (Cincinnati, St Louis, Pittsburg, Minneapolis, and elsewhere) the Board levies its own taxes within limits prescribed by state law; in others the municipal authorities raise the amounts which the Boards require; and in still other cases (even where, as in Boston, Detroit, and Rochester, the Boards are popularly elected) they can only expend such sums as the city councils may think fit to vote after consideration of estimates submitted by the Boards.[1]

SECTION 3

In all the smaller cities the Council consists of a single chamber, and this is the case also in a number of the larger municipalities, such as Chicago, New Orleans, Cleveland, Detroit, and Milwaukee; but Philadelphia, St Louis, Boston, Baltimore, St Paul, and a few others have adopted the bicameral system, whilst New York has recently abandoned it.[2] The members of the single chamber, or of the lower house, where there are two, are usually elected by wards, and hold their seats for one year in Boston and elsewhere, two years in most cases, and four years in the exceptional instance of New Orleans. The members of an upper house are elected sometimes by the same electoral districts as the ordinary councillors (but in smaller numbers),

The City Councils.

(i) Organisation.

[1] *Special Reports of Board of Education*, Vol. X., pp. 257-261.
[2] The two chambers are usually called "select" and "common." Where there is only one chamber its members are often styled aldermen; in other cases the title is given to members of the Select Council.

sometimes by larger areas, and sometimes on what is known as a "general ticket";[1] they are chosen for two, three, or (in St Louis) four years. There is no uniformity of proportion between the numbers in the two chambers; and the size of the councils varies greatly. Philadelphia has much the largest municipal assembly in America, with forty-two select and one hundred and sixty-one common councillors; New York, on the other hand, which has a very much larger population, has only seventy-two members in its single chamber. Generally it is a rule that the members of both chambers must be resident not only in the city but even in the ward for which they are elected, and this restriction is believed by many observers to have exercised a distinctly unfavourable influence upon the composition of the councils;[2] whilst the widely-accepted doctrine that municipal offices should be enjoyed by as many citizens as possible (of course of the predominant party) has produced in many cases rapid changes of membership and consequently the same lack of continuity as is shown (for the same reasons) by the lower houses of the federal and state legislatures. Occasionally the councillors are paid, receiving either a fixed annual sum or so much for each meeting attended.

[1] This corresponds to the French *scrutin de liste*, as opposed to the *scrutin d'arrondissement*.

[2] A plan much favoured by some reformers, and adopted in a few instances, is to have, in addition to the ward members, a few elected by the city "at large."

(ii) Character.

It is a matter of common repute that the city councils of the United States are far from satisfactory, and that their average composition is decidedly lower than is customary in English, Prussian, or French councils.[1] But the corruption and inefficiency of the councils of American cities as a whole have been somewhat exaggerated;[2] there are some very bad examples undoubtedly, but they are chiefly in a small number of great cities, and, on the other hand, there are a large number of smaller municipalities where the administration, though far from perfect, is at least not open to the charge of corruption. But it is true that the conditions of American municipal life do give abundant opportunities for the free play of evil influences. Reference has already been made to the rule of the party system and of "machine politics" in municipal elections, and the deterrent effect of this upon many of the better class of citizens. To an English observer, also, it would seem probable that the limitation of the work of the councils to deliberation and control, their exclusion from all share in the actual administration, and their comparative weakness over against the "mayoral autocracy" must tend to restrain able and energetic men from offering their services; but it may be that this particular argument has little weight

---

[1] Cf. Eaton, cc., xii.-xiii.

[2] Most of the literature on this subject with which English readers are familiar is written by the reformers of various schools, who in making out their case naturally seize upon the weak points.

with the ordinary American citizen, accustomed as he is to see the same careful distinction between deliberative and executive functions maintained in the federal and state governments as well as in the cities. However this may be, the dominance of the party organisation, with its not very scrupulous or refined methods, and the frame of mind which regards municipal office of any kind as part of the "spoils," together with the conditions as to residential qualification, do tend to place in the councils a considerable number of members who are susceptible to illicit influences, especially those of commercial companies struggling to get monopolistic concessions within the municipal areas.

(iii) Powers. It has already been pointed out that it is becoming more and more frequent for the councils to be debarred from any participation in the actual conduct of city administration; but this is true in the main only of the large cities. In the small municipalities the organisation and working of the councils are much the same as in the English corporate towns; some of the officials are directed and supervised by the councils as a whole, whilst others are under the control of committees. Very generally the appointment and dismissal of municipal officers (where they are not elected by the citizens) require the approval of the council. Where the separation of administrative and deliberative functions has been adopted, the work of the council is merely legislative; it

votes supplies (where there are two chambers
financial proposals must usually originate only
in the lower chamber) and passes ordinances for
the good government of the city; it may appoint
committees and sub-committees, but their duties
are simply to watch the work of particular departments, and to consider and report upon matters
referred to them by the councils. The exercise
of the ordinance power is hampered in various
ways; not only is it confined to subjects specified
in the municipal codes, but even in these cases
it is often subject to restrictions contained sometimes in general laws, but more frequently in the
state constitutions themselves.[1] Further, it is liable
to the Mayor's veto; and sometimes the ordinance
power in important matters is actually withheld
from the councils and given to administrative
Boards (*e.g.*, for police, parks, charities, etc.); and
finally, the right to organise administrative departments is often very limited in effect, since the
municipal codes contain the most elaborate
provisions for these matters. Conflicts between
the Mayor and the council are not infrequent,
but the Mayor is commonly in the stronger
position, and unless there is a sufficient majority
to over-rule him always, or the council is willing
to take the responsibility of refusing to vote the
necessary supplies, it is apt to sink into comparative insignificance.

A word must be said as to one particular Municipal
policy.

[1] For illustrations of this, *vide infra*, pp. 330-2 and 359-361.

o

group of municipal activities—known in England as "municipal trading." The policy of municipalisation has so far made but little headway in the United States. There we find "no city owning and operating its own tramways and street railways, probably less than half-a-dozen manufacturing gas, a very few engaged in supplying electric light."[1] But, on the other hand, the water supply is usually in the hands of the city councils; gas is supplied by private companies "at prices generally regulated by the state legislatures"; and in the case of tramways a system has been adopted in Boston and New York of making subways and then leasing them, "in which cases the municipalities insure themselves a net revenue for certain undertakings, by leasing to responsible private companies the subways for a series of years at a rate of interest from 1 to $1\frac{1}{2}$ per cent. higher than the city pays for the actual money expended on the undertaking; reserving as additional security a bond, and the entire equipment, to insure the public treasury against public losses." One reason for the very slow advance of municipal ownership in the United States is the debt limit fixed for municipalities, sometimes by ordinary laws and

[1] This, and the following quotations, are from a paper read to the British Association by Mr R. P. Porter in 1902. The *Fourteenth Annual Report of the U.S Commissioner of Labour* (1900) gives the following figures: Water supplies, 1,539 private, 1,787 municipal: gas undertakings, 951 private, 14 public; electric light undertakings, 2,572 private, 460 public.

sometimes by the state constitutions, which commonly make no distinction between renumerative and unremunerative enterprises. These enactments were the outcome of the financial mismanagement and disasters, not confined to the cities, of the middle of the nineteenth century. A second cause is the discredit into which so many of the American city governments have fallen, and the consequent disinclination to entrust to them large commercial undertakings and much wider patronage; and a third cause is the tremendous political power of the private companies. The result has been that hitherto, after a period in which rights and privileges within the municipal boundaries were granted to private enterprises almost without conditions of any kind, the municipal authorities have adopted the policy of granting the "franchises" for varying terms of years on specified conditions—payment of a rental, frequency and quality of service, limitation of charges, etc.; that is, they preferred control to ownership with financi ,ponsibility. But there is a growing moveme in favour of municipalisation, partly on general grounds, and partly because some of the reformers believe that the perils of corruption would be less than they are under the present system when rival companies are struggling to secure these municipal "franchises," which are in fact monopolies, and are not scrupulous in the methods which they employ to attain their object.

Municipal
reform.

Though the machinery of city government in the United States strikes an English observer as often unnecessarily cumbrous, yet the actual difficulties of working are neither so frequent nor so great as might be supposed. And the stories of corruption and inefficient administration should not be allowed to obscure the fact that the American municipal administrators are doing very much valuable, and in some respects pioneer, work.[1] The problems of the government of large urban areas are much the same all over the world, and there are no great differences between the public services required. With all their admitted defects, and in face of considerable indifference (until recent years) on the part of the best classes of the community, the municipal governments of the United States have made substantial progress; much good work is being done by a great number of students of city organisation both in Europe and America itself; the active propaganda of the various reform associations is bringing into existence a strong public opinion and a keen interest in the doings of the municipal authorities, and these are the first essentials of reform.

[1] Cf. Zueblin, *American Municipal Progress*.

CHAPTER V

THE HISTORY OF LOCAL ADMINISTRATION IN ENGLAND SINCE 1832.

SECTION 1

ALMOST all the historians and writers who have discussed the constitutional development of England have emphasised the fact that our parliamentary institutions have been so successful, in comparison with those of other states, mainly because they are the crown of a system of self-government, which in one form or another is as old as the nation itself, and has become an integral part of the national life. But once established, Parliament soon concentrated upon itself the greater part of the attention of the English people; and the gradual break-up of the old social organisation, resulting from the changes in economic conditions, brought about a steady decline in the effectiveness of the institutions of local government. The work of local administration was carried on, but without arousing any general interest — except in the disastrous instance of the Poor Laws—on the part of the community; "self - government"

Parliament and local institutions.

213

came to mean the rule of an ever smaller class,[1] until in the eighteenth century local institutions were as oligarchic as Parliament itself, and much less representative of public opinion.

The periods of reform.   The course of development was now reversed; political progress was to be made first in regard to parliamentary institutions, and afterwards in the sphere of local government. When the economic and social changes which followed in the train of the industrial revolution of the second half of the eighteenth century made reform absolutely necessary, it was in Parliament that the example was set. The two great constructive periods in the modern history of English local government followed as inevitable consequences upon the parliamentary reform of 1832 and the extension of the franchise to the great body of the rural population in 1884.[2] The Reform Act of 1867 did not bring quite such elaborate changes in its train; but it was followed by the establishment of a system of national education, and a greater activity in local government.

England in 1832.
(i) The Justices.   Up to the year 1832 the rural portions of

[1] "Its leading features (in the period between the Reformation and the Reform Act) are the foundation and abnormal growth of the Poor Laws; the progressive extension of magistrates' jurisdiction in counties; and the decay of municipal institutions in boroughs." Brodrick in Cobden Club's *Local Government in the United Kingdom* (1882), p. 8.

[2] "The English system of local administration represents the direct influence of the political and social ideas of democracy upon the organisation and functions of government." Redlich and Hirst, *Local Government in England*, I., p. 23.

England were administered by the country
gentlemen and clergy, who served as Justices
of the Peace. Under various forms their
authority dated back for nearly five centuries,
to the reign of Edward III.; and during that
period they had gradually drawn into their
hands almost all county affairs. In Petty
and Quarter Sessions they exercised judicial
functions defined by commissions whose forms
had been settled in the reign of Elizabeth;
and besides this innumerable statutes had
entrusted to them nearly the whole administrative work of the county. They were appointed
by the Crown, chiefly from the ranks of the
smaller landowners and rural clergy; the lay
justices were usually men of little education;
they were not very enterprising, but there
seems to have been little dissatisfaction with
their rule; and the office provided active men
with considerable experience and training in the
conduct of affairs.

The sole important division of the county The parish.
was the civil or "poor law" parish, which was
usually identical with the ecclesiastical parish,[1]
though the latter was in some instances divided
for poor law purposes. Each parish had its two
governing bodies—the vestry and the overseers—
definitely established since the enactment of the
Poor Law of 1601. The vestry was either
"open," in which case all ratepayers of the

[1] Odgers, *Local Government*, p. 44.

parish were entitled to attend, or "select," that
is, composed of duly elected representatives.[1]
The vestry dealt with all general parish affairs,
and met under the presidency of the rector,
with the churchwardens as its principal officers.
But the parish was also responsible for the
maintenance of its poor, and for this purpose

Poor Law. it had since 1601 elected "overseers of the
poor," who were authorised and required to
find work for all able-bodied poor in need of
assistance, and to provide any other necessary
forms of relief; and for these purposes they
were empowered to levy a local rate. The
churchwardens were overseers by virtue of
their office, and the vestry had the general
administration of the relief funds, the overseers
being the executive agents. Persons refused
relief by the overseers, or even without that
preliminary, could apply to the Justices of the
Peace, and in fact towards the close of the
eighteenth century — and particularly after
Gilbert's Act of 1782 had authorised the
grouping of parishes for poor law purposes,
with Boards of Guardians appointed by the
Justices[2] — the latter had come to be the real
controlling authorities for poor relief, as for
most other matters.[3]

[1] The "select" vestries were in those parishes (over 2,300 in 1831)
which had utilised an "Adoptive Act" of 1819. Redlich and Hirst,
I., 162.

[2] Redlich and Hirst, I., 102.

[3] Redlich and Hirst, I., p. 102.

By 1832 the whole rural administration was Condition of rural administration. in a most unsatisfactory condition. The only really serious task imposed upon the local authorities was the relief of the poor, and that task they discharged with the greatest possible inefficiency — in both rural and urban areas, for the poor law organisation was uniform throughout the country. The disastrous policy adopted during the long period of the Revolutionary and Napoleonic Wars had tended to pauperise the working classes completely; the poor rate had come to be regarded by employers in country and town alike as a source of grants in aid of wages; the distress after the war had increased the difficulty; the actual administration of relief was in the hands of small shopkeepers and farmers, untrained in business habits and afraid of unpopularity; there was no central control; and the result was general confusion, extravagance, and demoralisation.[1]

The corporate towns, of which there were The municipal boroughs. two hundred and forty-six in England and Wales in 1832, were in an equally bad plight. Each municipal borough had its mayor, aldermen, councillors and burgesses, who, however, commonly formed only a very small proportion

---

[1] "It is now our painful duty to report that the fund which the forty-third of Elizabeth directed to be employed in setting to work children and persons capable of labour, but using no daily trade, and in the necessary relief of the impotent, is applied to purposes opposed to the letter, and still more to the spirit of that law, and destructive to the morals of that most numerous class, and to the welfare of all." *Report of Commission to enquire into Poor Law*, 1834.

of the inhabitants of the town. The burgesses (or freemen) were a close body, enjoying in many cases exclusive rights of trade within the municipal boundaries, or exempt from various dues such as borough tolls; the remainder of the inhabitants, often the great majority, had no share in the corporate privileges, and no influence upon the municipal administration.[1] The Town Council was either elected by the small body of freemen, or recruited by co-optation, and its members held their seats for life; the aldermen were *ex-officio* Justices of the Peace for the borough. The Commission which enquired into the condition of the municipalties reported in 1835 that, "the corporations look upon themselves, and are considered by the inhabitants, as separate and exclusive bodies; they have powers and privileges within the towns and cities from which they are named, but in most places all identity of interest between the corporation and the inhabitants has disappeared." With the town government thus in the hands of an irresponsible oligarchy, confusion and corruption were almost inevitable; the corporate funds and municipal offices were openly used for the individual

---

[1] In Plymouth there were 437 freemen (including 145 non-resident) in a total population of 75,000. "In Ipswich, containing more than 20,000 inhabitants, the resident freemen form about one fifty-fifth part of the population. Of these more than one-third are not rated, and of those who are rated many are excused payment of their rates. About one-ninth of the whole are paupers." *Report of Commission*, p. 32.

benefit of members of the town councils, or other freemen; little was spent on actual municipal duties, and the work that was done was usually inefficient, and always gave opportunity for jobbery.[1] One result of the inefficiency of the corporations was that powers granted by local Acts of Parliament were frequently conferred upon special Boards of trustees or commissioners, so that the town councils often had little real work to do.[2]

SECTION 2

The policy of reform began with the Poor Law Amendment Act of 1834—the result of an elaborate and startling enquiry into the working of Poor Law administration, and the work in the main of Edwin Chadwick. The Act set up the organisation which exists, substantially unchanged, to-day; relief was no

Reform
(i) Of the
Poor Law.

[1] "In conclusion, we report to Your Majesty that there prevails among the inhabitants of a great majority of the incorporated towns . . . a discontent under the burdens of local taxation, while revenues that ought to be applied for the public advantage are diverted from their legitimate use, and are sometimes wastefully bestowed for the benefit of individuals, sometimes squandered for purposes injurious to the character and morals of the people." *Report*, p. 49. "In general the corporate funds are but partially applied to municipal affairs . . . but they are frequently expended in feasting and in paying the salaries of unimportant officers." *Do.*, p. 45. In reading the Report allowance must be made for the political predilections of the authors, but the evidence on the whole bears out their conclusions.

[2] *Report*, p. 43. This system led inevitably to conflicts of jurisdiction and administrative confusion.

longer to be given by the overseers except in rare cases, but by Boards of Guardians elected for the purpose by groups of parishes called Unions—to the elected members were added the Justices of the Peace for the district. The duties of the overseers were limited mainly to the making of assessments and the levying of rates. To secure uniformity the work of the Guardians was brought beneath the strict control of a central Poor Law Commission (afterwards Board) in London, armed with power to regulate the administration of relief even in the smallest details. An audit by officials of the central office put a check on illegal expenditure and extravagance, and the executive agents of the Guardians were to be appointed by them, but to be subject to the control of the central authority.

(ii) Of the municipal corporations. In the next year (1835) there came, also as the result of an elaborate enquiry, the Municipal Corporations Act, which completely changed municipal organisation throughout the country. After the great extension of the parliamentary franchise to the inhabitants of the towns in 1832, it was impossible to exclude them any longer from a part in the conduct of their own local affairs. The Act made the corporations into the legal personification of the whole local community;[1] broke down the old oligarchies by giving the municipal franchise to all rate-

[1] Redlich and Hirst, I., p. 124.

payers; made the councils elective, and abolished life membership; put an end to trading monopolies and privileges; provided for a better system of appointment to salaried offices; secured publicity for all proceedings of the new authorities; and withdrew all judicial functions from the aldermen as such.[1] Care was taken to ensure an honest and public use of the municipal property and revenue, by the establishment of an audit and of central control over the raising of loans and dealings with municipal property. The City of London was not touched by the Act.[2] The Municipal Corporations Act of 1882, which amended and consolidated the Act of 1835 and subsequent enactments, made no changes in principle.

The results of these two great pieces of legis- Effects of the lation were entirely satisfactory. The Boards reforms. of Guardians, under the direction of the new central department, speedily got to work, and soon changed the whole appearance of the administration. Whatever may be thought of the principles which influenced them or of the methods adopted,

[1] The Act limited the work of the new town councils almost entirely to the administration of police, and of the corporate revenues; the various bodies of trustees or commissioners existent in the towns prior to 1835 were not abolished, but were authorised to transfer their powers to the new town councils if they thought it expedient. Gradually this was universally done; but the town councils have not yet obtained the administration of poor relief. The councils could also promote Private Bills to obtain any desired additional powers.

[2] Sixty-nine of the old corporate towns ceased to be such on account of their insignificance.

it is certain that the relief of the poor thence-forward was orderly, fairly uniform, and free from corruption; and that the old abuses were swept away. In spite of much early unpopularity the new central and local authorities did their work courageously and well.[1] The change was as great in the corporate towns; the directly elected councils, working in the fullest publicity, were able to appeal to a civic enthusiasm such as had not existed before for several centuries, and local patriotism and the consciousness of popular support induced them to enter upon that course of municipal development which in little more than a generation was to make the English towns a model for the world.

Two policies.   These two changes were only portions of the results of the growth of Liberalism and the general awakening which had brought about the Reform Act of 1832; there were also the first grants for national education in 1833 and the establishment of a central education authority in 1839, and the beginning (in 1838) of the demand for sanitary legislation. But before examining subsequent developments it is important to notice the two different policies represented by the legislation of 1834 and 1835. The new Poor Law administration was highly centralised, and placed beneath a very strict control, in order to secure so far

---

[1] "The average annual expenditure on the relief of the poor in the five years preceding the Act of 1834 was £6,754,000, and in the five years succeeding the Act, £4,567,000. Redlich and Hirst, I., p. 110.

as possible uniformity and the maintenance of at least a minimum standard of efficiency; but to the new municipal authorities there was given a very full measure of local autonomy, and administrative control by the central departments was reduced to the lowest possible point. There was no contradiction between these policies at the time — they applied to wholly different sets of circumstances; but a real conflict between them was to arise later.

SECTION 3

Legislation after 1835 was less general and more detailed; it was concerned with making provision for special public services, and the customary policy was to lay the new duty upon the councils in the corporate towns, and elsewhere to create a special authority for each particular service, and often to give it a special area. Thus in 1835 the parishes were made responsible for the upkeep of the highways, but the "highway parish" was not always coincident with the "Poor Law parish"; and when in 1862 and 1864 the Quarter Sessions were empowered to group parishes into "highway districts," these new unions were not always identical with unions for other purposes.

Subsequent legislation.

(i) Highways.

The most important development of local government after 1835 was in regard to public

(ii) Public health.

health. The movement for reform in this direction was started by the Poor Law Commissioners in 1838,[1] and in the next ten years, under the stimulus of the danger of Asiatic cholera,[2] there were numerous enquiries by departments and a Royal Commission, the formation of voluntary associations for sanitary reforms, and attempts at legislation culminating in the Public Health Act of 1848—the first of a series of enactments destined to increase enormously the activities of local authorities.[3] A central Public Health Board was created, and empowered to direct the establishment of local boards in any district with an average death-rate for the preceding seven years of twenty-three per thousand, or on the petition of one-tenth of the ratepayers; these local boards were to have power to construct and maintain sewers, cleanse and pave streets, supply water, and enforce the sanitary laws generally. But the legislation was not very successful; the central Board was intended by its founders to exercise a strong control, but it was from the first unsatisfactory and unpopular—partly owing to defects of organi-

[1] By their letter to the Home Secretary on preventable disease as a cause of pauperism. The moving spirit in this, and in the subsequent report which they were directed to make, was Chadwick, the Secretary to the Poor Law Board.

[2] Simon, *English Sanitary Institutions*, pp. 168 *seq.* This work of one of the greatest English sanitary reformers remains the best account of the development of our public health administration.

[3] "The first compulsory measure of public health imposed by Parliament upon local authorities, if we accept an obscure and almost forgotten Act of James I., and the Vaccination Acts." Redlich and Hirst, I., 140. It was compulsory, but not universal.

children of school age were in receipt of instruction.

Two other developments during this period require notice. The first of these is the growth of central control. Reference has already been made to the establishment of the Local Government Board in 1870 ; it took over all the powers of control of the old Poor Law Board in undiminished stringency ; and though it was less completely equipped to deal with public health administration, it was authorised to issue directions,[1] to take the action necessary to enforce obedience to the law, and to watch the conduct of the local authorities generally ; and subsequent legislation[2] gave large additional powers to the Board. The Education Department was empowered to control closely the new School Boards, and all voluntary schools in receipt of state monies, and the Home Office had secured a strong, though indirect, authority over the police administration (which in the counties was in the hands of the magistrates, and in the municipal boroughs was under the town councils), partly by the necessity for its approval of police bye-laws, and still more by its power to withhold the central grants-in-aid.

Central control.

The policy of contributions from the central Exchequer (apart from educational grants) towards

Grants-in-aid.

[1] The Public Health Act, 1875, contains numerous clauses to the effect that "local authority *may*, and if required by the Local Government Board, *shall*" do particular acts.

[2] *E.g.*, the District Auditors Act, 1879.

the expenses of local authorities began also in the period now under review. The motives were two — the encouragement of due provision for certain public services on the part of the local authorities, and the relief of the localities and especially of the agricultural ratepayer by the transference of some part of their burden to central funds. The latter was the original motive; the plan was first adopted by Sir Robert Peel in 1846 to compensate the agricultural classes in some measure for the losses they were expecting to sustain from the repeal of the import duties on corn.[1] Since that time the demand for fresh relief has constantly come from the same class;[2] it has been consistently successful, until the policy culminated in 1896 in the arrangement that the Exchequer should pay annually half the amount of the rates on agricultural land in that year. The first suggestion of grants to encourage local authorities seems to have been made in 1839, when a Royal Commission recommended the establishment of constabulary forces, and that one-quarter of the cost should be defrayed by the central government. Nothing, however, was done until 1856, when, as it had become evident that without more encouragement the local authorities would make little use of the permission to establish constabulary forces, the duty

[1] Hamilton, *Memorandum on Imperial Relief of Local Burdens*, p. 12 (in volume of *Memoranda* issued by the Royal Commission on Local Taxation, 1899).

[2] Hamilton, pp. 12-19.

was made obligatory, and the central government undertook to pay one-quarter (increased in 1874 to one-half) of the cost of paying and clothing each county or borough force certified as efficient by the Home Secretary. A similar policy was adopted in regard to public health, and in a lesser degree in Poor Law administration; in 1846 the central authority undertook to pay the salaries of teachers in the Poor Law schools, and half the cost of medical relief; in 1872 it agreed to pay half the salaries of medical officers of health and sanitary inspectors, if appointed upon approved terms; and it made some other contributions. The total amount so paid in 1888, prior to the rearrangement of the system, was £2,600,000.[1]

SECTION 4

The result of all this piecemeal legislation, and of many smaller matters necessarily omitted in the above sketch, was by 1888 a chaos of areas and authorities, unintelligible to all save a few.[2] A simplification was absolutely necessary,

[1] Hamilton, p. 20.

[2] See the list of 27,361 authorities in 15,039 areas, in Gomme, *Principles of Local Government*, pp. 12-13. "The result of such legislation was shown to be that an inhabitant of a borough or local board district lived in a four-fold area for the particular purposes of local government, and was ordinarily governed and taxed by a six-fold authority, and might be subject to four or five different rates and as many separate debts incurred by different local bodies. The same was in general true of the inhabitant of a rural parish; while both in town and country there were a multitude of minor

and the third period of development, which commenced in that year, is characterised therefore by the extension of local self-government upon democratic lines, and also by attempts at the reorganisation and co-ordination of authorities. As a result, something approaching to order and coherence has been attained.

Reform of county government.

The first step was the necessary sequel to the extension, by the Representation of the People Act, 1884, of the parliamentary franchise to practically the whole rural population. It was impossible to leave the county administration any longer solely to the justices, who, though they did the work entrusted to them fairly well, yet represented, or were supposed to represent, a particular social class. Various schemes for the reorganisation of county government had been put forward from time to time, but the question was now felt to be urgent; the Local Government Act of 1888 withdrew from the Justices almost all their administrative powers and transferred them to elective bodies—the county councils—and thereby completely changed the whole character of rural government.[1] But it was thought necessary to go further, and the Local Government Act of 1894 carried on the work. Throughout the

matters in respect of which the districts, authorities, and rates might be additionally multiplied and complicated in all the above cases." Wright and Hobhouse, *Local Government and Local Taxation*, p. xi.

[1] Some of the old counties were divided into "administrative counties," and boroughs of more than 50,000 inhabitants form "counties of boroughs."

country district councils, urban and rural, were established; they were founded (with some re-adjustments of boundaries) on the urban sanitary districts (not being municipal boroughs) hitherto administered by improvement commissioners or Boards of Health, and the rural districts which for public health matters had been under the Boards of Guardians. More important was the attempt made in this legislation to revive the parish (with parish council and meeting) as the unit of local self-government; the new parochial authority received all the civil powers of the old vestries, with additions. The general result of these two Acts may be described as the establishment of new popularly elected authorities for rural administration, and the immediate or gradual abolition of all authorities except the County, Municipal, District and Parish Councils, the Boards of Guardians, and the School Boards.[1] The processes of simplification, and of the concentration of powers and duties, were carried still further by the Education Act of 1902, which abolished the School Boards and transferred their work to the County, Municipal, and Urban District Councils. Something still remains to be done in the rectification of boundaries, and in the reorganisation of Poor Law administration by making the areas and authorities identical with the areas and authorities for general local purposes, i.e., by completing the

Simplification of authorities.

---

[1] The Act of 1894 abolished some 8,000 authorities. Gomme, p. 13.

abolition of the so - called authorities *ad hoc*; but even as it is the legislation of 1888 and the following years has given us a coherent and fairly intelligible system.[1]

The government of London.

Meanwhile attempts had been made from time to time to reorganise London, which had been untouched in 1835. The name "London" had a very uncertain application; strictly it applied only to the 1 square mile of the city, but it was used loosely for that area and the surrounding belts of more or less thickly populated parishes. In 1855 the Metropolis Management Act created the metropolis by defining it as the area contained by the City of London and a number of specified parishes. The city was left unchanged: the parishes were divided into two classes. In the first class, each elected a vestry; parishes of the second class were grouped into districts, each with a Board elected by the vestries of the component parishes; these Vestries and District Boards dealt with streets, lighting, and public health administration, and could make use of the Adoptive Acts and any powers which they could obtain under Private Acts. For the whole of London there was a central authority, the Metropolitan Board of Works, elected by the Vestries and District Boards, and not directly elected by the ratepayers; it was to provide a

---

[1] A number of miscellaneous authorities still remain scattered about the country, but only in a few cases are they important. *Vide supra*, p. 52, n.

number of public services for the metropolis generally. In 1867 the Metropolitan Asylums Board was established, to concentrate some part of the work of the thirty Boards of Guardians in the metropolitan area. Some changes of detail were made subsequently, but nothing of importance was done until 1888; by that year the Metropolitan Board of Works, though it had done much valuable work, had fallen into discredit. The Local Government Act abolished the Board, and transferred its work to a new central authority, the London County Council, invested with far wider powers, and directly elected by the ratepayers. No further organic change was made till 1899, and to that year London suffered from the confusion from which the rest of the country had been freed; more than five hundred authorities of various kinds, with doubtful and conflicting jurisdictions in many cases, ruled the metropolis. The London Government Act, 1899, was a great measure of simplification; the "central" authorities (County Council, Corporation of the City, Metropolitan Asylums Board) were untouched; so also were the Board of Guardians; but all the rest were swept away, and replaced by twenty-eight municipalities, with mayor, aldermen and councillors. The London School Board came to an end under the Education Act, 1903, which transferred its powers and duties to the County Council; but in the following year an indirectly elected

Metropolitan Water Board was established, for an area five times as large as the administrative County of London.

SECTION 5

Victory of central control. It has already been pointed out that in the legislation in regard to local government which followed the Reform Act of 1832, two different policies were adopted. The municipalities were given a very large measure of independence, and in the main were subordinated only to Parliament,[1] and of course to the Courts of Law—the administrative or departmental control over them was very slight; the Poor Law authorities, on the other hand, were placed beneath the strictest supervision, and formed part of a highly centralised organisation. These two conflicting policies are apparent at work ever since; but whilst in the middle of the century it seemed (in the failure of the Board of Health) as if the opposition to central control would be successful, since 1870 the authority of the government departments has steadily increased. This has been due to the recognition of the fact that in the interest of the whole nation it is necessary to secure that local authorities shall maintain a minimum standard of efficiency, and that there shall be

[1] That is, their powers are defined by Parliament, and at any time they may go to the legislature for fresh powers.

uniformity in the conduct of at least some public services; and consciously or unconsciously, we have been endeavouring to obtain this efficiency and uniformity by the development of the regulating, inspecting, and enforcing powers of the departments, and by the system of conditional grants-in-aid. It is noteworthy that, though the Act of 1888, and a recent amendment to it, provide for the transference to any or all of the county councils of any powers, duties, and liabilities of the central departments connected with local administration, practically no use has been made of this provision. Yet it seems to be clear that the central departments are becoming overburdened, and that it is desirable that there should be some considerable decentralisation, or at least deconcentration, of control. The municipalities and county councils might be left subject to the central departments as now, but the limited supervisory powers already exercised by the county councils over the smaller authorities might be greatly extended— the councils acting in this as the agents of the departments. The problem is a difficult one: we have to relieve the pressure on the departments without lessening the means of securing the minimum standard, and it is of the utmost importance also that in extending central guidance and control nothing shall be done tending in any way to diminish that local interest, responsibility and initiative without which the

Need of re-
arrangement
of areas.

institutions of local self-government are merely an empty form. Possibly the solution, or at least a part of it, may be found in some rearrangement of areas, which is becoming more and more necessary. For many purposes—means of transit (roads and tramways), all services in which electric power is employed, even poor relief and education—most of our existing areas are much too small.[1] The growth of greater London has made the boundary of the administrative county into little better than an artificial boundary which has already been ignored for water - supply and police, and is a hindrance to the effective administration of many important services. The formation, by grouping of authorities or in some other way, of large districts, for the purposes of actual administration or of supervision, would make the maintenance of a standard and the work of control much easier, would assuredly promote economy whilst increasing efficiency, and need not in any way whatever impair that interest in the work of local self-government which is so much more real and general in Great Britain than in any other European state.

[1] Cf. Wells, *Mankind in the Making*, Appendix I.

CHAPTER VI

THE HISTORY OF LOCAL ADMINISTRATION IN FRANCE SINCE 1789.

SECTION 1

THE history of France since the great Revolution of 1789 has been so varied, and its central political institutions have undergone so many changes, that it would be natural to suppose that the principles and methods of its administrative organisation have been much altered from time to time. Yet it is not so. In spite of the four revolutions since 1815, the fundamental ideas upon which French administration is based, and many of its forms, are to-day as they were left by the first Napoleon; and his policy was in many respects a return to the ways of the old monarchy. Republican France is the direct descendant of Napoleonic, and even pre-revolutionary, France; and during its descent its characteristics have not been greatly modified.

The Revolution of 1789 was the result of a century and a half of absolute monarchy. Ever since Richelieu had overthrown the political power of the Protestants and reduced the

Development of the French Monarchy.

independent authority of the nobles, and his successor Mazarin had crushed the hostile "parliaments"[1] and great lords in the struggle of the Fronde, there had been no institution in France capable of withstanding, from whatever motive, the arbitrary power of the Crown. This unlimited authority, destroying all initiative and responsibility amongst its subjects, led France straight to the Revolution. But, nevertheless, the monarchy had created France. From the time of Hugh Capet, through Philip Augustus and Louis XI., to the reign of Louis XIV., the territories of the French Crown were steadily extended, and within the widening boundaries a united state was slowly created. The struggle against feudalism waged from the foundation of the monarchy, victorious under Philip Augustus and Saint Louis, and again under Louis XI. in his war against the League of the Common Weal, seemed ended in favour of the monarchy at the accession of Francis I. But it began again when the Reformation as a political movement came to arouse the slumbering passions of the nobles; and it was not until a century later that the monarchy, guided first by Henry IV., then by Richelieu and Mazarin, ultimately triumphed. The States-General, after three centuries of a troubled existence, were no more

[1] The French "parliaments" were the Law Courts, become heredi-tary: the Parliament of Paris had the task of registering Royal Edicts, and by protesting, or by the suggestion of amendments, could impose some check upon the Crown.

convoked, and by 1660 Louis XIV. was absolute master of France. His long reign thenceforward falls into two periods: in the first, Colbert strove with some success to reorganise the administration, and to carry out economic reform; in the second, the foreign policy of Louis involved France in a series of wars which left her by 1715 utterly exhausted, financially ruined, and in administrative chaos. In spite of the efforts of a few able men the French state thenceforward simply drifted to the catastrophe.

What then was the condition of France on, the eve of the Revolution?[1]   The monarchy was absolute, and ruled the country by means of agents drawn, not from the nobility, but from the middle classes of society. It was unapproachable, irresponsible, ignorant or careless of the true condition of its subjects; yet it had drawn to itself the immediate control of all administration, central and local. For administrative purposes the old provinces were retained only for military affairs, and their noble governors were only military authorities. The country was divided into thirty - two *généralités*, each controlled by an Intendant. These officials had been placed by Richelieu at the side of the old provincial governors to act as agents of the Crown, and gradually they had drawn into their own

The "Ancient Régime."

---

[1] The best accounts are De Tocqueville, *L'Ancien Régime et la Révolution*, and Taine, *Les Origines de la France Contemporaine* (ed. 1900), Vols. I. and II.

hands the whole work of taxation and general administration. Chosen from the middle classes, generally lawyers, and moved from one generality to another at the will of the central authority, they were free from all local connection, untouched by local influences, and directly and solely responsible to the Controller - General at Paris. Beneath them were the " sub-delegates," who in smaller districts carried on the work of the Intendants. It should be noticed, however, that there was a distinction between the " Pays d'États," and " Pays D'Élection." In the " Pays d'États," provincial estates still met to vote the provincial share of taxation, and to supervise its assessment and collection; here the Intendant exercised little more than the authority in matters of police—in the widest meaning of the word. On the other hand the " Pays d'Élection" were those where the contribution was fixed simply by the King, and assessed and collected by agents who had once been elected, but had become later the nominees of the Crown ; in these districts the Intendant controlled everything. And it is scarcely necessary to add that these " Pays d'Élection" were much the more numerous ; they formed three-quarters of France.

In the towns and communes there were mayors and syndics, councils, and parish meetings. The municipal and parochial offices had been for a long time elective, but shortly before the Revolution they had become hereditary, and could be

purchased. In most towns and villages therefore the local offices had fallen into the hands of
a small group of families, which, as they could
not be ousted, administered for their own purposes.
They had only to keep on good terms with the
Intendant; and in fact they had speedily become
little more than his agents; for the tutelage
exercised by these agents of the central government over the communal administration, even in
the considerable towns, was exceedingly strict, and
extended to the most minute local affairs.

France was then in the grip of a vast
bureaucracy, which could rarely move without
authority from the centre, and strove to bring
all local administration into line.   In itself this
was a good purpose—nowhere was its realisation
more desirable than in France—but the method
adopted crushed all local life, and the extreme
centralisation had by 1789 resulted in the utter
congestion of all administration.

Combined with these disastrous administrative **The burden of taxation.**
methods was an equally bad system of finance.
A vast number of exemptions, freeing the two
wealthiest classes, the nobles and the clergy, from
all taxation, threw practically the whole financial
burden of the state upon the two lower classes,
the *bourgeoisie* and the populace.   They bore
the whole (the burden weighing most heavily
upon the peasants),[1] yet were without political
rights; while, on the other hand, the nobles and

[1] Taine, *Les Origines*, II., pp. 199 *seq.*

Q

clergy had ceased to earn their exemption by any service to the state. The great nobles did not reside on their estates; the small nobles did, but had no share in the local administration, except to a slight degree in the extreme western part of France. Not only was the taxation heavy, but it was imposed—as for example in the case of the salt-duty—in the most vexatious and irritating way. Direct taxation was favoured rather than indirect, and the army of financial agents which this required was in constant conflict with the people. Everywhere the agents were regarded as the messengers of evil, and their chiefs, the Intendants, were universally the object of popular hatred.

And while they were thus harried by the state the agricultural classes were also oppressed by the feudal dues, often heavy and always vexatious. Famine and the failure of harvests brought the lower classes to the verge of utter ruin; even the Royal Treasury could extort no more from them. The schemes of Turgot (1774-76) and Necker (1776-81) to restore financial order had alike broken down before the opposition of class interests; less capable men were doomed from the first to failure, and when Necker was recalled it was too late. The final crisis had come; only heroic measures could succeed, and the meeting of the States-General was summoned.

Original character of the Revolution of 1789.

It is quite clear that when the States-General met at Versailles in 1789, republicanism as a political force did not exist in France. The vast mass of the people held a creed of *Royalisme irraisonné*.[1] The complaints against the tyranny of ministers and the harshness of the administration came from the nobles and the *bourgeoisie*, and they condemned the monarchy only because it did not keep its agents sufficiently in check. The peasantry also, traditionally regarding the Crown as their ally against the nobles, looked to the King and a reformed administration to free them from the feudal dues which weighed so heavily upon them. And so the first effect of the summoning of the States-General was an outburst of enthusiasm for the monarchy: the nation rallied to its support. The national demands as formulated in the Cahiers drawn up in the local assemblies of the various estates preliminary to the despatch of representatives to Versailles, were four in number: (1) a fixed constitution; (2) a unification of law, and its impartial administration; (3) reforms in administration; (4) the abolition of the feudal dues.[2] The need of the two last of these reforms has already been shown. As to the second, the unification of law, it is necessary only to point out that, broadly speaking, France was divided into the countries of written law and customary law; but the former was sometimes modified by local usages, and the latter varied greatly, for

---

[1] Aulard, *Histoire politique de la Revolution Française*, p. 7.
[2] Cf. Champion, *La France d'aprés les Cahiers de* 1789.

sixty districts and three hundred towns were governed by their own special "customs." And the first demand of all, that for a constitution, sprang inevitably from the other three, for, as the clergy of Provins rightly remarked, "the abuses against which the nation protests have one common origin—arbitrary power. It is only by bringing this power into its proper limits that there can be any hope of re-establishing order in the various departments of the administration." But there was no thought of a *republican* constitution; in all the lists of local grievances and of necessary reforms, drawn up in the local assemblies in preparation for the great meeting of the States-General, we find no trace of this, but only a universal demand for the four reforms already enumerated. The Revolution in its early stages was simply and solely a movement for economic and administrative changes; in fact France did not become republican even in form till it was apparent that no help could be found in the monarchy.

SECTION 2

Stages of the Revolution.
Between 1789 and 1804 the movement of events in France was tremendously rapid. When it appeared certain that, owing to the attitude adopted by the monarchy, gradual reforms were almost out of the question, the growing violence

of the opposition swept everything before it. The ground was cleared — but what was to be the nature of the new edifice? Every kind of theory was in the air; every sort of scheme was propounded, and change followed change with kaleidoscopic rapidity. But there are three chief periods which can be distinguished between 1789 and 1799.[1] In the first year of the Revolution a limited monarchy, with a limited suffrage, was established. This was followed in August 1792 by a republic based on universal suffrage, and the period of the democratic republic commenced. But again a change came. In 1795 the people as a whole gave up its power to a particular class; the republic ceased to be democratic. This is the period of the directory, which endured until 1799.

By that year France had become utterly weary of faction and of change. Not one of the three forms of government had proved itself able to maintain order, and to reorganise the state in a satisfactory manner. In 1789 (as Taine has remarked) France was on the verge of bankruptcy, and discontented with the old *régime*; in 1799 she was absolutely bankrupt, and dissatisfied with the Revolution. She needed two things; an internal reorganisation which should prevent the exploitation of one class for the benefit of the others, as the old *régime* had exploited the *bourgeoisie* and the people for the benefit of

---

[1] Aulard, p. vi.

the Crown, the nobles and the clergy, and as the Revolution had exploited the nobles and clergy for the benefit of the *bourgeoisie* and people; and a strong and single policy in foreign affairs. And so, as in 1795 the power was surrendered to a small group of men, in 1799 it was surrendered to one man, Napoleon Buonaparte. Nominally, the republic endured till 1804; practically it had ceased to exist in 1799.

There was then no real contradiction between the action of France in 1789 and 1799. In neither year had she sought liberty, save in a very limited sense. At both dates she sought chiefly a Government strong enough to reorganise the state, and to maintain order; she had sought it in a limited monarchy, in various forms of republicanism, and at last she found it in a despotism. A strong Government was needed, but not an arbitrary one; monarchy and republic were alike weak and arbitrary; the despotism of Napoleon was, in internal affairs at least, always regular and unquestionably beneficial.

Here we are concerned chiefly with his changes in the system of local government, and it is necessary, in order to understand them, to notice briefly the experiments made during the earlier stages of the Revolution.

Changes in local administration. The condition of affairs has already been described; France presented an example of the most extreme centralisation. From the first days of the Revolution attempts at wide-reaching reform were made; but revolutionary legislation had some characteristics which did not promise satisfactory results. It was theoretical and extremely optimistic; it failed to grasp facts, and to realise the extreme complexity of the problem by which it was faced. The French people were utterly inexperienced, totally devoid of political training; and the legislators of the Revolution seem to have believed that political experience was unnecessary — reason alone was needed, and every man had that. The consequent legislation was idealistic, not practical; and the result was chaos.

The Constituent Assembly began by abolishing the Intendants, who, as already stated, were extremely unpopular. Then it abolished the provincial divisions, and in their stead divided France into eighty-six departments. This may, perhaps, have been desirable as a necessary step towards internal unity, for in the old provinces there were local traditions, local patriotisms, local customs and privileges.[1] In their place were henceforward the departments, bearing geographical names, following no traditional boundaries, and often violating them; they were subdivided into districts. As to the communes, the old classification into cities, boroughs, towns, and villages, was abolished; henceforward there

---

[1] An instance of this survival of provincial particularism was seen as late as the war of 1870, when the South of France cared little about the fate of the North.

were to be only "communes." In all three areas—department, district, commune—there were elective councils, and in all three (except in the smallest communes) the administration was in the hands of an Executive Board, and not (as had been the case with the Intendants and their delegates) of a single official.[1] These local authorities, though they were charged with some matters which were considered as the functions of the central authority, could be neither controlled nor dissolved by the central government; the result was that the local bodies, during the rapid changes of the revolutionary years, were often in opposition to the central power, and a general collapse of local administration soon became inevitable. The Convention, however, was resolved to make itself obeyed, and everywhere it appointed agents to watch the local administration, and strove to enforce obedience to the central government, while maintaining the decentralisation established by the Constituent Assembly. Its agents were rabid republicans, and the system was that of the Terror. But it failed, and in 1795, at the commencement of the Directory, a new experiment was tried. In each department a directory of five was established, with all powers, both deliberative and executive; the departmental councils had been abolished two years before; and the division into districts was abandoned. The communes

[1] Law of 14th December 1789.

were also reorganised : every one with five thousand inhabitants formed a municipality; those with more were divided, those with less were grouped together into municipal cantons. The control of the central government was strengthened by its power of suspending and dismissing members of the local directories and municipalities, and by the appointment of representatives of the central government to supervise the local administration. Thus, after the state had from 1789 practically *The return to autocracy.* abdicated all its functions to local bodies, and administrative anarchy had been everywhere the result, it found itself gradually forced back to the centralised system of the old monarchy.[1] The Directory had gone a considerable way towards re-establishing this system before it surrendered its functions to Napoleon, who immediately completed the work. The departments were retained, and subdivided into arrondissements; the communes returned (as regards area) to their condition before the days of the Directory. Everywhere executive and deliberative authorities were placed side by side; but everywhere the executive officials (the prefects, subprefects, and mayors) were the direct nominees of the First Consul or Emperor, and absolutely subject to his will; and the members of the

[1] "These measures simply revived the centralisation of the *ancien régime* under a panoply of new names, and with the accompaniment of the modern American spoils system." Young, *Administrative Centralisation and Decentralisation in France* (American Academy of Political Science), p. 29.

councils were appointed by the central government from select local lists. In the smallest matters the central control was rigorous, and no local feeling could resist it.[1] The new official, the Prefect, was only the Intendant revived, though entrusted with a smaller area; the centralisation was as elaborate and complete as it had ever been. It will be observed that local government had followed precisely the same evolution as central government during these years; both had fallen first into utter confusion, and from that they had passed by way of the administration by boards (the Directory period) to "one man rule" and extreme centralisation.

From the Napoleonic period France derives her whole administrative, judicial, financial, military, ecclesiastical, and educational system of to-day. In spite of parliamentary government, in spite of many revolutions, in spite of the extension of democracy, modern France is in its main features still the Napoleonic state. But it has inevitably been somewhat liberalised; the ideas which found their expression not in 1789 so much as in 1830, 1848, and 1870, have succeeded to some extent in making their influence felt upon the mechanism of the state, and where the

---

[1] "Les citoyens n'avaient plus aucune action sur l'administration de leur village, de leur ville, de leur département; les intérêts qui les touchaient de plus près dependaient du bon plaisir du préfet, agent docile du pouvoir, et dont les maires et les conseils n'étaient que les dociles subordonnés." Rambaud, *Histoire de la civilisation contemporaine en France*, p. 71.

mechanism has not been changed its working has been modified.

SECTION 3

The republican party failed to hold the power which it obtained in 1792, because it was only a minority in the country. Popular support was lacking: the weakness of the central power, and the confusion arising from a system of decentralisation which required much political training where none whatever existed, made the French nation willing to accept the rule of Napoleon. When he fell, the whole administration was firmly established upon the principles of extreme centralisation. That remained: the immediate task was to reorganise the central government, for only when a stable constitution had been found could time and attention be given to the local institutions.

Subsequent development of central government.

The restoration of the Bourbons was accepted without enthusiasm, but without active hostility. It was not the restoration of the old monarchy; there was a formal constitution and something of parliamentary government, though with a very limited franchise; and there remained the two great results of the Revolution, equality of all before the law, and uniformity of administration.[1]

(i) The Restoration Monarchy.

[1] "La restauration de 1814, amenée par un accident de politique étrangère, n'a été qu'une restauration incomplète. Elle a conservé l'organisation sociale démocratique créée par la Révolution et l'organisation administrative centralisée laissée par Napoléon. A

Louis XVIII. tried to steer a middle course between the extreme royalists on the one side and the revolutionaries (republican and imperialist) on the other. But he failed; the ultra-royalists came to power, and under his successor, Charles X. (1824-30), who was identified with them, their violence greatly increased. At last the ordinances of 1830, attacking the Parliament, the franchise, and the Press, brought the Revolution of July, and the substitution for the Bourbons of the House of Orleans in the person of Louis Philippe. The change was like that of 1689 in England; Louis Philippe was the head of the younger branch of the Royal Family, but his kingdom was based less on hereditary right than on an agreement with the nation.

(ii) The Monarchy of July.

The rising in Paris which had overthrown Charles X. was the work of the republicans, but they were not strong enough to take the power, and were compelled to leave it to the moderate Liberals, whose most conspicuous leaders were Guizot and Thiers. The Monarchy of July lasted eighteen years, but at no time during that period was its position at all secure. Louis Philippe relied entirely upon the middle class, and the Government considered only the interests of that class; its policy was simply to oppose the growing revolutionary and even reform forces at home, and

cette société démocratique et à cette administration bureaucratique elle a superposé un mécanisme politique monarchique d'importation anglaise." Seignobos, *Histoire Politique de l'Europe contemporaine*, p. 205.

to maintain peace abroad; beyond that it had no
ambitions.   It abolished the censorship of the
Press, it extended the system of national education,
it doubled the electorate ;[1] but it was not inclined
for further reform.   And consequently it was
faced by an ever-increasing opposition, formed of
very diverse elements ; the more advanced Liberals,
the discontented monarchists, the republicans
(rapidly growing in strength) all combined to
attack the "bourgeois monarchy." They attacked
on three points—the personal power of the King
and the ministries chosen by himself alone, the
centralised administration and the use of officials
for political purposes, and the limitation of the
franchise.   Meanwhile the agitation of the avowed
republicans was becoming ever more dangerous,
under the inspiration of the historians, such as
Michelet and Lamartine, who idealised the great
Revolution of 1789 ; and at the same time men
began to seek an economic reorganisation of
society, and socialism appeared.   The socialists
lacked coherence, and the teaching of St Simon,
Fourier, and Proudhon had little direct political
influence, but the particular form of socialism
represented by Louis Blanc was soon to become
an active force.   The Government made some
reforms,[2] but in the main clung to the policy of
resistance: the result was that it alienated all

---

[1] But even then the electorate numbered only 200,000, out of a
total population of about 34,000,000.

[2] See the list in Guizot, *Mémoires*, c. xlix.

sections of the population except the wealthier middle classes, who were too weak to give any effectual support. A street riot in Paris in February, 1848, led to its downfall without a single blow being struck in its defence. It was the final failure of monarchy in France.

(iii) The Second Republic.

The Provisional Government of 1848 set up a republic, but in the ranks of the republicans themselves there was a division. Though they had tried, they had not in 1830 been strong enough to erect a republic, and they had been forced to accept the "bourgeois monarchy": now they were strong enough to establish their desired form of government, but not strong enough to maintain it. For they were hopelessly divided into republicans and socialists: the former, led by Lamartine, sought political reforms; the latter, led by Louis Blanc, attempted sweeping economic changes. The elections by universal suffrage to the Constituent Assembly gave the republicans a strong majority; the socialists began to alarm their bourgeois allies, and from the executive commission of government the socialists chiefs were excluded. Then a struggle ensued, followed by street fighting; the socialists were crushed for a time, and the republicans were free to arrange their own form of government. They decided upon a single chamber, and a President of the Republic; both were to be elected by universal suffrage. Now the grant of universal suffrage transferred the voting power to the peasants, and the immediate result was an overwhelming majority for Louis Napoleon. In the new assembly there were numerous parties—imperialists, monarchists of the legitimist and orleanist schools, republicans, democrats or socialists, and moderates. Few cared for the new *régime*; and the *coup d'état* of Napoleon and his subsequent assumption of the imperial dignity were easily accomplished, and were readily ratified by a great majority of the nation in the plebiscites.

It was the story of 1789 over again. A particular form of government having been overthrown, a party which formed only a minority of the nation—much larger and more intelligent in 1848 than in 1792, but still a minority—had taken possession of the central power and established a republic. In each case the republicans then proceeded to quarrel amongst themselves, and gave no promise of a stable government; the majority of the nation was hostile or indifferent, and finally, desiring above all things order, turned to imperialism, and deliberately elected a dictator. The tradition of the great Napoleon and his work carried his nephew to power; and the institutions of 1852 were those of 1804. All power was in the hands of the Emperor, and he alone could initiate legislation, make war or peace. The legislature met or was dissolved at his pleasure; the ministers were his ministers, not those of the legislature. The legislature could accept or reject Bills prepared by the Council of State;

(iv) The Second Empire.

it could not ordinarily amend them. Thus an autocracy was again established; but the autocracy retained the instruments which had raised it to power—it kept the universal suffrage; but the elections were always manipulated, as they had been under all the previous Governments, and the extreme centralisation of the administration was maintained for political purposes.

But the Liberals though overthrown were not crushed, and they soon became again important. From 1860 onward the Empire found itself forced to incline more and more to the moderate Liberals, especially when diplomatic and military failures had greatly diminished its prestige. It yielded more power to the legislature, it gave it the right of initiating laws; and when the legislature had become overwhelmingly Liberal, the Emperor turned to the constitutional Liberals, *i.e.*, those who were prepared to retain the Empire, and to secure their support called their leader, Ollivier, to power. But there was another and perhaps stronger section of the Liberals who were resolved to overthrow the Empire, and meanwhile a new form of socialism was making rapid progress among the workmen. The doctrines of modern socialism had been formulated by Marx; by 1864 the "International Association" was at work, and by 1870 the new movement had become a political factor which caused the Government serious alarm. Against on the one side the advanced Liberals and the socialists, on the other side the monarchists,

the Empire found support only in the moderate
Liberals; these might conceivably have saved it,
with considerable modifications, but there was no
time. They had been called to office in 1870,
and in that same year the disastrous foreign policy
of the Empire brought about its abrupt collapse.

The Republic established in 1870 has now (v) The Third
Republic.
endured for thirty-five years; like its two pre-
decessors, it originated in a Paris-made revolution,
and there was for a time every prospect that it
would not endure. But there was absolutely
nothing to take its place, and the nation had
learned by previous experience. It went to work
soberly and steadily, and a set of institutions was
established, which were accepted willingly by a
very considerable minority, and from necessity,
though with reluctance, by the majority. And
so time was given for the institutions to make
their working felt, and to grow into the life of
France; and it appears to be certain, in spite of
the troubled career of the Third Republic, that
the considerable republican minority of 1870 has
become a very great republican majority to-day.

One event, however, of the early days of the
republic must be briefly noticed, and that is the
Commune. The history of that movement is
extremely uncertain, but it seems to be clear that
the revolt was to some extent at least a protest
against over-centralisation—a demand for a greater
amount of communal liberty. It was the effort
of the socialists; to most of the towns it would

R

have been disastrous.   And so, whereas in every previous revolution Paris had imposed her will on France, in the matter of the Commune the provinces imposed their will on Paris.

SECTION 4

Changes in local adminis- tration. We now have to notice briefly what changes have come over the local administration during these constant variations in the nature of the central government in France.[1]   It has already been suggested that these changes have in sum been very small, but the growth of Liberalism was bound to exercise some influence.   France still keeps from the Napoleonic period her judicial organisation, and the systems of education and finance ; whilst the ecclesiastical arrangements made by the first Emperor are about to be abandoned.   In the local administration she has kept the departments administered by prefects and sub-prefects, and the strict tutelage of the communes ; and she has kept the "administrative courts."   The remarkable series of changes in the central government would in fact have been impossible but for this continued existence of the highly centralised bureaucratic machinery by which France was actually administered ; the new authority had only to secure the central offices,

[1] There is a useful sketch in Rambaud, *Civilisation Contemporaine en France*, cc. xvi. and xxvi.

and the subordinate agents throughout the country obeyed it as a matter of course.

But there have been certain changes of a Liberal and decentralising nature. The first is that the municipal authorities and departmental councils have become—though very gradually—representative of the localities; and their powers have been increased under administrative supervision. Under the Monarchy of July the councils of the communes (1831) and departments (1833) were made elective, but the franchise was confined (as for parliamentary elections) to the limited class of large taxpayers and officials upon whom the government of Louis Philippe relied, and the mayors and adjoints were appointed by the central government from the persons elected as councillors.[1] The Second Republic in 1848 retained this arrangement for the larger communes, but in those with less than 6,000 inhabitants it permitted the free election of the communal officers. Next, the Second Empire, which owed its existence to the universal suffrage, established that form of election for the councils, and during the last years when it was seeking everywhere for support it increased the powers of these bodies (1866 and 1867); but

[1] Cf. Thiers: "Savez-vous pourquoi la Restauration, en nous faisant un mal moral et politique immense, n'a cependant pas frustré les intérêts materiels? C'est qu'elle a respecté la vieille administration de l'Empire, qui en savait plus qu'elle, et qu'elle a laissé aller. . . . Ce n'est pas nous qui sommes rétrogrades, c'est nous qui défendons la Révolution vivante. En affranchissant les grandes communes, vous debruissez l'unité; vous portez un coup de hache au pied de l'arbre." Quoted in Rambaud, *Civilisation Contemporaine en France*, p. 340.

as regards the mayors and adjoints it returned in 1852 to the methods of the monarchy. Finally, under the Third Republic the mayors were made elective first in the smaller communes in 1871, and then (after a brief return to the old plan in 1874 under the reactionary rule of Macmahon) in 1876 and 1882 in all the communes; the municipal code was rearranged and extended (1884); and the departments have become of greater importance. But decentralisation has not gone very far; and the central control is in reality as strong as ever.

The maintenance of centralisation and bureaucratic authority.

One reason for this is that for very obvious reasons no political party has really cared for decentralisation; with the highly organised bureaucracy any party which can get hold of the central offices can control the whole country, especially as it is a recognised thing that administrative officials may be used for political purposes. The machine is too valuable a weapon for any political party lightly to throw it away. Decentralisation has been constantly advocated; as early as 1863 a conference at Nancy urged that the communes should be strengthened, the cantons revived, the tutelage of the departments reduced, and the administrative tribunals abolished; and the first three of these reforms have been persistently urged by some prominent politicians, whilst a Government Commission on the subject was appointed in 1895. But there is no sign of any changes of real importance; neither the politicians or the people really want them. The socialist municipalities naturally call for a greater amount of autonomy; they desire to be released from the strict administrative control which hampers their experiments. But their demand is not likely to be granted until the socialist party is much more powerful than it is at present; and it must be remembered that it has no hold upon the peasants, who form the great majority of the people of France.

There seems then every probability that the organisation of local administration will continue in something closely akin to its present form, at least for a considerable time. But what of the central government? Is the republic to be the definitive constitution of France? The course of French history is a warning against prophecy, but there are some points which may be noticed. The first is the growth of republican sentiment; the party was in a minority in 1870, and also in 1875 when the constitution was adopted, but in every election since its strength has increased, until to-day it has undisputed control in all except a few districts of France. The second point is that its long existence (nearly twice as long as that of any previous Government since 1789) has enlisted on its side the peasantry, who are the great conservative force. Thirdly, the socialists, who had long been in constant opposition, have recently been banded with the republicans in defence of the existing order, though it remains to be seen if, in saving the republic, they will

Growing strength of the Republic.

not greatly change it. And, finally, one of the most striking things in recent French politics is the decline in the influence of Paris; up to 1870 the capital had for centuries imposed her will upon the provinces, but in 1871, by the repression of the Commune, the provinces imposed their will upon Paris, and they have repeated this since in the cases of the Boulangist and the Nationalist agitations. The reasons for this are of course to be found in the growth of the great mercantile and industrial towns, and the improved means of communication; and the change must assuredly make for the greater stability of the central political institutions of France. Changes in the local institutions will probably come, but the process is certain to be very slow; France is accustomed to centralised and bureaucratic government, and is not ready for anything else.

CHAPTER VII

THE HISTORY OF LOCAL ADMINISTRATION IN PRUSSIA SINCE 1806

SECTION 1

THE modern Prussian state began with the general reorganisation which followed the military collapse before Napoleon I. at Jena in 1806, and the political disaster at Tilsit in the following year. The administrative system which Frederick William I. had founded, and the great Frederick had wielded with such extraordinary success, had revealed its inability to meet new requirements, and to cope with the new forces set in action throughout Europe by the French Revolution. The necessity for drastic and far-reaching reform could no longer be obscured, and the entry into office of the Freiherr vom Stein in October, 1807, began the second great constructive period of Prussian history.

The Prussian realm in 1806 was a quite recent recreation. It had originated in the Mark of Brandenburg, founded between 1134 and 1170 by Albert the Bear, as one of the

The formation of the Prussian state.

"marks"[1] intended to guard the eastern border of Germany against the Slavs.[2] Gradually, and for centuries only very slowly, its rulers extended their territories, but always towards the east. The development became rapid only after the close of the Thirty Years' War, with the reigns of the Great Elector and his successors. The Elector (1640-88) took up vigorously the task of reorganisation after the ravages of the long war, and in particular devoted himself to economic improvements. His son, Frederick I., raised Prussia to the dignity of a kingdom. The next King, Frederick William I. (1713-40) elaborated an administrative system, highly centralised but extremely efficient, and subordinated everything to the maintenance of a powerful army. Frederick the Great (1740-86) and his nephew, Frederick William II. (1786-97), made use of the weapons prepared for them, and by the acquisition of Silesia and part of Poland more than doubled the extent of the Prussian kingdom. But still the gains were chiefly towards the east; in 1806 Prussia included a few scattered territories west of the Elbe, but its capital, Berlin, was between the Elbe and the Oder, and the great mass of its provinces

[1] By "mark" in this instance was meant a border-territory intended for defence, and therefore having the whole administration concentrated in the hands of a military ruler. Cf. the English "palatine counties."

[2] A similar "mark" to the south was the Bavarian "East-Mark," destined to grow into the Austro-Hungarian Empire.

lay to the east of the last-named river. And then suddenly by the Treaty of Tilsit its western possessions, and much else, were torn from it; it was reduced by almost one-half, and seemed to have sunk into its old unimportant position in Europe.

It had collapsed, and the task of reconstruction was extremely difficult. Prussia was still in the feudal stage of society. Nearly one-half of the land was royal domain, that is, the actual private estates of the King; and in these, as almost everywhere else throughout the kingdom, the manorial system had firm hold. The whole of the social and economic life of the country was determined by a strong caste system, which gave a status to land and prevented its easy transfer — since land once held by a noble could never be alienated to a member of another social class; and at the same time prohibited the rise of a peasant to the citizen class, and of a citizen to the ranks of the nobles. The towns were controlled by a narrow guild-system which, while it excluded the greater number of the inhabitants from any share in the municipal government, had fallen to the lowest depths of incompetence, so that the real authority had come to be exercised, in fact though not in law, by petty royal officials. At the same time the towns were oppressed by a system of taxation which was based first on a distinction between town and country, and, secondly, on a system of exemptions and privileges for nobles and manorial lords; it laid therefore a most disproportionate burden upon the towns.

Administrative organisation in 1806.

The central government was in the most complete confusion.[1] There was no distinct separation of powers; the King was sole law giver, he was chief of the civil administration, and head of the army, and only a man of exceptional ability could keep control; just as was the case in France in the eighteenth century, all power was concentrated in the hands of the monarchs, and their task was become impossible. In the local government the old provincial assemblies had fallen into disuse with the growth of the absolute monarchy, and the chief organs for local administration were the Offices for War and Domains (*Kriegs-und Domänen-Kämmern*), of which each province had one or more. Created in 1723 as local agents of the General Directory (*Generaldirektorium*), which Frederick William I. had established as the one supreme administrative body for the whole kingdom, these authorities were originally intended to control only military and financial matters; but gradually they had drawn to themselves all the more important of local affairs. Beneath them were

---

[1] The chief authorities for the administrative history of Prussia are Bornhak, *Geschichte des preussischen Verwaltungsrechts* (3 vols.), and Isaacsohn, *Geschichte des preussischen Beamtentums* (3 vols.).

the Circles (*Kreise*), which from the reign of Frederick the Great had been the real units of Prussian local government. At the head of each Circle stood the Landrath, whose office first appears in the Mark of Brandenburg in the sixteenth century. Originally the representative of the landowners, he became about the end of the seventeenth century the chief local administrative official, and under the absolute monarchy he was by 1806 the chief agent within the circle of the central power, though still elected by the landowners from their own number. The representative body of the Circle was the Circle Assembly (*Kreistag*), composed of the owners of manors; and thus the whole administration was in the hands of the land-owners.[1] As regards the communes, the code prepared under Frederick II., and published by his successor,[2] drew no distinction between manorial and non-manorial villages, and the free villages of the western part of the kingdom received the same organisation, with Schulz (steward), assessors and assembly, as the unfree villages of the eastern provinces. Finally, the bureaucracy, once the most skilled in Europe, was now become decrepit, and had broken down beneath the burden of over-centralisation. The

---

[1] The powers of the Circle Assembly varied according to the provinces; in some instances it had only advisory powers, whilst in others it had some control over local finances. Bornhak, *Geschichte des preussischen Verwaltungsrechts*, II., p. 289 *seq*.

[2] Das allgemeine Landrecht.

whole system had failed completely, and the chief reason for this, as Stein and most of his abler contemporaries perceived, was that it left no room for individual or local initiative. The Prussian people was accustomed to be ruled, it was in the habit of looking to the central government for guidance even in small matters; it had no desire and no ability to rule itself. And in the eastern provinces, that is to say, in far the greater part of Prussia, the rural population was in a condition of almost complete economic dependence.

SECTION 2

The reformers.

Stein had at first advocated administrative reform alone. Finding his ideal of local administration in the English system at the close of the eighteenth century, he thought to initiate reforms upon that model; but he speedily perceived that changes of a far more sweeping character had become necessary. His contemporary Hardenberg is as a reformer entitled to a much higher rank than Stein; he was the first Liberal statesman of Prussia, and almost of Europe, after 1789. He recognised clearly that thorough economic and social reforms would have to accompany, and in some cases to precede, administrative and political reorganisation; and his schemes were consequently much more comprehensive than those put forward by Stein, who always remained essentially a Whig. But in his attempt to rebuild the state the latter was forced to somewhat the same conclusions as Hardenberg, though he was never ready to go so far. The objects of the reformers were then the abolition of all that remained of the feudal and caste systems; the creation of some degree of union between the various classes of society; the introduction of a system of local self-government which should give all classes an interest in the conduct of local affairs; the reform of the central government, of taxation, and of the army. As regards the central government, Stein abolished the General Directory in 1808, and divided the work between five departments, each under a single minister; unity of policy was secured by the establishment of the Ministry of State, composed of the heads of departments under the presidency of the Chancellor.[1]

Here we are chiefly concerned with the development of the institutions of local government.[2] One great economic change had necessarily to come first, and this was brought about by the Emancipation Edict of 1807 and its complement, the Edict of 1811. These established freedom of sale of land and of choice of occupation, abolished

The Emancipation Edicts.

[1] The office of Chancellor was not filled after the death of Hardenberg; the head of the Ministry was thenceforward styled Minister-President, and had much less authority over his colleagues.

[2] Meier, *Reform der Verwaltungsorganisation unter Stein und Hardenberg*, passim. A useful account is in Seeley, *Life and Times of Stein*, especially Pt. III. cc. 3-4, and Pt. V., cc. 1-3.

serfdom, and made it possible for a peasant to free his holding from heavy duties and turn it into hereditary property. Though only a small number of peasants could avail themselves of such an opportunity at first, yet the legislation as a whole gave personal, and a chance of economic, freedom, and so founded the class of peasant proprietors in modern Prussia.[1]

The reforms. (i) Municipalities.

In all this Stein had no particular share, though he approved of it. Apart from the reform of the central administration, the chief monument of his fifteen months' tenure of office (practically a dictatorship) is the Municipal Edict (*Städte-Ordnung*) of 1808. It was the realisation of a mere fragment of his schemes, for he had intended a general reform of all urban and rural communes, but was compelled to limit his work to the towns. Of the condition of these we have already seen something ; for further evidence we may turn to the evidence of a contemporary observer, who writes :—

"The magistrates in some places filled up their number by co-optation, but for the most part they were nominated by the Government, and since the second half of the eighteenth century the citizens had no influence worth mentioning either in this or in regard to the taxes, accounts, etc. Thus the town fell into two entirely unconnected parts. The completely disfranchised part submitted grudgingly,

---

[1] But the eastern group of provinces remained (and remains) on the whole a land of great estates.

seeing in the magistrates, often quite justly, nothing but partial and interested opponents, and at the same time these apparently unlimited despots did not at all enjoy their power. In the first place, many posts of Burgomaster, Treasurer, Councillor, were treated as comfortable berths for invalid Quartermasters and Sergeants: . . . secondly, these men were under the strictest Government tutelage, scarcely allowed to make or carry out the most trifling decision without its approval. Besides this, almost all the towns were subject to the oversight of a Supervisor of Taxes in the neighbourhood."[1]

Stein's Edict set up a complete municipal system, with Burgomaster, Magistracy (*i.e.*, an Executive Board) and Town Council—all to be elective authorities. It swept away the oligarchy of the guilds, widened the franchise, and whilst opening office to all citizens laid down the principle that unpaid service to the community was obligatory upon every citizen from whom it might be required. In a natural reaction against the over-control of the previous *régime*, it gave the towns almost complete independence even in the matter of taxation, only laying down certain general rules, and retaining a modified right of supervision.[2] In general the control of the state over the administra-

[1] Von Raumer (quoted by Seeley, *Life and Times of Stein*), Pt. V., c. II., 3.

[2] The administration of justice was separated from municipal affairs, and given to royal officials; and the central government kept control of the "police," either through its own directly appointed agents, or through municipal officials who in this matter acted under its direction and supervision. Bornhak, III., pp. 20-22.

tion of the towns was unduly weakened, and this was one of the objections to the new system. Another was its want of elasticity, and a third was the absence of any means of ensuring harmony between the Magistracy and the Town Council. In the course of the next two decades these evils became apparent, and an attempt to remedy them was made by the Edict of 1831, which authorised the issue of a special statute (practically a special charter and constitution for each town) at its own initiative, widened the franchise, raised the qualification of councillors in order to secure a better class, settled the relations of the various bodies between themselves, and placed the towns beneath a stricter central control. The approval of the central authorities for all local taxation was also made necessary. The new Edict was to some extent reactionary, but it removed most of the previous difficulties; and though issued only for the province of Brandenburg, it was gradually extended to several of the other provinces. With these changes, consolidated and re-enacted in 1853, "the municipal government founded by Stein's great law in 1808 is as yet the only real and living piece of self-government in Prussia. It has, after nearly seventy years of a fruitful existence, driven its roots deep into the soil, and satisfactorily solved the great problem of local government, viz., the combining the administration of affairs which are partly private, partly public, in the same hands: it has established itself as the type which all future attempts at creating self - governing institutions must follow."[1]

Neither Stein nor Hardenberg touched the (ii) Communes. constitution of the country communes. But the way for change was prepared by the economic reforms and also by the introduction, during the Napoleonic occupation, of the French communal system into all the Prussian territories west of the Elbe. This survived until the Westphalian and Rhineland Edicts of 1841 and 1845. The nearly uniform system which these established was, however, much under the influence of the Napoleonic institutions, and is so to this day.

Since the reign of Frederick II. the division (iii) Circles. into Circles had been extended into all newly acquired territories. It rested, as did all local administration, on the politically privileged position of the great landed interest, and on the caste system. The Edicts of 1807 and 1811 swept away this basis, and some slight further reforms were made. In the reorganisation after the Congress of Vienna the Circle arrangement was imposed on all the conquered or reconquered territories. The most important changes subsequently made were in the position of the Landrath, who, as chief executive officer of the Circle, was to be at once a royal representative

---

[1] Sir Robert Morier, in the Cobden Club's *Local Government and Taxation* (1875), p. 424. By "partly private, partly public" Sir Robert must have meant "partly state, partly local."

S

and the official head of a corporation (for the
Circle now for the first time received the
position and rights of a body corporate); in
the reorganisation of the Circle Assemblies
(1825-28), which became representative of the
three estates of the large and small landowners
and the municipalities; and in taxation, when in
1841-42 the Circles received the power of taxation for their own local purposes, and full
control of their local finances.[1] The system
thenceforward remained unchanged until the
Bismarckian legislation of 1872.

(iv) Govern-
ment
Districts.

The Offices for War and Domains were
displaced in 1808 by the Government Boards
(*Regierungen*), and after 1815 the whole
kingdom was divided into twenty-six Government Districts (*Regierung-Bezirke*), each with
a President and Board of officials appointed
by the central authority; and, of these twenty-
six, twenty - one remain to-day practically
unaltered. In these Boards the collegial
system, under which all matters of any
importance must be settled by a majority of
votes of members of the Board, was retained;
whilst in the lower authorities the bureaucratic
system, under which almost all matters may
be settled by a single official, also continued.
It will be remembered that, with one or two
exceptions, these Government Districts do not
form corporate bodies; they exist only for

[1] Bornhak, III., pp. 50-71.

purposes of state control and for general, as opposed to local, matters. The plan was afterwards extended to the territories acquired by Prussia between 1860 and 1870, that is, to Schleswig-Holstein, Lauenberg, Hanover, Electoral Hesse, and Nassau.

The revival of the old provincial organisation (v) Provinces. began in 1815, when the kingdom was divided into ten Provinces, each to include two or more Government Districts. In each province a Chief President was appointed to exercise general control over all matters affecting the province as a whole. During the reaction after Hardenberg's death in 1822 the old provincial assemblies, based on the representation of the three estates of nobles, citizens, and peasants, with the first class predominating, were revived and given increased powers; Hardenberg himself had refused to touch them. But the attempt to galvanise them into life met with small success.

SECTION 3

The reorganisation of local administration The Constitutional carried out by Stein and Hardenberg has been Reform movement. described at some length, because the system then created remained in its essential features unchanged for half a century. When Hardenberg died in 1822 the constructive period had come to an end. Neither the idea of a general representative body, as Stein had conceived it, nor of a constitution, for which Hardenberg had persistently toiled, had been realised, although both had been publicly promised by the King in the crisis of the War of Liberation. The government was still an absolute monarchy, working by means of a powerful bureaucracy.[1] On the whole, it was probably well that there should be a long delay. After the Vienna Congress the Prussian statesmen had to face the same difficult and complicated task as Frederick II. after the conquest of Silesia. They had to attempt to weld together the various Prussian territories into a solid state, and to introduce some measure of uniformity into their administration. To a considerable extent this task had been accomplished when Hardenberg died; and it may be, as Treitschke holds, that for the future of Europe this was the most important event in the ten years after Waterloo. Till its accomplishment a system of general representation would have been of little or no use; when it was completed the forces of reaction had grown too powerful, and the nation had lost its former enthusiasm.

[1] " Der von allen Schranken befreite absolute Beamtenstaat unter Leitung des allmächtigen Staatskanzlers stand in seiner höchsten Vollendung da. Keine gesellschaftlichen Interessen wirkten auf das Beamtentum ein, Grundbesitz und Kapitalismus waren gleich einflusslos auf dasselbe. . . . Es war die zweite Blütezeit des preussischen Beamtentums, welche die unter Friedrich Wilhelm I. noch zu übertreffen schien." Bornhak, III., pp. 9-10.

The constitutional movements in Germany and their partial success in the South-German States (Bavaria, Würtemburg and others), and the "young German" agitation in the universities, had thoroughly alarmed the well-meaning but weak King. The Court party was hostile to all idea of a constitution, and the powerful influence of the Austrian minister, Metternich, worked unceasingly in the same direction. One result of this has been already noticed—the re-establishment of the provincial assemblies, based on a theory of social organisation which no longer corresponded to the facts. Another was a long period in which the growing commercial and industrial classes, outside the towns, were excluded from all share in the government, which remained the monopoly of the land-owners. The hostile forces were only held in check by the rather unreasonable amount of respect inspired by the old King; and immediately after the accession of Frederick William IV. the agitation began in earnest. The two parties, Liberal and Conservative, were now definitely organised; between them stood the bureaucracy, a distinct class, dependent solely upon the Ministry. It was the only class which as yet had shown any political ability; it was disliked equally by both political parties, and was again beginning to break down beneath the immense amount of work and authority necessarily assigned to it by Hardenberg in order to carry out his far-reaching social and economic reforms. The new King desired a constitution based upon the system of provincial estates, and was strongly opposed to the rule of the bureaucracy. But his attempts at compromise were certain to fail. He himself was not strong enough and had no capable adviser; the Liberals were encouraged and roused to action by the growing weakness of the governments of continental Europe; and the attempt to realise the King's idea by the summoning of the United Landtag (or general meeting of all the provincial assemblies) in 1847 began the struggle which ended with the victory of the Liberals and the publication of the Constitution of 31st January, 1850. This was, however, preceded by the establishment of the "three-class system" of elections (1849), which, while it accorded with the ideas of the Liberals in that it gave the preponderance of voting power to wealth, whatever its form, and not to land alone, at the same time robbed the new national representation of much of its value. Moreover, the new constitution (which is still in force and is almost unchanged) did not give "parliamentary government." The ministers are still the nominees of the monarch, and need not have the support of the legislature; the latter body is an advisory, informing, and legislative authority, with control over the budget; but its powers are very small compared with those of the British Parliament, for it

The Constitution of 1850.

cannot overthrow the ministers, and its conservative character renders it peculiarly amenable
to royal and official authority. We have already
seen how these two features — the conservative
nature of the membership and the submissive
attitude towards the bureaucracy—repeat themselves in the local institutions.

The Prussian Revolution of 1848-50 had been Reaction.
a triumph for the industrial and commercial classes,
a successful protest against the system by which
all the power of the state had been wielded for
the benefit of one particular class. When they
secured a majority in the new Landtag, and the
appointment of a favourable ministry, their whole
legislative efforts were directed towards the abolition of all special rights and privileges of the
landowners. In spite of the emancipation edicts
and economic reforms, these rights were still very
extensive; it was only in 1849, during the constitutional struggle, that the manorial courts, both
for civil and criminal matters, came to an end.
The Liberals had captured the Government for a
time, but a strong reaction was certain, for while
many of their proceedings were justified, in others
they undoubtedly went too far, and popular support
fell away. The Conservatives threw themselves
into alliance with the bureaucracy; they soon
secured the upper hand, and made their action
felt especially with regard to the rural communes
in a series of laws and edicts between 1853 and
1856. The importance of these lay chiefly in the

fact that they avowedly set aside the principles which since the Municipal Edict of Stein had never wholly lost influence, and reorganised the communes so as best to suit the interests of the great landowners. For this very reason they troubled little about the towns, except to strengthen the state control of the municipal administration; the Municipal Edict of 1853 is still in force for the eastern provinces. In the country communes of the western provinces they also did little, for, as they were modelled upon the French institutions set up by Napoleon I., they were closely dependent upon the bureaucracy. But in the eastern provinces, the peculiar strongholds of the great landowners, they restored as far as possible the old patrimonial administration, as authorised by the code of Frederick II., and made it almost completely free from state control. As the Liberals had sought to manipulate the local franchise to secure the preponderance of their own particular social classes, so did the Conservatives now.

Such rapid changes, and the constant struggle of each party to secure advantages for itself at the expense of the other, without regard for national interests, were only possible during the existence of a weak monarchy such as that of Prussia under Frederick William III. and his eldest son. With the accession in 1861 of William I., who had been the object of violent popular hostility during the struggle for the constitution, the whole position changed. The first sign of the new era was the appointment in the following year of Otto von Bismarck to be Minister-President, and the great constitutional struggle of 1860 to 1864 over the Army and Budget questions revealed the strength of the new rulers. They had come to their posts possessed of a distinct policy alike in home and foreign affairs— a characteristic lacking in Prussian ministries for more than a generation. The first decade after the accession of William I. was too fully occupied with foreign politics and war for serious attention to be given to matters of home administration; but immediately after the close of the Franco-German war Bismarck began the task of reform. In the hour of Prussia's greatest triumph he took up the work which Stein had commenced in the time of her severest misfortunes.

SECTION 4

The objects which Bismarck and his fellow-reformers now set before themselves had been learnt in the party struggles of the last twenty years.[1] The first thing necessary was to put an end, if it were in any way possible, to the system which had allowed the whole machinery of local government to be captured from time to time by a particular social class for its own benefit; and

The local government reforms of Bismarck: its aims.

[1] *Vide* Bornhak, III., p. 296 *seq.*

to devise some method by which all classes might participate in the work of local administration. About this time the works of Professor Gneist exercised great influence upon German political thinkers, and gave a theoretic basis to the practical proposals of Bismarck.[1] Gneist sought to explain the failure of parliamentary government in Prussia, and its success in England, by the fact that while in Prussia much thought had been given to the new parliamentary institutions, no regard had been paid, except in the one instance of the Freiherr vom Stein, to those local institutions which alone had in England rendered parliamentary government possible. To these, and to the organisation of local administrative authorities, elected in the towns and composed in the country districts of unpaid persons drawn from the upper and middle classes, with the landed gentry predominating, Gneist attached the very greatest importance. But at the same time he desired for Prussia a stronger administrative control than existed in England, and he thought it possible to combine in the administrative authorities unpaid lay or non-official persons and paid officials—the laymen to be elected.[2] Gneist promulgated that doctrine of self-government which still holds in

[1] His chief works in this connection are: *Geschichte des self-government in England* (1863); *Verwaltung, Justiz, Rechtsweg* (1867); *Die-preussische Kreisordnung* (1871); and *Der Rechtsstaat* (1872).

[2] Cf. Lowell, *Parties and Governments in Continental Europe*, I. pp. 309-310. But Lowell over-estimated the direct influence of Gneist upon legislation.

Prussia, that is, that "self - government is the performance by locally elected bodies of the will of the state," not necessarily of the locality which elects them—the local bodies are in the first place agents of the state, and only secondarily of the locality.[1] And in these bodies he found a training-school for administrators, and the means of developing a sense of responsibility which seemed altogether lacking at that time in the conduct of Prussian local government and in the Parliament. Led by these ideas the reformers, while retaining the bureaucracy (and in fact Bismarck believed that all development of local government must necessarily bring an increase in the bureaucracy) yet sought to carry through an extensive decentralisation of powers. They wished to transfer many of the powers of the central government to local elected bodies, and to weaken the power of the bureaucracy by the introduction of a large class of laymen into local administration. In this way they hoped to develop the political capabilities of the people; but at the same time the lay element was to be drawn in the main from the landowning classes (or at least from the large taxpayers) and these classes were to be given a more than

[1] "Preussen, wie im wesentlichen auch Deutschland, hat den Mittelweg eingeschlagen zwischen dem streng zentralisirten Frankreich, das die Selbstverwaltung nur als genau umschriebenes und eng eingegrentzes Glied der staatlichen Verwaltung kennt, und dem frei-gestalteten England, das die gesammte örtliche Verwaltung bis auf die Justiz und einen Teil der Polizei in Gemeinde und Grafschaft verweist und dem Staate nur eine ergänzende Tatigkeit belässt." H. de Grais, *Handbuch*, p. 96n.

numerically proportionate share of representation. For the first time in Prussian history, central[1] and local affairs were to be entrusted to a class of non-professional administrators.

But it was also necessary to establish some form of judicial control over the bureaucracy and the local administration generally. To this end the reformers proposed to set up a series of what are known as "administrative courts"; these, in the highest instance, should be composed of lawyers and officials, but in the lower instances should resemble the English Justices of the Peace, in that judicial and administrative functions alike should be entrusted to the same local bodies, consisting chiefly of unpaid laymen.

Obstacles to reform. There were great difficulties in the way: the vast majority of the people were indifferent, the bureaucracy hostile, the Conservatives in violent opposition. Only the steady support of the King availed to break down the resistance, and even then the position of Prussia made it necessary to proceed slowly and with caution.

For the first time in its history the kingdom of Prussia, after its conquests in the period from 1860 to 1870, possessed a connected territory extending from the Rhine to beyond the Vistula. But within this territory the local differences were very great; the Prussian ministry had again to face the problem of 1815. There was as yet no united Prussian nation. In the east, Posen after

---

[1] In the Regierung-Bezirke, for example, *vide supra*, pp. 139-142.

eighty years of Prussian rule still cherished its Polish national feeling as strongly as when it had impressed Heine in 1822;[1] and in spite of the settlements made by the German Government in its midst, the hostility there to Prussia and to all things German is to-day exceedingly great, as it is also in a part of Westpreussen. In the north-west, Schleswig-Holstein was newly acquired, and not yet assimilated to the Prussian state; south of that, in Hanover, whatever the mass of the population felt, there was a noble class which was not inclined to yield its rights without a struggle; and still further south there was a group of terri-tories, Hesse and Nassau being the chief, newly acquired and not yet organised or fully incor-porated into Prussia. But still greater than the political were the economic and social diversities. Between the provinces of the extreme east where, as in Ostpreussen and Posen, three-quarters of the population were engaged in agriculture, and the whole organisation of society rested on that basis; and the most westernly provinces, Rhineland and Westphalia, where already the industrial classes predominated and the industrial organisation was fast gaining ground—between these two extremes almost every variety of social and economic organisation could be found.

It was therefore necessary to proceed slowly. The new organisation. The first enactments, for the Circles in 1872 and the Provinces in 1875, were issued only for those

[1] Cf. Heine, "Ueber Polen," in *Reisebilder*.

territories which had formed the old monarchy—
that is, for the eastern group except Posen. In
that province the anti-Prussian feeling rendered a
strictly bureaucratic administration almost inevitable. The enactments were gradually extended,
with various alterations and additions to meet
local peculiarities, to the remainder of the kingdom
during the next ten years. Further legislation
was necessary to harmonise the system, and after
Bismarck's dismissal the work was continued by
the great Landgemeinde-Ordnung (which may be
described as a Parish Councils Act) issued for the
seven eastern provinces in 1891. Finally, the local
authorities received their due share of attention in
the financial reforms carried out by Dr von Miquel.

General
character-
istics.

In regard to all these administrative reforms it
will be noticed that they have almost always been
imposed from above. If we except the agitation
for the constitution, there has never been in
Prussia a strong popular movement for political
reform; and this phenomenon is apparent in local
government also. Like its great rival, the Prussian
state has been created by its monarchs, aided by
a powerful bureaucracy; and like that rival, over-
centralisation has brought it to the verge of ruin.
But in both countries the lesson has been only
partially learned. In both a system of decentralisation and self-government has been introduced, and
in neither is it very real. We have seen the
characteristics of France; of Prussia it must be
said that the bureaucracy still rules, and that the

ordinary citizen is neither able nor inclined to take much part in the work of local administration except under the guidance and direction of officials. In the towns there is something of a healthy civic spirit, and the work of municipal management is admirably done, as is in fact the administration generally; but the fact remains that the initiative comes from the officials. But the mass of citizens seem satisfied, and whatever complaints may be heard regarding the omnipotence of officialdom there is no energetic protest against it, except occasionally from the great cities. The strong socialist party has done little in the matter; unlike France, Prussia has no examples of socialist municipalities—official control is much too strong, and the " three-class system " is an almost insuperable obstacle. But it must be said that the bureaucracy does its task extremely well; it has developed in many matters an almost perfect method of working. It has encouraged municipal activity and enterprise to an extent unsurpassed except in England, and in some things not equalled even there. If it has kept affairs in its own hands, it is because the Prussian people do not care to take the responsibility. They prefer to have something done for them rather than to do it themselves; they expect to be guided, not to find their own way. Which simply means that tradition is stronger than education, and that the Prussians are acquiring only very slowly the art of self-government and all that it involves.

CHAPTER VIII

ADMINISTRATIVE LAW

SECTION 1

"Administrative law" in continental countries.

THE English student who undertakes an investigation into the administrative organisation and methods of the countries of continental Europe speedily encounters a definite body of legal principles and enactments, called in France *droit administratif*, and in Germany *Verwaltungsrecht*. He also finds that this particular body of law is not entrusted to the guardianship of the ordinary courts of justice, but to a set of special tribunals constituted in a quite different manner. He knows that no such courts exist in England, and he will find that no such carefully distinguished system of law is recognised by English legal writers.

Its contrast to the "rule of law" in England.

If now he turns to Professor Dicey's "Introduction to the Law of the Constitution" he will read there that one of the chief features of English polity since the Norman Conquest has been "the rule or supremacy of law," and that this involves "three distinct though kindred conceptions." [1] There is first the exclusion of arbitrariness or even of any wide discretionary powers on the part of the Government; that is, no man can be lawfully made to suffer "except for a distinct breach of law established in the ordinary legal manner before the ordinary Courts of the Land." Secondly, constitutional law is not so much the origin as the result of individual rights defined and enforced by the Courts. And thirdly, there is "the equal subjection of all classes to the ordinary law of the land administered by the ordinary Law Courts." This supremacy of law in England is contrasted with the conditions prevalent in other European countries, where the state governments have very considerable discretionary powers which can be, and often are, used in an arbitrary manner, unchecked by ordinary courts of justice, or sometimes by any courts at all; where the political rights of individuals are the result of constitutions often granted by governments as an act of grace; and where an important section of the community (the official class) is to a large extent withdrawn from the control of the ordinary judicial authorities. As a particular instance of these things, and especially of the last, reference is made to France, where "officials are, in their official capacity, protected from the ordinary law of the land, and exempted from the jurisdiction of the ordinary tribunals, and subject in many

---

[1] Dicey, *Law of the Constitution* (6th edition), c. iv., *passim*.

T

respects only to official law administered by
official bodies." In this respect there is a striking
contrast with England, where " every act of
public authority, no matter by whom, or against
whom it is directed, is liable to be called in
question before an ordinary tribunal, and there
is no other means by which its legality can be
questioned or established." [1]

The system of law thus indicated as existent
in France, and in most continental countries, is
so little known in England, and a proper appreciation of its true nature is so important in any
study of continental administration, and especially
of the control of authorities, that it is necessary
to try to understand clearly what a foreign jurist
means by the term " administrative law." [2] Without entering unnecessarily into detail, and without discussing the numerous problems which arise
both in theory and practice, it will be sufficient
here to state the general principles on which
administrative law is based.

Definitions.

We may take first two definitions, one from a
French, and the other from a German, authority.
Aucoc writes:

" Le droit administratif détermine : 1. La constitution et les rapports des organes de la société

---

[1] Redlich and Hirst, II., p. 365.

[2] Dicey remarks (p. 323) that the expression "administrative
law," which is the most natural rendering of *droit administratif*,
is unknown to English judges and counsel. This seems to be true,
mainly because of the absence in England of any scientific classification of law, in which the term must take its place. Cf. Holland,
Elements of Jurisprudence (3rd edition), pp. 305 *seq.*

chargés du soin des intérêts collectifs qui font l'objet de l'administration publique, c'est-à-dire des différentes personnifications de la société, dont l'Etat est la plus importante; 2. les rapports des autorités administratives avec les citoyens."[1]

And the German jurist, von Rönne, writes:

"Die Rechtgrundsätze, welche sich auf die Bildung jener Einrichtungen, sowie auf die Bestellung und Instruktion jener Organe beziehen, also der Inbegriff der Normen über die Ausübung der Staatsgewalt und der einzelnen Hoheitsrechte innerhalb der Grenzen der Verfassung, bilden das Verwaltungsrecht."[2]

The constitutional laws of a country do not ordinarily do more than formulate the general principles on which the political system of that country is based, and draw its main outlines. They define the relations to one another of the three branches of government — the legislative, the executive, the judiciary; they may also indicate in detail the methods by which these three are to be formed, and they establish certain political rights of the individual citizens. But there remains after that a multitude of further details to be settled — the application of the principles of the constitution, and provision for the realisation of the aims of the state, amid the ever-changing economic and social conditions of national life. The laws which do this are

---

[1] *Conférences sur le droit administratif*, I., p. 6.
[2] *Preussisches Staatsrecht.*

subsidiary to the constitutional laws, and are
their necessary complement, since they prescribe
the manner in which the institutions created by
the constitutional laws are to work from day to
day.[1]

But this is the widest possible meaning of the
term; used in this way it would include all the
rules of procedure adopted by the legislature and
the courts of justice, whether determined in the
latter case by the judges themselves or imposed
upon them by the legislature. But the term has
come to be employed generally in a more limited
sense, and to be applied only to those laws and
regulations, enforceable in some court of justice,
which relate to the organisation and working of
the national executive, both central and local.
Thus the laws concerning the formation and
powers of government departments, the whole
body of laws which establish local authorities
and direct their working, enactments concerning
the civil service, the regulations issued by various
authorities under any legal sanction—all these are
part of administrative law.[2]

[1] Holland (p. 305) remarks that constitutional law describes the
organs of the sovereign power at rest, whilst all laws which prescribe the manner of their action form administrative law in its
widest sense. Cf. Berthélemy, p. 2: "Comment l'appareil est con-
struit, c'est le droit constitutionnel qui nous apprend; comment il
travaille, comment fonctionne chacune de ses pièces, c'est la matière
du droit administratif."

[2] Administrative law is then "that part of the public law which
fixes the organisation and determines the competence of the administrative authorities, and indicates to the individual remedies for the
violation of his rights" by them. Goodnow, *Comparative Administrative Law*, I., pp. 8-9.

SECTION 2

As it is evident that such a body of law does exist in England, there arises the question why it does not occupy so distinct and separate a place, in the minds of lawyers and ordinary citizens alike, as it does upon the Continent of Europe. The answer is to be found in a number of facts, all closely related to one another. Reasons for the absence of any such definite body of law in England.

The first is that, owing to the peculiar course of our national development, we have no definite body of constitutional laws, no formal constitution such as is possessed by almost every other civilised state; we have no one law, or even small group of laws, regulating the three branches of the national government; and much of our constitutional practice is based on custom which no court of law could enforce. One result of this is that many writers on the English Constitution[1] include in their survey a large number of matters which would certainly be omitted by a foreign jurist writing on the constitution of his own country; and it is extremely hard here to say what is, and what is not, to be included under the term "constitutional law." But if we examine the constitutional laws of another country (*e.g.*, the United States, Switzerland, Prussia, or the German Empire) we shall (1) No formal constitution.

---

[1] *E.g.*, Anson, in his *Law and Custom of the Constitution*, Part II. ("The Crown").

find that they are comparatively few in number, often contained in a single document of very limited size, and that they do not do much more than has already been indicated; they announce a number of general principles, especially the rights of individual citizens; they organise, in outline, the legislature, the executive, the judiciary; but they leave the arrangements for practical working to be made, sometimes by each branch of the government for itself, or else (and most usually) by the legislature for all three. This distinction between fundamental and subsidiary laws is rendered still more emphatic by the fact that the latter can be changed by ordinary legislative processes, whilst constitutional laws often require for their enactment and amendment a special and sometimes very elaborate procedure.

(2) No codification of laws. Secondly, this difficulty of distinguishing between the two sets of laws is enhanced for the English student by the absence of any scientific codification of the law, and the indifference towards questions of classification shown by most of our ordinary legal writers.[1] If, however, we take the scheme adopted by French jurists, the place of administrative law, and its general character, at once become clear.[2] All law is either private or public. Private law regulates the relations of individuals between themselves; they may be members of the same

---

[1] Goodnow, I., pp. 6-7.
[2] Cf. Bœuf, *Droit Administratif*, p. 1.

state, in which case their relations are governed by private (national or civil) law; or they may be members of different states, and then they are subject to private international law. Public law, on the other hand, regulates the relations between the individual citizens in a state and the state itself, or between different states. In the latter case it is public international law, and is said to be external to any particular state; in the former case it is internal, and falls into three divisions. The first of these is constitutional law, which is concerned with the establishment of the principles and forms of government; the second is administrative law, which is the supplement and detailed application of the first;[1] and the third is criminal law, which deals with the definition and punishment of criminal acts.[2] The general classification adopted by German writers is much the same.[3]

---

[1] "Le droit constitutionnel pose les grands principes de l'organisation sociale et politique, fixe la constitution de l'état, la forme de son gouvernement, les conditions de l'exercice de la souveraineté, et organise les grands pouvoirs publics qui président sur la marche de la société. . . . Le droit administratif, réglementant et développant les principes du droit constitutionnel, fixe les rapports des particuliers avec les diverses autorités administratives, qui relèvent du pouvoir exécutif, et détermine les sacrifices qui l'intérêt public réclame de l'intérêt privé pour la satisfaction des besoins généraux. . . . Le premier se préoccupe surtout des droits garantis aux citoyens . . . le second a principalement pour le but de déterminer les devoirs des citoyens." Bœuf, loc. cit.

[2] Ecclesiastical law—enforceable in the state courts—is only a part of administrative law.

[3] Cf. Kahl, in his *Grundriss zu Vorlesungen über Verwaltungsrecht*: "Innerhalb des Rechtssystems dem öffentlichen Rechte, innerhalb dieses dem Staatsrecht im weitesten Sinne angehörig und von ihm als wissenschaftliche Disziplin nur aus den Bedürfnissen geistiger

(3) No special tribunals.   Thirdly, a practical reason for the non-recognition of administrative law, as a separate branch, is the fact that we do not possess any special tribunals to which it is entrusted. For in this country all disputes in any branch of law go to one set of courts of justice; controversies between two individual citizens, between two public authorities, or between a public authority and a private person, are all determined by the same courts. The ordinary practice of the courts applies generally, though with some exceptions, to all three kinds of cases; consequently, as the legal remedies for the infringement of rights are almost identical, there is nothing to mark off the rights of citizens against public authorities from their rights against each other. In countries which have adopted the system of administrative law, that is not the case; it may be stated, in general terms, that there disputes between public authorities, and still more conflicts between authorities and ordinary citizens, are decided by a special set of courts, and that the remedies given by these courts for the infringement of individual rights by the authorities are quite different from those given in other cases by the ordinary tribunals.

Arbeitsteilung getrennt, umfasst das Verwaltungsrecht die Rechts-regeln über die Organisation der Verwaltungsbehörden, sowie über wesentlich diejenigen Funktionen des Staats und der Kommunal-verbände, welche im spezifischen, wiewohl nicht ausschliessendem Gegensatz zu Gesetzgebung und Gerichtsbarkeit den Inhalt der regierenden Tätigkeit der öffentlichen Gewalten im Staate bilden."

And this brings us to the last reason for (4) **Different principles as to the legal relations between the administration and the individual.** the absence of any distinction here between the two kinds of law. Administrative law, as the term is understood upon the Continent, is in fact, as Dicey points out, something more than the legal enactments as to the powers of public authorities; it includes also a number of principles as to the nature of the relations between the administration and its agents on the one side, and the private citizen on the other. We have next to examine the precise nature of the disputes which are withdrawn from the cognisance of the ordinary judicial tribunals; to point out the reasons advanced in defence of this withdrawal, and for the existence of the special courts, and to show how this contrasts with the English rule.

SECTION 3

The acts done by a public authority may be **The sphere of the administrative courts.** of two kinds. There are some which can be done only by an administrative authority as such, and others which could equally well be done by private persons. For example, the making of bye-laws, or the assessment of taxes—these acts are possible only to the central administration or one of the local authorities acting in accordance with powers definitely conferred upon it;

they are acts of authority (*actes de puissance publique, Ausübung der Staatsgewalt*). But there are also a number of actions of an altogether different kind, taken by a local authority or even by a central department as agents of a corporate body. Thus a town may own land, houses, or other property, and its council (as its agent) may let or buy or sell such property; these are acts which any private person could do, and are unofficial (*actes du person privé*). Now, in general it is the principle, in both France and Prussia, that all actions which are possible to an authority, *because it is an authority*, are removed from the competence of the ordinary courts of the land; the judges in these can take cognisance only of the business acts which arise from the fact that the authorities—representative either of the locality or the state—form bodies corporate, and have a certain amount of corporate business.[1] There are some exceptions to this, some matters which under it would come before the ordinary courts have been transferred to the administrative courts by legislative enactment, and, on the other hand, disputes in regard to the expropriation of land for public purposes, which is clearly an *acte de puissance publique*, go in France to

---

[1] "On ne doit pas considérer comme échappant de plein droit de la compétence judiciaire tout acte émané de l'administration, toute opération accomplie ou prescrite par elle en vue d'un intérêt général, mais seulement les actes ou les opérations qui se rattachent à l'exercise de la puissance publique, et qui excèdent, à ce titre, les facultés des citoyens." De Laferrière, *La Jurisdiction Administrative*, I. p. 199.

the ordinary judicial tribunals. But the rule which governs the division of cases, as a whole, is the one just stated.

It should be observed, however, that penalties for the infringement of the law by the citizens are enforced by the ordinary police tribunals, and not by the special courts; and this may mean that one of these ordinary courts may find itself called upon to determine the validity of an order or bye-law issued by a central or local authority. It can do so, and if it considers the order or bye-law invalid, it will refuse to impose any penalty for disobedience. But it cannot formally annul the order or bye-law — that can be done only by an administrative court.[1]

One very important result of this distinction is a difference between England and continental countries in the legal position of authorities and officials over against the citizens. Here, if a private individual suffers damage from an official in the execution of an order which is illegal, or in consequence of an act which is beyond the official's authority, he has a remedy in the ordinary courts, and against the particular official concerned; he may sue him for damages, or, in certain cases, prosecute him. It may be that the official acted in obedience to orders, but that fact does not enable him to escape responsibilty—it only causes him to share responsibility with his superiors. And the ordinary courts of justice,

[1] Berthélemy, pp. 33-34.

in deciding upon the liability of the official, really decide upon the validity of the order or act in question. That is to say, the English principle makes the official personally responsible, though he may have acted in perfectly good faith, from a mistaken idea of duty or even in obedience to orders from his superiors, and his liability is determined by the ordinary courts.[1] But in continental countries the case is different, and we may take France as the best example.

"La garantie des fonction- naires." From the year 1799 French officials were protected by the so-called *garantie des fonctionnaires*, which forbad the bringing of any action against any administrative official except with the consent of the Council of State.[2] With

---

[1] "In England the idea of legal equality, or of the universal subjection of all classes to one law administered by the ordinary courts, has been pushed to its uttermost limit." Dicey, p. 185. "There is no exception in England to the rule that every public proceeding, be it the issue of a warrant to arrest, or a demand for rates, or a summons to pay money due to a public authority, or an order of justices, is just as much a matter of ordinary law, and is liable to be questioned in the same way, as a private suit or action brought by one individual against another. In either case the question as to what is lawful has to be decided by the ordinary courts." Redlich and Hirst, II., p. 365.

[2] "All servants of the State, below the rank of a minister, may be taken before an ordinary court of law to answer for an official act only by a decree of the Council of State." *Art.* 75 *of Constitution of* 1799. Dicey (pp. 347-48) compares this with the old English writ *De non procedendo rege inconsulto*, obsolete already in the sixteenth century, of which Bacon wrote: "The writ is a mean provided by the ancient law of England to bring any case, that may concern your Majesty in profit and power, from the ordinary Benches to be tried and judged before the Chancellor of England. . . . *And your Majesty knoweth that your Chancellor is ever a principal counsellor and instrument of monarchy, of immediate dependence upon the King; and therefore likely to be a safe and tender guardian of the regal rights.*"

the permission of that body the action could be brought before the ordinary courts. The guarantee did not apply to acts committed by officials not in the exercise of their authority; if the act complained of was a personal fault of the official—that is, if it was the result of a malicious use of lawful powers or of a malicious excess of powers—the Council of State would authorise the action; but if it was a *faute de service*—that is, an unintentional excess of the legal authority possessed by the official, or a mistaken application of that authority—then the administration was responsible, but not the official personally, at least so far as the aggrieved citizen was concerned, though of course he would be subject to the disciplinary control of his superiors. But this power of the Council of State to prevent actions against officials was liable to abuse, and was abolished in 1870. There has been much discussion as to the exact effect of the abolition; but it appears now to be definitely established that, without any permission, actions can be brought against officials in the ordinary courts; but if the administrative authority hold that the act was not a personal one on the part of the officer concerned, but was committed by him in pursuit of his duty and as a part of his duty, then they can invoke the Tribunal of Conflicts and have the matter removed to the administrative courts, where it may be that the complainant has no very satisfactory remedy. But for personal faults the official remains liable in the ordinary courts. Thus if an officer commits an illegal act in the supposed execution of his duty, or in obedience to orders, he is answerable to the administrative tribunals only; but should the abuse of power have been conscious and deliberate, and not in obedience to orders, then the case falls within the jurisdiction of the ordinary courts.

The German view.   The sketch just given summarises the general doctrines of the French jurists, and is based upon French authorities; it will be well to set beside it an outline of the general position in Prussia. The laws and regulations relative to the public administration may be violated by subjects or officials, and they are protected therefore in two different ways. Against violation of the law by the subject, there are the ordinary police powers to enforce obedience, and these, as in France, can be exercised usually only by the ordinary courts.[1] But in the case of officials the remedies differ, according as the act is a conscious neglect of duty, or a mistaken or illegal use of authority. The first of these is clearly a matter of discipline—the official is subject to the customary bureaucratic control. For the other cases there are three remedies. The first is the right which one authority has to supervise the actions of another;

---

[1] The administrative courts then are not concerned with the action taken by local authorities against private citizens to compel them to obey the law, but solely with actions against the authorities themselves. This rule applies alike in France and Prussia.

for example, a Landrath may interfere on his own initiative with the acts of an Amtsvorsteher within his Circle. Secondly, a complaint may be lodged by the person aggrieved with the superior authority, which then hears and decides the matter. And thirdly, an action may be brought against the official or officials whose conduct is challenged ; and such action comes before the administrative courts.[1] The control in the first two cases is administrative; in the third it is judicial. As a rule, where one of these last two remedies can be employed, recourse may not be had to the other ; but in some cases an option is allowed, and in others an action can be brought only when a complaint has been lodged and the complainant is dissatisfied with the result. The basis of a complaint may be either that the act which is challenged is not adapted to the end in view,[2] or is not in accordance with the law ; an action may be brought only on the ground of illegality. But in a large number of instances the particular remedy to be employed is settled by the Competence Law,[3] which states positively in what cases the action may be brought, and, therefore, negatively in what cases the complaint is the only remedy. Beyond this the doctrine of

[1] The technical German terms for the three forms are : (1) das Aufsichtsrecht; (2) die Verwaltungsbeschwerde; (3) die Verwaltungsklage.

[2] *Unzweckmässig.*

[3] Das Zustandigkeitsgesetz. The text of this will be found in Anschütz, *Organisationsgesetze der inneren Verwaltung in Preussen.*

Prussian administrative law agrees with that held in France, that actions against officials for anything done by them in the real or intended exercise of their authority can be brought only in the administrative courts; but that those acts done by public authorities, which are equally within the power of private individuals, and deliberate excesses or abuses of power, are normally within the sphere of the ordinary tribunals.

There must of course constantly be cases where it is very uncertain which set of courts has jurisdiction, the more so as the content of administrative law is perpetually changing. Therefore in both France and Prussia special courts have been set up ("Tribunal des Conflits," "Kompetenzgerichthof") on which both the ordinary and administrative courts are represented; their task is to settle all doubtful questions of jurisdiction.

SECTION 4

The argument for administrative courts.

There remains the question as to the reasons alleged in support of this system. Viewed from one standpoint, it is simply an extreme application of the theory of the separation of powers, which holds that the three branches of the state government must be absolutely distinct, each confined within its own particular sphere of action. A

(i) Separation of powers.

necessary consequence is that the judiciary may not interfere with the executive in the exercise of the latter's authority, which is based only partially on legislative enactment; and is largely discretionary. But there must be some restraint on the executive, some way of preventing merely arbitrary action; therefore within the executive a special judicial authority should be established. The principle was not necessarily bad in itself; the danger lay in the fact that the special courts might become the creatures of the administration. In modern Prussian legislation an attempt has been made to guard against this peril by a system of popular (though indirect) representation upon the lower administrative courts, and by security of tenure for the judges in the highest court; and, on the whole, the effort has met with considerable success. In France the composition of the courts tends to place them much more under the control of the executive, or at least less likely to take an independent line, than in Prussia; but, nevertheless, there does not appear to be any serious complaint as to their working.

Professor Dicey has observed that the fundamental idea of continental administrative law—that " affairs or disputes in which the Government and its servants are concerned are beyond the sphere of the civil courts, and must be dealt with by more or less official bodies "—is " alien to modern Englishmen." Whilst this is in the main undoubtedly true, it must be remembered that even in England the citizen is not entirely unhampered in any dispute with a public authority.

U

He cannot sue the Crown except on the grant of
a petition of right, and that petition is granted
by the Crown on the advice of the Attorney-
General, who is himself a political officer.   There
are cases also in which a department, for example
the Local Government Board, is authorised to
determine disputes as to the powers and duties
of local authorities, and in so doing may have to
decide doubtful legal questions.[1]   These exceptions
to the general rule in this country are indeed few
in number, but they should help to make the line
of argument which has prevailed elsewhere in
Europe intelligible to English students.

(ii) Discre-
tionary
powers of the
administra-
tion.

The state exists for one general purpose in
the pursuit of which it engages in a number
of diverse activities.   Now in regard to these
activities two things must be recognised.   The
first is that to the administration, that is, to the
recognised executive agents of the state, a greater
or smaller amount of discretion must often be
allowed as to the exact course to be adopted to
obtain a desired result.   The legislature may
attempt to regulate the action of the executive
in every detail, or it may be content to authorise
the executive to take whatever action may seem
to it advisable under particular circumstances.   It

---

[1] These "quasi-judicial" functions of the Local Government Board
"do not really encroach upon the unity and sovereignty of the law.
Nevertheless they have been sufficient to cause uneasiness to English
jurists and statesmen, who have bestirred themselves to throw
obstacles in the way of the extension of these functions."   Redlich
and Hirst, II., p. 365.

may give departments power to issue rules, regulations, and orders, or to make bye-laws, or to
elaborate legislative outlines, and to decide the
manner in which enactments shall be applied in
detail. All this is discretionary power. This
executive discretion is comparatively small in
England, though more extensive than is commonly
supposed; it is much greater in Prussia, and
perhaps greatest in France (of the countries now
under discussion). The second consideration is
that the state, in whatever it undertakes, cannot
be regarded as engaged in ordinary business, or
as holding the same relation to the citizens as
they hold to one another; it has special rights
and responsibilities, it has the discretionary power;
the officials, being its agents, are more than the
agents of a private individual, as the state itself
is more than a private individual, and cannot be
subject to the same rules of law. A distinguished
American authority writes :—

"The result of the position of the administration as the representative of the sovereign is that
the law which governs the relations into which it
enters as such representative is quite different in
many respects from the private law. In this law
contract and tort play a very subordinate rôle.
While contract and tort lie at the basis of a large
part of the private law, in public law, and therefore in administrative law, there is hardly any
room for them at all, it may be said, except
where the government is treated as *fiocus—i.e.*,
as a subject of private law. For the relations
into which the administration enters are not as

a rule contractual relations, but find their sources and their limitations rather in obligations or powers conferred by the sovereign power through its representative, the legislature ; nor are the injuries which the administration as administration commits often torts, but are rather to be classed as *damna absque injuria*." [1]

The relations between the administration and the citizens being then different from those which exist between the citizens themselves, it is not unreasonable that the rules governing them should also be somewhat different, and in that case it is well that cases arising under them should be decided by special judges. For the ordinary judges are engaged chiefly with cases arising out of private law, and they will be inclined to apply, as they have applied in England, the same principles in cases of public law ; and this may be harmful in some cases to the effectiveness of the administration and the realisation of the very purposes for which it exists. [2]

[1] Goodnow, I., pp. 11-12.

[2] For a general summary (from a sympathetic standpoint) of the whole argument see Goodnow, I. Bk. I. Cf. Sidgwick, *Elements of Politics* (edition 1891), p. 482. " My fear is that a tribunal, not specialised by containing as one element persons who have had experience of executive work, will hardly be well qualified to interpret the limiting rules of law wherever a somewhat indefinite standard has to be applied. There is, however, a considerable difficulty in constructing a tribunal of this kind that will command general confidence and not be widely suspected of undue bias in favour of the executive. If this difficulty be found insuperable, it may be necessary for the effective performance of governmental work, to give the executive somewhat wider powers than it ordinarily requires, trusting to public opinion and parliamentary criticism to keep the exercise of those powers within somewhat narrower limits than those enforced by the judiciary."

Such is, briefly, the argument; and the result is the erection in France and Prussia of the special administrative courts, which apply a distinct set of principles to cases arising under the laws regulating the action of the executive. Such courts would not be alarming to Englishmen if they were established as a separate branch of the Supreme Court of Judicature; they are alarming chiefly because they bear a name which suggests that they are the servants and tools of the executive, that they are used often to give a false appearance of legality to arbitrary acts, and that they are inclined to wrest the law to the purposes of the administration. It is true that the remedies given to the citizen under the English system are in some ways more effective, but apart from that it cannot now be said (whatever may have been the case originally) that the administrative courts show any marked tendency to favour the executive unduly. Everything depends on the principles guiding the action of these special courts; if they attempt to decide not merely upon the legality, but also upon the policy, of any particular act which comes before them, or if (to put it in another way) they are inclined to declare any act legal because the administration deems it expedient, then it is evident that they may become instruments for the support of arbitrary action and the oppression of the citizens. But, though they unquestionably have

in the past sometimes been so used, they are
coming more and more to limit themselves to
the consideration of the legality of any act
brought before them; and in both France and
Prussia the courts and the jurists together have
built up an elaborate system which is based
upon the strictest principles of legal interpretation, and upon a regard for precedent (for
administrative law is largely "case law") as
strong as that entertained by the civil tribunals.
The remedies which they give may not be
completely satisfactory, viewed from the English
standpoint, but their action is regular and very
little influenced by any special regard for the
convenience of the executive. Professor Dicey
writes of France (and his remarks would apply
with even more force to Prussia):

"*Droit administratif* with all its peculiarities and
administrative tribunals with all their defects have
been suffered to exist because the system as a
whole is thought by Frenchmen to be beneficial.
Its severest critics concede that it has some great
practical merits, and is suited to the spirit of
French institutions. Meanwhile *droit administratif*
has developed under the influence of lawyers
rather than politicians; it has during the last
half century more and more divested itself of its
arbitrary character, and is passing into a system
of more or less fixed law administered by real
tribunals. . . . These tribunals are certainly very
far indeed from being mere departments of the
central government." [1]

[1] *Loc. cit.*, pp. 500-1.

CHAPTER IX

LOCAL AUTHORITIES AND THE LEGISLATURE

SECTION 1

IN the previous chapters an attempt has been made to describe briefly the organisation and principles of local administration in England, France, and Prussia, and to sketch its development in relation to the constitutional changes which each state has undergone. An account has also been given of some characteristic features of American city government. It remains for us now to consider somewhat more in detail the general nature of the relations between the elected authorities of the local self-governing communities and the representatives of the central power; and it will be convenient to commence by examining the ways in which the powers possessed by the localities are conferred upon them. *The grant of powers to local authorities.*

There are two possible policies which a legislature may adopt towards local authorities, apart from the imposition of compulsory duties upon them. There is first the plan of grants of general power to all local bodies of a particular *(a) General.*

311

class—that is, the legislature may establish a set of authorities and empower them to do anything which in their judgment will tend to promote the satisfactory administration and general well-being of their areas, so long as any particular powers which they may propose to use are not expressly prohibited or reserved to other authorities. But as this liberty might easily in some cases be abused, there is necessarily the restriction, of greater or less extent according to the country and the nature of the authorities in question, that the actual exercise of these general powers shall be subject to the approval of an administrative department of the central government, or its agents. Or, on the other hand, the legislature may grant

(b) Specific. only specific powers to local authorities—that is, it may give them permission to do all or any of a number of enumerated things, with or without the approval of central departments; and then nothing else may be done by the local authorities unless permitted by fresh legislative enactments.

Contrast be-
tween British
and Continen-
tal methods.   Now, speaking in general terms, it may be said that continental legislatures have been inclined to adopt the first of these two methods, and to give the local self-governing communities power to do anything for which they can get administrative approval. In Great Britain, the British self-governing colonies, and the United States, the practice has been the opposite one—

local authorities may do only specified things; but in order, in spite of this, to allow free play to local initiative and enterprise, provision has been made to enable local authorities to obtain additional powers by means of special legislation promoted by themselves.   This difference between what we may conveniently call the English and continental methods has this very important result, that in England and the United States the development of the activities of local authorities is conditioned and controlled by the temper and ideas of Parliament—that is, of the elected representatives of the nation;[1] whilst in France and Prussia the deciding influence is exercised by a bureaucracy whose general ideas of policy in these matters may or may not be coincident with those of the majority of the nation.   It is impossible to generalise as to the effect of this in practice: it may fairly be doubted if, under a system of bureaucratic control, there would have been so great an extension of some branches of local, and especially municipal, government, as we have witnessed in England in the last thirty years; though there is the example of Prussia to show that bureaucratic rule may be very enlightened, and ready to encourage and aid, in every way, the growth of local action and experiment.   But against this there is the case of France, where (rightly or

---

[1] There are some modifications of this, but they are not sufficient to affect the principle seriously.

wrongly) the bureaucracy has steadily resisted most of the schemes put forward by the more enterprising municipalities.

A further consequence is the existence in England of an elaborate system of Private Bill legislation, not confined to local authorities but very largely used by them, and with a procedure quite different from that followed by Public Bills. The distinction between the two classes of Bills has been thus defined by an eminent authority :[1]

"A Public Bill is introduced as a measure of public policy in which the whole community is interested, and originates on the motion of some member of the House in which the Bill is introduced. A Private Bill is a measure for the interest of some person, or class of persons, whether an individual, a corporation, or the inhabitants of a county, town, parish, or other locality, and originates on the petition of the person or persons interested. The object of a Private Bill is, in fact, to obtain a *privilegium*, that is to say, an exemption from the general law, or provision for something which cannot be obtained by means of a general law, whether that general law is contained in a statute or is common law."[2]

This system of Private Bill legislation employed here, which, as will be seen later, is partly legislative and partly judicial, is peculiar

---

[1] Ilbert, *Legislative Methods and Forms*, p. 28.

[2] The "petition" character of a Private Bill is marked by the words in which the royal assent is given—*soit fait comme il est désiré* as compared with *Le roi le veut* for Public Bills.

to this country and its self-governing colonies.
In continental countries the grant of general
powers renders it unnecessary for local authorities
to have recourse to the legislature, and the
wide discretionary power of the administration
is substituted for parliamentary control in the
case of proposals both by local bodies and
private individuals or companies.[1] Consequently
any foreign local authorities who may be desirous
of extending the sphere of their activities, are not
troubled by the necessity of a costly, cumbrous,
slow and somewhat doubtful procedure : and the
time of the legislature is not occupied so much
as in England by questions of purely local interest.
That the British Parliament could be made more
effective for dealing with imperial and national
questions by relieving it of the burden of Private
Bill legislation may be doubtful, and it is certainly
not desirable to substitute a merely official control
over the development of local action for that
which now exists ; but it should not be impossible
to devise an arrangement which would combine
the advantages of un-bureaucratic control with
the rapidity and cheapness of the continental
system, and an account of the present methods
may serve to suggest some of the lines on which
this object could be attained. The experience of
the States of the American Union in regard to

---

[1] In a few cases relating to finance French local authorities
promote Bills, which proceed, however, in the same way as other
legislation in the French Parliament.

Private Bills, or what is there called "special legislation," is so instructive as also to deserve a brief examination.

SECTION 2

Legislative enactments concerning local government.

English local authorities exercise their powers under legislative enactments of various kinds. There are first what may be called the "Constituent Acts," which create the various classes of local government authorities, and arm them with the powers necessary for the fulfilment of the duties intended to be discharged by them.

(1) Constituent Acts.

(2) General Acts.

Secondly, there are "General Acts" dealing with one special subject or group of subjects of administration (such as the Public Health Act, 1875, and the Education Act, 1902), and giving powers for that particular service either to all authorities or to all of a class. Thirdly, there are the "Adoptive Acts," a favourite device of British legislators; they are laws conferring on all or specified local authorities powers which, if they wish to do so, they become entitled to exercise simply by formally "adopting" them, with, in some cases, the approval of a Government department. Instances of this are the Tramways Act, 1870, the Burial Acts, 1852-1885, and the Public Libraries Acts, 1892. In some cases parts of Acts are mandatory, imposing duties on the authorities, and other parts are

(3) Adoptive Acts.

"adoptive," with or without special formalities. It also frequently happens that laws in all these three groups prescribe the particular machinery by which the powers shall be exercised, the commonest plan being to direct, in the Act itself, the establishment of a committee (called therefore "statutory") of each local council concerned, and to lay down regulations as to its methods of working, and its relations to the council as a whole.[1]

All these three groups of laws are Public Acts, and are paralleled more or less in all countries which have parliamentary and local government institutions. But there are also two other groups: Private Acts, the outcome of a partly legislative and partly judicial process; and Public Local Acts, which are the product of a peculiar semi-legislative, semi-administrative procedure.

Private Bills, as already pointed out, still (4) Private Acts. formally originate on the petition of the promoters, which is incorporated in the preamble of each Bill.[2] They may be promoted by the councils of municipal boroughs and urban districts, which have always been active in acquiring additional powers by this means, and by county councils only since

[1] The most recent example of this is the Education Committee (with co-opted members), required to be appointed by authorities under the Education Act of 1902.

[2] On Private Bill legislation see Clifford, *History of Private Bill Legislation*; Wheeler, *Practice of Private Bills*; and Redlich and Hirst, II., pp. 338-351. Cf. also Lord Onslow, *Rise and Development of Local Legislation by Private Bill*, in *Journal of Royal Statistical Society*, March 1906.

1903. In the case of municipal boroughs and urban districts the approval of the ratepayers is required, either at a town's meeting or by poll, for spending public money on a Bill;[1] and this, though often a mere form, yet sometimes (if there is any strong opposition in the town to any of the proposals contained in it) amounts to a *referendum*.[2] The consent of the Local Government Board to the promotion of the Bill is also necessary, but is withheld only if the object could be obtained in other and simpler ways, *e.g.*, by Provisional Order. The contents of a Private Bill may relate to either the general business of local government, *e.g.*, authority to make bye-laws dealing with particular matters, additional public health powers, markets, expropriation of land for various purposes, etc.; or to public works, such as sewerage, waterworks, tramways, ferries, electric light and power works, gas works, and similar undertakings. There is, however, a growing tendency to deal with this second group of proposals by the simpler method of Provisional Orders. And there are certain limitations as to the subject matter—no Bill imposing any duties upon a Government department may be introduced as a Private Bill; and it is open to the principal

[1] Under the Borough Funds Act, 1872 (as amended in 1903). By the amending Act provision was made for the rejection by the ratepayers of part of a proposed Bill without rejecting the whole.

[2] Recent examples of the refusal of the ratepayers to allow the Town Council to proceed with a Bill are furnished by Birmingham (1902) and Oxford (1906).

authorities of the Houses of Parliament who deal with Private Bill legislation (the Lord Chairman of Committees in the Lords and the Chairman of Committees in the Commons), or for either of the Houses themselves by resolution, to declare that the proposals contained in the Bill are of such importance, either in extent [1] or in the principles involved, that they must be introduced only as public measures.

The Private Bills must be deposited about two months before the commencement of the parliamentary session, and copies must be sent to any Government departments interested or concerned in any way with their contents. The Bills must comply with the Standing Orders fixed by each house, which relate partly to procedure (notice to persons and authorities affected, deposit of plans, estimates of expenditure, etc.), and partly to clauses which must be included in each Bill of a particular class.[2] Non - compliance with the Standing Orders of either House (unless excused by the Select Committee on Standing Orders of that House) prevents a Bill from proceeding further. The Bills are considered by the Lord Chairman and the Chairman of Committees in the Commons, with their legal advisors, and any clauses to which they object are discussed with

Procedure.

---

[1] Bills affecting the whole of London are therefore often introduced as Public Bills.

[2] *The Standing Orders of Lords and Commons relative to Private Bills* are published sessionally.

the promoters, who practically must give way on the various points. The Bills are then divided, for the sake of convenience; some commence in the Commons, and the remainder in the Lords. They then follow the ordinary course of first and second readings, committee stage, and third reading.

Persons, companies, or authorities interested in a Bill, may petition to be heard in opposition to it, and the course taken by a Bill, after the second reading, depends on its being opposed or unopposed. Unopposed Bills go in the Lords to a committee which consists solely of the Lord Chairman; in the Commons they are referred to a committee consisting of the Chairman of Committees or his Deputy, the member introducing the Bill,[1] and one other member not personally interested.

The Select Committees.   In the case of opposed Bills, there is not usually any contest on the first or second readings, though sometimes there is opposition at the second stage in the House of Commons. Each Bill then goes to a Select Committee, consisting of four members in the Commons and five in the Lords— the members are chosen in each House by a Committee of Selection, and may not have any especial interest in the Bills which they are to consider. The committee stage is of the nature of a semi-judicial enquiry; counsel are heard and

---

[1] The petition being allowed, some member is "ordered to prepare and bring in the Bill"—often as a mere formality.

witnesses examined.[1] A committee may reject the whole Bill, usually by finding the preamble not proven; if they accept the principle they may make whatever amendments they think desirable, and the promoters must either accept the amendments or abandon the Bill.[2] After successfully enduring this ordeal the Bill is reported back to the House, passes the third reading formally, and goes then to the other House. In that House it is possible for the opposition to be renewed at the committee stage, but this rarely happens.[3] The Government departments are required to report on all Private Bills with which they are concerned in any way; these reports go to the Select Committees, and the Commons' Committees are required to inform the House in what manner the recommendations in the reports have been dealt with by them.

There is, of course, danger that the Select Committees may not adopt a uniform line of action in regard to Bills of the same kind, and attempts have been made to obviate this difficulty in various ways, by instructions in the

[1] Each committee of the Lords decides for itself what persons or authorities shall be permitted to appear in opposition to a Bill; the committees of the Commons have the matter decided for them by a special Committee of Referees.

[2] In the years 1891-95, 746 Private Bills affecting England and Wales (exclusive of purely Personal Bills and Provisional Orders Confirmation Bills) were introduced, and 580 passed; for the period 1896-1900 the numbers were 1,028 and 861; and for 1901-05, 989 and 807. Vide Onslow, loc. cit.

[3] Courtney, Working Constitution of the United Kingdom (edition 1901), p. 206. According to Lord Onslow, loc. cit., about 7 per cent. of Private Bills are so opposed in both Houses.

X

Standing Orders to the Committees as to the points which they are specially to consider, and the course to be taken about them, and by referring several Bills of a kindred character to the same committee. Particularly all Bills containing sanitary or police clauses go—so far as those clauses are concerned—to a Special Standing Committee of the Commons, appointed annually. Probably, however, the most effective guarantee for something like uniformity, without unduly checking local experiments, and also against the authorisation, by Private Acts, of anything contrary to public policy, is the examination of Bills by the Government departments, which has become more complete and careful in recent years, and the attention which their reports receive from the Select Committees.

Defects.   This system of Private Bill legislation is slow and costly: a Bill resolved on in March of one year (*i.e.*, after the commencement of one session) could not be introduced till the next year, and probably would not have passed through all its stages until from fifteen to eighteen months after the local authority had decided to promote it. Parliamentary agents must be employed; there are fees required to be paid to Parliament; if there is opposition, councillors and officials must be in London during the progress of the Bill, counsel employed, and expert witnesses engaged, and if the contest is a long one the sums expended may be very large. Moreover, much time of

members is taken up by the work of the Select
Committees, and, in some cases at least, might
perhaps be more profitably employed in other
ways.   Consequently attempts have been made,
in two ways, to lighten the burdens which Private
Bill legislation casts upon both local authorities
and Parliament itself.

SECTION 3

The first of these plans is the system of (5) Provisional Orders
Provisional Orders, which are orders granted by
a Government department, but requiring the
approval of Parliament before they can come
into force; the method was first adopted in
1845, and is now very extensively employed.
The cases in which the departments may issue
such orders are all specified by Parliament in
various enactments; they relate partly to local
government in the old and narrower sense, and
partly to industrial enterprises of various kinds,
whether promoted by local authorities or by
trading companies.   Thus the Local Government
Board may, by Provisional Order, combine
sanitary districts for the purposes of water
supply;[1] confirm improvement schemes made
by local health authorities for insanitary areas;
authorise county councils to incur debt amount-

---

[1] For regulations as to the grant of Provisional Orders by the
Local Government Board, see the Public Health Act, 1875, secs.
297-298.

ing to more than one-tenth of the rateable value
of the county; transfer to all or any of the
county councils such of the powers, duties, and
liabilities of certain Government departments as
relate to matters arising within the areas of the
councils;[1] authorise the purchase of gasworks;
make alterations in the boundaries of local government areas; and do many other similar things.
The Board of Trade grants Provisional Orders
for the erection of electric light and power works
by municipalities or private companies, for docks
and quays, tramways, light railways, waterworks,
etc. Other departments also may issue Orders
upon matters within their spheres.

The Orders are granted after an enquiry (held
locally if the department thinks it necessary), of
which public notice must be given, and at which
evidence is taken and opponents heard. If the
Order is refused, there is no appeal; if it is
granted, it is incorporated in one of the several
Provisional Orders Confirmation Bills which are
introduced in Parliament every session by the
departments. Any particular Order contained in
such a Bill may be again challenged, and in
that case the Bill goes to a Select Committee,
as if it were an opposed Private Bill. But
opposition is seldom of much use, though it
may secure some modifications of the Order in
question; Parliament has always shown itself
extremely ready to accept the decisions of the

[1] Local Government Act, 1888, sec. 10 (1).

Government departments.[1]　The method of Provisional Orders is much quicker and cheaper than Private Bill legislation, but though the supremacy of Parliament is maintained, the substitution of an administrative for a parliamentary enquiry, and the willingness of the legislature to accept the decision of the department based upon the results of that enquiry, combined with the absence of appeal against the refusal of an order, all tend somewhat to the substitution of administrative for legislative control.

In 1899 an Act was passed which made a sweeping change in the procedure in regard to private legislation for Scotland, by substituting Provisional Orders for Private Bills, but modifying the English system by giving the task of enquiry to a committee of Members of Parliament or unofficial persons instead of a department.[2]　A draft order is presented by the petitioners to the Secretary for Scotland, and to any Government offices concerned in its contents; the draft is referred to the Lord Chairman and the Chairman of Committees, and if the proposal relates only to Scotland, does not raise large general questions of policy, and is not of great magnitude, they authorise procedure by Provisional Order; otherwise a Private Bill becomes necessary.　If there is no opposition the Secretary for Scotland may grant the Order, either without

Private legislation for Scotland.

---

[1] In 1903-4 the Local Government Board granted seventy-two Orders: only seven of these were challenged, and *all* were confirmed by Parliament.　33*rd Report*, pp. cxxxvii.-cxxxviii.

[2] Private Legislation Procedure (Scotland) Act, 1899.

or with enquiry, as he may think fit. If there is opposition, the proposal is referred to a committee drawn from a body of commissioners consisting of fifteen members from each House of Parliament, and twenty other persons who are, "qualified by experience of affairs" and appointed by the Lord Chairman and the Chairman of Committees in conjunction with the Secretary for Scotland. The enquiry is held in Scotland at a place selected with due regard to the subject matter of the proposed order and the locality to which it relates;[1] and in the report presented to the Secretary for Scotland notice must be taken of the recommendations made by the parliamentary authorities or any public department. The committee may suggest the grant of the order as proposed, or its modification, or its complete refusal. If the last course is adopted by the Secretary of State there is no appeal from his decision; if he decides to grant the order, either as proposed or as amended, he introduces a Confirmation Bill into Parliament, and it may be challenged in the manner previously described. The plan, which seems to have given satisfaction in Scotland, has the advantages of the English Provisional Order system, with the additional merit that it does not leave the enquiry (and practically the decision) solely to the permanent

[1] The "extra-parliamentary panel" is to be drawn upon only when the necessary committees cannot be formed from the parliamentary members of the Commission; but the requirement that the enquiry shall be held in Scotland causes them to be much used.

officials of a Government department. There seems to be no obvious reason why, in any considerable extension of the Provisional Order system for this country, this device of enquiry by a committee, drawn from a commission attached to a department but composed of unofficial persons, should not be widely used.

SECTION 4

Reference has already been made, in a previous chapter, to the fact that in the States of the American Union the control of the central governments over the local authorities is exercised only by the legislature and the courts of justice, in the absence of strong state executive departments which could be entrusted with the task, even if the strength of the feeling for local independence allowed it. The state-executives are ill-organised and weak; and local self-government has been carried to its extreme limits. Professor Woodrow Wilson writes: [1]

Legislatures and local authorities in the United States.

"The governor, therefore, is not the 'executive'; he is but a single piece of the executive. There are other pieces co-ordinated with him over which he has no direct official control, and which are of less dignity than he only because they have no power to control legislation, as he may do by the exercise of his veto, and because his position is more representative, perhaps, of the state govern-

[1] *The State* (edition 1899), p. 500.

ment as a whole, of the people of the state as a
unit.   Indeed it may be doubted whether the
governor and other principal officers of a state
government can even when taken together be
correctly described as 'the executive,' since the
actual execution of the great majority of the laws'
does not rest with them but with the local officers
chosen by the towns and counties and bound to
the central authorities of the state by no real bonds
of responsibility whatever.   Throughout all the
states there is a significant distinction, a real
separation, between 'state' and 'local' officials ;
local officials are not regarded, that is, as state
officers, but as officers of their districts only,
responsible to constituents, not to central
authorities."

As there are no central offices which can be
armed with the supervising, directing and authorising powers possessed in respect of local administration by the English Government departments,
and as therefore it would be impossible, without
producing undue varieties particularly of municipal
organisation and action, to give the local authorities
wide grants of general powers, the American state
legislatures have found it necessary to make laws
dealing with the details of local government to an
extent never attempted by the British Parliament.[1]

[1] " We are just beginning to grasp the idea that the municipality
is an agent of the state and also an organisation for the satisfaction of
local needs.   Our past failure to comprehend the truth has led us to
adopt a legislative system of control, and although instances may be
found of a tendency to substitute central administrative for legislative control, the regulation of local authorities, whether dealing
with state or local needs, has been almost entirely through judicial
action or legislative statutes.   As to questions of legislative policy or

This they do alike by general and "special" Extent of
legislative
legislation, corresponding to British Public and interference,
Private Acts.   In general laws the smallest
matters of municipal administration are provided
for, whilst "special" Acts are passed every year
in vast numbers, and often dealing only with
comparatively trivial points.   All this would not
necessarily be bad in itself, though it is a cumbrous
method to adopt ; but the unfortunate conditions
of so many American municipalities, and the
unsatisfactory character of most of the state
legislatures[1] have made it into a serious evil.
The irresponsibility of the legislative bodies,
which have little or no effective control over the
executive, the fact that the party system has
almost complete sway in municipal affairs also,
since the "spoils system" makes the control of
a city government a means whereby a party may
strengthen its general position, the pressure exercised by private interests upon legislators, all these
have led to the serious abuse of legislative control and its abuse.
and intervention in the affairs of the cities.   This
extends to form and functions alike.   The British
Parliament, when it has established local authorities,
is slow to change their constitution, and gives them
an almost free hand in the organisation of their

administrative expediency, we have either left the local authorities
to do as they pleased or undertaken to direct them by general or
special acts. Beginning with the granting of charters or the conferring of powers by special acts, we soon fell into the habit of
regulating everything by special act." Malbie, *English Local Government of To-day*, p. 242, speaking of the United States.

[1] Bryce, *American Commonwealth*, cc. xliv.-xlv.

work and the formation of their official staffs. But the American state legislatures are constantly making changes in municipal organisation, partly from a mere desire to try experiments (often without regard to the interests or wishes of the cities concerned), and, what is far more serious, the forms of city government are often manipulated in particular cases for the purposes of the party which chances to be predominant in the legislature.[1] The result is that municipal law is constantly being changed, and it is therefore very confused and uncertain. Further, there is much interference with the functions of municipal authorities; "franchises" in the cities are granted to private companies without any regard to the wishes of their inhabitants, whilst on the other hand proposals of the city councils are often rejected not on their merits, but owing to the pressure of private interests, or the hostility of a political party, or the mere jealousy felt among the rural population towards the growing power of the cities.

Attempted remedies. The results of this interference have been so bad that attempts have been made in various ways to check it. One plan widely adopted is to deal with the organisation of municipal government, and to lay down its main lines in greater or less detail, not by ordinary general laws but in the actual state constitutions, which can be changed **(1) Constitutional Laws.** only by a slow and elaborate process. This does

[1] *Vide supra*, pp. 189-190.

prevent the frequent changes, but it is impossible
to anticipate all the wants of a developing city,
or the particular needs which may arise in regard
to its official machinery; and consequently this
device frequently means either that the cities are
unduly hampered, or that it is necessary to revise
the constitutions at frequent intervals. To quote
again a distinguished American authority:[1]

" Not only do the constitutions of the states go
very much more into detail in their prescriptions
touching the organisation of the Government; they
go far beyond organic provisions and undertake
the ordinary, but very different, work of legislative
enactment. . . . The motive is dissatisfaction with
legislation, distrust of legislators, a wish to secure
for certain classes of law a greater permanency and
stability than is vouchsafed to statutes, which
stand in constant peril of alteration or repeal. A
further motive is the desire to give to such laws
the sanction of a popular vote. . . . The practice
perhaps discovers a tendency towards devising
means for making all very important legal provisions dependent upon direct popular participation
in the process of enactment.

The objections to the practice are as obvious as
they are weighty. General outlines of organisation,
such as the Constitution of the United States
contains, may be made to stand without essential
alteration for long periods together; but in proportion as constitutions make provisions for interests
whose aspects must change from time to time with
changing circumstance, they enter the domain of
such law as must be subject to constant modification and adaptation. Not only must the distinctions

[1] Wilson, *The State*, pp. 474-475.

between constitutional and ordinary law hitherto recognised and valued tend to be fatally obscured, but the much to be desired stability of constitutional provisions must in great part be sacrificed. Those constitutions which contain the largest amount of extraneous matter, which does not concern at all the structure or functions of government, but only private or particular interests, must of course, however carefully drawn, prove subject to most frequent change. In some of our states, accordingly, constitutions have been as often changed as important statutes. The danger is that constitution-making will become with us only a cumbrous mode of legislation."

(2) Prohibition of special legislation.

Another scheme of reform was the prohibition (by clauses in the constitutions of many of the states) of all special legislation affecting local bodies.[1] But this was quite impracticable; cities are of all sizes and conditions; there is the utmost variety of needs; and to deal with them by general law, especially in regard to functions, soon proved to be impossible. The result was elaborate manœuvres to escape the restriction, and they were soon easily successful. The plan of classifying cities according to population, and of legislating separately for all the cities of any one class, was introduced, and in itself was a thoroughly

[1] For an example, see the clause from the Constitution of Pennsylvania quoted above, pp. 188-9. Cf. the Constitution of California (1879), Art. IV : "The legislature shall not pass local or special laws in any of the following enumerated cases: . . . (9) regulating county or township business or the election of county or township officers . . . (28) creating offices, or prescribing the powers and duties of officers in counties, cities, townships, election, or school districts."

sound and desirable arrangement. But it was soon realised that the device could be used for much more than this—that it was possible to enact that the cities should be classified in such a way as to put only one city in a particular class, and then in the same law to confer powers upon the governments of "all cities" in that class, or grant franchises in them, or modify their organisation. In this way what were practically special laws were passed in the form of general laws, and the courts of justice held that they were valid. Another evasion was by means of Bills which, in the interests of single cities, professed to amend a general act, and were therefore held to be themselves general. Consequently legislation of this kind became extremely abundant, and the results were much the same as if the constitutional prohibition had not existed.[1] There is a growing dislike of this special legislation and the abuses which in America seem inseparable from it, but none of the schemes for reform are really satisfactory.[2] Special legislation must continue, unless state boards of control (with considerable powers over against the local authorities) can be established, and of that there is little probability. That being so, the United States are in an unfortunate position. The distrust felt of the state legislatures has resulted in the incorporation in the constitutions of provisions relating to the details of local

Failure of the attempts.

---

[1] Maltbie, *loc. cit.*, p. 243.
[2] For examples see Bryce, *loc. cit.*, cxlv.

organisation and functions, and this tends to inelasticity; so long as there are not strong central offices with powers of control, grants of wide powers seem undesirable; and with the present political conditions both general and special legislation are liable to abuse. Much could be done by the adoption of a procedure modelled on that which, on the whole, has been so successful in England; but any reform, to be really effective, must commence with the composition and character of the legislative authorities themselves.

CHAPTER X

THE ADMINISTRATIVE CONTROL OF LOCAL AUTHORITIES

SECTION 1

UNDER the term "administrative control" are included all the various powers possessed by the departments of the central government in any country for the general direction and supervision of the action of the authorities for local self-government, with the exception of the powers relating to finance, which are sufficiently numerous and important to be considered separately. There is the further limitation that the term applies only to those powers of the central offices which are complete in themselves, and are exercised subject only to the surveillance of the legislature; it therefore does not include that part of the work of control which, though it may originate with the departments, yet in order to be effective requires the co-operation of the courts of justice.

Character of "administrative control."

It will be apparent from what has been said in previous chapters that this administrative control is much greater abroad than it is here, since the continental conception of local self-government is in many respects very different

Its greater extent abroad than in England.

335

from our own.   Perhaps the most striking illustration of this is furnished by the position of the professional officials in local administration, and their relations to the central departments.   In England the conduct of local affairs is absolutely and solely in the hands of the elected and unpaid representatives of the locality, and the salaried permanent officials are merely their agents and servants ; the central offices have to deal with the councils, and cannot normally interfere with the local officials, who are in no way responsible to them.   There is, it is true, one striking exception to this rule ; in the administration of the Poor Law not only do the appointments and dismissals made by the boards of guardians require the approval of the Local Government Board, but the latter authority can also dismiss any paid agent of the guardians even against their wishes. This central power is, however, like so many others, quite peculiar to the Poor Law, and is now used only very infrequently ; and apart from this there is no instance in English local government of the permanent officials being dependent for the retention of their posts upon the goodwill of the central department alone.   Confirmation by the Local Government Board is necessary for the appointment and dismissal of those medical officers and sanitary inspectors whose salaries local authorities wish to be borne partially by the Exchequer Contribution Account ; but this is solely as a guarantee that the persons appointed

The position of professional local officials.

(1) In England.

shall be properly qualified and have something like security of tenure in the discharge of their very difficult work, which may often bring them into conflict with influential local interests. The appointments of chief constables must be approved by the Home Secretary, and of public analysts by the Local Government Board. But in none of these cases is there, as in the Poor Law, any central control over the action of the permanent officials; that is directed solely by the elected councils, who alone bear the responsibility.

When we turn to continental Europe the situation is very different. The central offices have naturally complete control over their local delegations, whether paid or unpaid, professional or lay; but it will be remembered that in many cases the local delegates of the central government are also the executive agents of the local governing corporations. They may be originally central officials, with the character of local executive agents superimposed upon them, as is the case with the French Prefect; or in other instances the chosen agents of the locality have been entrusted with certain powers and duties by the central government and act as its representative within their area — this is so with the Prussian Landrath, Circle Committee, and Town Magistracy, and to a lesser degree with the French Mayor. Now in so far as they are central agents they are under bureaucratic control, and, even if they are not (as the French Prefect) entitled in

(2) In France and Prussia.

Y

some cases to ignore orders from the local councils
of which they disapprove, their position as central
officers subject to disciplinary action inevitably
reacts upon their attitude towards local affairs.
The Prefect is primarily a central agent; his con-
currence is required for the validity of many
resolutions taken by the departmental Council-
General, or he must reserve them for consideration
by the ministry at Paris; he has to decide, or
obtain a decision, upon questions not merely of
legality, but of expediency, and his own view of
expediency will naturally be determined by the
views of the ministry, upon whom his position
depends. A more curious situation is that
occupied by the Prussian Landrath. He is
appointed by the Crown on the nomination of
the Circle Assembly, which pays his salary; but
in his added character of a central agent he can
be suspended or dismissed by his superiors in the
bureaucratic hierarchy. Consequently, as his career
and chances of promotion are determined mainly
by the approval of these superiors, he is anxious
to avoid any conflict between the two masters
whom he has to serve; and should a dispute arise
he will naturally side with the central government
—in fact, it is understood to be his duty to do so.
The indirectly-elected lay members of the Circle
Committee also, so far as they are entrusted with
"central" functions, are subject to the same
administrative control; but as they are not
members of the bureaucracy, they cannot be dis-

missed from office save by the decision of an administrative court.[1] In the same way the burgomaster and other members of a town magistracy, and the headman (Vorsteher) of a country commune, in Prussia can be removed from their posts only by a similar decision. On the other hand, a French mayor, if he fails to carry out properly any duty devolving upon him at law or laid upon him by the central government, can be suspended for one month by the Prefect, or for three months by the Minister of the Interior, or finally dismissed by presidential decree. He is therefore much less protected than his Prussian colleague against arbitrary action by the central offices.

In England if the elected councils come into conflict with the central departments in any way, either for exceeding the law or for neglecting or deliberately refusing to carry out its requirements, almost the only thing which the central authority can do is to call in the aid of the courts of justice. Under the Elementary Education Act, 1870, if an elected school board refused to act, or was negligent or incompetent in its work, the Board of Education could dissolve it, and either order a new election to take place or nominate persons to whom all the rights and duties of the dissolved board should be transferred. These powers were

Central dissolution of elected authorities.

[1] This applies also to the unprofessional members of the provincial councils, since, though charged with purely central functions, they are elected and unpaid.

used with some frequency in the early years after
1870,[1] but they gradually fell into disuse and were
abandoned by the Education Act of 1902. The
same power of dissolving elected authorities exists
in France and Prussia, and is still occasionally
employed. In the former country the departmental councils and commissions may be dissolved
for persistently refusing to discharge their legal
duties. A communal council may also be dissolved,
but its successor must be elected within two months,
and although during the interregnum a temporary
commission is appointed to carry on the municipal
administration, it may deal only with urgent
matters, and may not prepare the local budget.[2]
These dissolutions must be by presidential decree,
and are on the whole very infrequent, though they
occur occasionally in small communes, and have
sometimes been talked of as possibilites in a large
town when its council has shown (as is often the
case) marked political hostility to the government
of the day. But the step of dissolution is rarely
taken on political grounds, since, should the fresh
election in a large town return the same anti-
government majority, the position of the ministry
(under the present conditions of French politics)
would become extremely difficult. In Prussia
provincial and circle assemblies, and town and

---

[1] In the first fifteen years (1871-86) there were thirty-two cases
of boards dissolved and substitutes appointed by the Board of
Education, and eight of boards dissolved and fresh elections ordered.
Maltbie, *English Local Government of To-day*, p. 168.

[2] Municipal Law, 1883, sec. 43-45.

communal councils, are all liable to be dissolved by royal edict; elections must then be held within three months for the provincial assemblies, within six months for the circle assemblies and town councils, and within six weeks for the councils of the rural communes.[1] But the use of such drastic measures is even less frequent than in France, for usually the desired end can be attained in other ways.

SECTION 2

Reference has already been made in a previous chapter to the very large extent to which the approval of the central departments is necessary for action proposed to be taken by local authorities in France and Prussia, and it has been pointed out that this is due in the main to the way in which powers are conferred upon the localities. English legislators have attempted to specify all the powers which a local authority may require, and to permit their use under various conditions; whilst abroad the plan has been adopted of avoiding incessant legislation for local government matters by giving very wide powers to the localities, but with the requirement that in the great majority of instances they must obtain administrative approval for any exercise of these general powers. It would be troublesome and unnecessary to require that all

Central approval of local action.

[1] Städte-Ordnung, 1853, sec. 79; Landgemeinde-Ordnung, 1891, sec. 42.

proposed actions should be formally authorised; and so the method generally employed is to specify a few matters in which central approval shall not be necessary at all, and to direct that the resolutions on all other matters shall be valid in some cases only after formal sanction (this applies chiefly to resolutions in regard to finance, or subjects in which the central government has a particular interest), and in others unless disallowed within (a) In France. a fixed time.[1]   In France this approval is purely bureaucratic—that is, it is given by the prefect on his sole responsibility (in only a very few cases does the decision rest with the prefectoral council), (b) In Prussia. or by the central ministry.   In Prussia the control is exercised (according to the authority seeking approval) usually by the district committee or circle committee, on both of which lay members predominate; and only in provincial affairs does the ministry concerned decide.   From the circle committee an appeal is generally allowed to the district committee, and from the latter (when it decides in first instance) to the ministry.

(c) In England. In England the impossibility on the one hand of legislating for every separate authority, and on the other of allowing all authorities of the same class to exercise the same powers—since authorities identical in form often [differ greatly in circumstances, financial resources and administrative

---

[1] Cf. the Provinzial - Ordnung, 1875, sec. 118-121, and Kreis-Ordnung, 1872, sec. 176, with the French Municipal Law, 1883, sec. 61-69, and Law of 1871 on the Councils-General, sec. 46-48.

ability—has led to the grant by Parliament of the same authorising power to the central departments, though it springs from other motives and has a quite different character, since the cases in which it may be exercised are all minutely specified. Thus the bye-laws made by local authorities under the various Public Health Acts need to be confirmed by the Local Government Board,[1] and bye-laws relating to police matters must be confirmed by the Home Secretary. For many other things connected with public health administration, such as the formation of special drainage districts, joint burial boards, housing schemes, the acquisition or establishment of water-supplies, authority must be obtained from the Local Government Board, which also may grant to a rural district council all or any of the special powers of an urban sanitary authority. Rural authorities are generally required to obtain the consent of the same office for the use of the various Adoptive Acts; and practically the issue of Provisional Orders by the central departments to local councils may be classed under this same head, since, as we have seen, their decision in any case is almost always accepted, and indeed unquestioned, by Parliament. The Local Government Board may combine or divide parishes, or

---

[1] In 1903-4 the Local Government Board approved 500 series of bye-laws issued under General Acts, and 36 series under Local Acts. They applied to such diverse matters as lodging-houses, recreation grounds, locomotives, pleasure - boats, slaughter - houses, shooting-galleries, hop and fruit pickers, and hackney-carriages.

readjust boundaries, generally by Provisional Order. All public works under General Acts, and not infrequently those under Private (local) Acts also, need the sanction of the Local Government Board or the Board of Trade; but this, as it is concerned chiefly with expenditure out of loans, will be considered in the next chapter.

Central direction of local action. The powers of directing action possessed by our central departments are also very large. The Board of Education has wide discretionary powers in regard to most things connected with elementary education, and deals with them in great detail in the code. The Local Government Board may direct any local sanitary authority to undertake services not otherwise compulsory, though the services which may thus be commanded are all carefully specified in legislative enactments;[1] and in case of plague or epidemics it can issue orders which are immediately binding on all authorities concerned. The local councils which are authorities for dealing with outbreaks of diseases amongst animals must carry out all instructions received from the Board of Agriculture in that matter. But the greatest example of the directing powers of a central department is supplied in England by the Poor Law administration, where the Local Government Board can issue orders — "general" or "special," according as they are sent to all the boards of guardians or to a single one—dealing with every conceivable detail of the work; in the

[1] Cf. Public Health Act, 1875, sec. 42 and 141.

year 1903-4 alone no less than eight hundred and
fifty-two orders of one kind or another were thus
issued.   This very wide directing power, combined
with the control of officials already mentioned,
makes the Poor Law administration of this
country into as highly centralised a service as can
be found in any state of Western Europe.   The
direction by central departments abroad of the
action of local self-governing authorities is not
quite so extensive as in England, since the services
in which foreign central governments are at all
keenly interested are generally classed as " state "
matters, and therefore entrusted to agents who
are subject to the (more or less ordinary) bureaucratic control.

A more difficult matter is the enforcement of Central en-
action — that is, the task of compelling local forcement of
authorities to discharge the duties laid upon them
either immediately by the legislature or by the
central offices under Parliamentary sanction.   In
England the powers of the departments in this (a) In
respect are comparatively limited, and a distinction England.
must be made between the actual neglect of work
by local authorities, and its inefficient performance.
In the former case, in matters of Public Health
administration the Local Government Board may,
if it chooses to do so, authorise other persons to
act, at the cost of the defaulting authority;[1] but

[1] Public Health Act, 1875, sec. 299 and 106.   In case of default
by a Rural District Council, its County Council may intervene and
do the work.

it usually prefers to take the alternative course, and to go to the High Court of Justice for a writ of *Mandamus* directed to the recalcitrant authority. This is its sole available course in other matters; the Board of Education is armed now only with the same weapon.[1] For inefficient performances of some services (police and education) there is the possibility of withholding the Government grants, wholly or in part; and, since the local authorities have usually spent money in the expectation of receiving the grant, this amounts to the imposition of a fine upon the locality. But it is not a very satisfactory method, though the threat that the grant, though not withheld at the time, may not be given in the ensuing year unless an improvement takes place is sometimes effective. Where such a grant, conditioned by efficiency, does not exist, almost the only thing which a central department can do is to hold an enquiry, urge reforms upon the local authorities, and endeavour to shame them into action by publishing their deficiencies abroad.

(b) Abroad.
An unsatisfactory local council in France or Prussia may be dissolved, as we have seen, by the superior authority, or the latter may in some cases step in and do the work itself. But there is one curious power employed in both countries which calls for special mention. In France, if a local council does not make sufficient provision in its

---

[1] Cf. Public Health Act, 1875, sec. 299, and Education Act, 1902, sec. 16.

annual budget (which is submitted for administrative approval at the commencement of the financial year) for various compulsory services, the supervising authority (Prefect or Ministry of the Interior) may insert in the budget the necessary additional expenditure—this is the so-called *Inscription d'office*—and, if necessary, impose extra taxation to meet it.[1]   The same power is exercised by the various supervising authorities in Prussia.[2]

SECTION 3

It is obvious that to carry on properly this work of superintending and directing the action of the local authorities, and also to be able to give them any guidance and advice of which they may stand in need, the central departments

The machinery of control.

[1] Or the superior authority may order a sale of communal property for this purpose (in the case of a debt).   Berthélemy, *Droit Administratif*, pp. 158 and 511.

[2] *Das Zustandigkeits-Gesetz*, sec. 19.   Cf. the power given to the Local Government Board (though never used) by sec. 300 of the Public Health Act, 1875: "Any sum specified in an order of the Local Government Board for payment of the expenses of performing the duty of a defaulting local authority . . . shall be deemed to be expenses properly incurred by such authority, and to be a debt due from such authority, and payable out of any monies in the hands of such authority or of their officers, or out of any rate applicable. . . . If the defaulting authority refuses to pay any such sum . . . the Local Government Board may by order empower any person to levy, by and out of the local rate, such sum. . . . Any person or persons so empowered shall have the same powers of levying the local rate . . . as the defaulting authority would have."   As a result of the recent action of some of the Welsh County Councils an Act was passed in 1905 authorising the Board of Education to make to the managers of elementary schools payments to which they may be legally entitled, but which are withheld by the local education authorities, and to deduct such amounts from the central grants payable to the authorities.

must have some means of keeping a constant watch upon them and of maintaining an intimate acquaintance with the conditions and needs of their areas. In England the attempt to attain this result—an attempt not altogether successful—is **(a) The English inspectorate.** made chiefly by means of the inspectorate, which is a peculiarly English institution. Attached to each of the Government offices concerned in local administration is a staff of inspectors, who may be divided into two groups according as the inspection which they conduct is regular or occasional. In the first group are (1) the Poor Law inspectors, who have power to visit all institutions for the relief of the poor, may attend the meetings of all boards of guardians and their committees, and are expected to make themselves thoroughly acquainted with the general conditions of their areas so far as they affect Poor Law administration; (2) the auditors, who examine once or twice a year the accounts of all local authorities except town councils (whose education accounts are alone subject to this central inspection); (3) the inspectors of the Board of Education, who visit and report on all schools which are in receipt of public money; and (4) the small number of inspectors of constabulary forces, who are attached to the Home Office. To each inspector of the first three of these classes a particular district is assigned. The second group includes (5) the medical inspectors of the Local Government Board, who are sent down from time to time to hold enquiries into the causes of the outbreak of disease, or into complaints as to local sanitary administration;[1] (6) the engineering and other inspectors of the Local Government Board and the Board of Trade, who hold enquiries into proposed public works which necessitate loans, or for any other reason require central approval; and (7) the inspectors of the Board of Agriculture. These inspectors have no authority of their own, and cannot decide matters (except the auditors, from whom there is an appeal); their function is simply to inspect, observe, make enquiries, and report to their respective departments.

It will be noticed that except in the case of the Poor Law—and there only by chance discoveries on the part of the inspectors—the central departments in England have no machinery for detecting any proposals for illegal action made by the local authorities, or for the discovery of illegal action when actually taking place; the audit finds it out only after it has occurred, and not then unless it involved special expenditure. For the prevention of any transgression by a local authority of its legal limits we depend then almost solely upon individual initiative, on proceedings taken in a court of justice either by a private citizen having a legally recognised interest in the locality concerned, or by a central authority

[1] The medical inspectors may attend the meetings of local sanitary authorities only if directed to do so by the Local Government Board.

acting at the instigation of such a citizen. In
France and Prussia, on the other hand, the
detection of any proposals for action beyond the
sphere of a local body is rendered comparatively
easy by the deconcentrated central control. The
central agents are bound to watch the proceedings
of all local authorities within their areas, and
they are able to do so partly because those
areas are fairly small ; partly because the central
agents are also, in the larger areas, the executive
agents of the localities, and are required in their
former character to report to their administrative
superiors any order received by them from the
local councils ; and partly because it is customary
in any case to require that a full report of the
proceedings of any local council must be trans-
mitted to the supervising authority.

This system of deconcentrated central control, as
carried out in Prussia, has some distinct practical
advantages. It secures first that the responsibility
for the supervision of a host of local government
authorities shall not rest only upon two or three
departments consisting chiefly of officials stationed
at the national capital ; but that the work shall be
done by delegations scattered about the country
and able to acquire a more detailed knowledge
of local conditions than a department can obtain
in any other way. Secondly, the supervision is
not solely by officials, but also by responsible
and experienced persons who command local
confidence. The general results are, first, that

the actual "headquarter's staff" of a government department is relieved of much of that minute and detailed work which falls upon the English Local Government Board, and therefore can give more time to the study of administrative problems and the consideration of questions of policy;[1] secondly, that the control is rendered much less purely bureaucratic; and thirdly, that it is much more expeditious.

In England it is beyond question that the Local Government Board is greatly overburdened with detailed work relating to all authorities, even the very smallest; with the natural result that the office tends to become stereotyped alike as to aims and methods. The Board of Education, also, seems to be occupied excessively with minute matters of administration. The attempts hitherto made at the decentralisation of control have been very slight. The county councils have been given some powers over the rural district councils in respect of sanitary administration, and over the parish councils in regard to a considerable number of matters of general local government (boundaries, loans, Adoptive Acts, etc.); whilst in the Metropolis the consent of the London County Council is required for the raising of loans by the borough councils. But beyond this little has been done, and the transference to the county councils of powers exercised by the

Decentralised control in England.

---

[1] The same deconcentration, and the liberation of the central office from much burdensome detail, is the aim of the French organisation of education.

central departments, which was contemplated by
the Local Government Act of 1888,[1] has been
scarcely attempted in fact.   Yet that some deconcentration of control—or at least something to
Possibility of relieve the pressure upon the Local Government
further de-
concentration Board—is desirable is generally agreed; and the
of control
in England. only possible policy appears to be an extension
of the supervisory powers and duties of the
county councils.   The municipal boroughs cling
jealously to their privileged position, and would
strongly oppose anything tending to give the
county councils greater authority in their areas;
the larger urban districts would also resist.   But
there seems no adequate reason why the county
councils should not be entrusted with the control
of the parishes and rural districts, and the smaller
urban district councils; and the Local Government Board itself would then be left to deal
with the Poor Law authorities, the county and
borough councils, the ordinary municipalities and
the larger urban districts.   This, though not a
great step, would yet be a distinct improvement;
and something further could be obtained by
the abolition of the separate boards of guardians
and the transference of their functions to other
authorities.   In the case of the Board of Education it is possible also that something might be
done, by getting rid of the system of separate
grants to, and therefore separate reports upon,
each individual school.

[1] Section 10.

CHAPTER XI

THE CONTROL OF LOCAL FINANCES[1]

SECTION 1

THE control exercised by the central governments over the financial operations of local authorities is partly legislative and partly administrative, for it consists of the enforcement of two sets of limitations—one imposed by statutory enactments, and the other by administrative discretion. The legislature may indicate, as in England, the objects upon which alone local money may be expended ; but whether it does that or not, it often sets limits to local taxation and indebtedness, or leaves a certain discretion to be exercised in the case of each separate authority by a government department. It is then the task of the central administrative offices to watch the finances of the local authorities, in order to detect the employment of public money for illegal purposes, and to decide upon any proposals for local expenditure in regard to which a discretion is allowed them.

Nature and objects of the financial control.

In England, for the detection of illegal expenditure we depend mainly upon the audit of

Central audit of accounts.

---

[1] Some passages in this chapter are quoted from an article by the present writer in the *Economic Journal*, June 1902.

the accounts of the local authorities by agents of
the central government.   The auditors of the
Local Government Board examine yearly, or half-
yearly, the accounts of all local bodies except
municipal councils, and the education accounts of
such municipal boroughs as are authorities for
that purpose, and they have power to disallow
illegal or improper expenditure, and to surcharge
it upon the individual members of the offending
authority.   From the decision of the auditor there
is an appeal either to the Board itself (which may
involve a departmental interpretation of the law),
or to the High Court of Justice.[1]   The general
policy of the Board, where it upholds the auditor's
decision (as is generally the case), is to relieve
the members of the local authority from the consequences of their illegal action in the particular
instance, but to warn them that such relief will not
be given again.[2]   The Local Government Board
may, however, in certain cases, on the application of local authorities, authorise in advance
expenditure which otherwise the auditors would
be compelled to disallow; and it does this in a
fair number of cases each year.[3]   This central

---

[1] The use of this second alternative by persons surcharged is,
however, now very infrequent.

[2] In 1903-4 3,809 disallowances and surcharges were made by the
auditors, nearly one-half being in respect of items of Poor Law
expenditure.   There were appeals to the Board in 1,042 cases; in
52 the auditors' decisions were reversed, in 907 the decisions were
confirmed, but the surcharges remitted, and in 63 the decisions were
confirmed, but the surcharges not remitted.   The remaining 20 were
"dealt with according to merits."

[3] Local Authorities' Expenses Act, 1887.

audit is a very useful institution in many ways, but it has certain distinct defects. Experience has shown that the auditors may continue for years to pass items which are clearly illegal, simply because their attention is not specially drawn to them. Secondly, the audit does not prevent illegal expenditure, but only stops its recurrence; and, finally, it would be a great improvement if the audit were to be made not merely a search for illegalities, but also a real consideration of the whole financial position of a council and of its various separate undertakings. The Local Government Board may prescribe the way in which the accounts of local authorities— other than municipal boroughs—must be kept, and the forms in which all authorities must make returns to the Board for the purpose of the annual summaries which it publishes.

The accounts of English municipal boroughs *Audit of municipal accounts.* (except those relating to education) are exempted from the governmental audit, and are examined by three persons, of whom one is appointed by the Mayor from the members of the town council, and the other two are elected burgesses. Their powers are considerably smaller than those of the Local Government Board auditors, since they have no power to disallow or surcharge, and can only draw attention to doubtful items; their examination is generally not very efficient;[1] very

[1] But most of the important councils voluntarily have their accounts examined and certified by competent accountants.

little interest is taken, as a rule, in the election of the auditors, and they need not possess any appropriate qualifications whatsoever. The town councils are opposed to the introduction of the government audit of their accounts, partly because of their jealous regard for the maintenance of their independence, and partly on the ground that the official auditors are not properly trained accountants, and, further, are inclined to take too narrow a view of the law, and thereby to check desirable experiments.[1] The ratepayers of a municipal borough are, however, to some extent protected by the fact that an order for any payment made by a town council may be taken (on the application of any person interested) by the writ of *certiorari* before the High Court, and there quashed if invalid.[2]

The examination of estimates.

In France, the accounts of local authorities are examined at the end of the year, but that operation is less important than in England, because the French local authorities are required to prepare a budget for each financial year, and to secure approval for it either from the Prefect, or from the Ministry of the Interior. The budgets of the councils of all the large towns, and of the departments, must go directly to the Ministry.

---

[1] There are about three cases of boroughs subjected to the Local Government Board Audit, Select Committees of the Houses of Parliament having made this a condition of the grant of additional powers.

[2] Municipal Corporations Act, 1882, sec. 141. The same course is possible in cases of expenditure by county councils (Local Government Act, 1888, sec. 80 (2)), but is rarely taken.

This presentation of the local budget in France (and also in Prussia, where the same system prevails) gives the controlling authority an opportunity, not merely to strike out illegal expenditure, or expenditure which it deems inadvisable, but also, as was pointed out in the previous chapter,[1] to enforce proper provision for all compulsory services. English county councils are required to prepare estimates of receipts and expenditure at the commencement of each financial year,[2] and this is done by many other authorities voluntarily; but the estimates so prepared are not submitted to any higher authority for approval.

SECTION 2

The legislature has often deemed it necessary to place restrictions upon the amount of taxation which may be levied, or debt incurred, by local authorities for purposes which in themselves are recognised as altogether desirable—such restrictions being sometimes absolute and sometimes capable of modification by the central departments. Almost the only example of the restriction of rates levied for general purposes in England is supplied by the parish councils, who may not levy rates (exclusive of those under the Adoptive Acts) of more than threepence in the pound except

Legislative restrictions upon local taxation and debt.

---

[1] *Vide supra*, pp. 346-7.
[2] Local Government Act, 1888, sec. 74 (1).

with the consent of a parish meeting, and even then may not go beyond sixpence. The limitation of rates for special purposes is much more common; there are maximum amounts fixed for most of the Adoptive Acts. As regards debt, a board of guardians may not borrow beyond one-fourth of the rateable value of their union, though this limit may be raised to one-half by Provisional Order; the loans raised by county councils for general purposes may not exceed one-tenth of the rateable value of their areas except by Provisional Order or Act of Parliament; and there are other instances. The same kind of restrictions is frequent upon the Continent, the customary plan in the case of taxation being to fix a rate beyond which the local authority may not go without approval. Thus a town council in Prussia may not for local purposes impose an addition of more than 100 per cent. to the state income tax without the permission of the supervising authorities. In France the maximum of the ordinary additions which may be made by local authorities to the state direct taxes is fixed by the annual Budget Law, and for some further increases (" *centimes extraordinaires* ") made by the communes the councils - general fix limits, each for its own area.

Legislative restrictions in the United States. The most elaborate attempts at the legislative restraint of taxation and indebtedness have been made in the United States, where administrative control does not exist. But the desire to impose some check upon the often reckless expenditure of the cities has not always been quite satisfactory in its results. To such regulations as that imposed by the constitution of the State of Pennsylvania, that " every city shall create a sinking fund, which shall be inviolably pledged for the payment of its funded debt," there can be no possible objection ; the obligation to establish a sinking fund is frequently imposed in this way in England. But the tendency is for many of the regulations to be inelastic. Thus an Act of 1885 in Massachusetts orders that " the taxes assessed on property,[1] in any city, except the city of Boston, exclusive of State Tax, County Tax, and sums required by law to be raised on account of the city debt, shall not exceed in any year twelve dollars on every one thousand dollars of the average of the assessors' valuations of the taxable property therein for the preceding three years," and " the limit of indebtedness of cities shall hereafter be two and one-half per cent. on the average valuation " prescribed above. Such limits can only be exceeded by legislative authority, which is not always easy to obtain. But it is a simple task in comparison with the difficulties encountered when the limits of taxation and indebtedness are imposed not merely by ordinary legislative enactments, but by the constitutions of the States, which can only

---

[1] All American city (as all internal) taxation is raised by Taxes on the total (not annual) value of real and personal property. *Vide* Ely, *Taxation in American Cities.*

be amended by a very complicated process. The failure of the legislatures and state constituent conventions to distinguish between remunerative and unremunerative expenditure also tends to hamper municipal enterprise in the direction of the ownership of public services, though in view of the general want of confidence in American city councils this is perhaps not unreasonable.

Perhaps the most satisfactory piece of legislation in this matter, avoiding inelasticity and allowing for municipal ownership within limits, is to be found in the constitution adopted in 1889 for the State of Washington, which may be quoted in full:

"No county, city, town, school district or other municipal corporation shall for any purpose become indebted in any manner to an amount exceeding one and one-half per cent. of the taxable property in such county, city, town, school district, or other municipal corporation without the assent of three-fifths of the voters therein voting at an election to be held for that purpose, nor in cases requiring such assent shall the total indebtedness exceed five per cent. of the value of the taxable property therein . . . provided that no part of the indebtedness allowed in this section shall be incurred for any purpose other than strictly county, city, town, school district, or other municipal purposes," and "that any city or town with such assent may be allowed to become indebted to a larger amount, but not exceeding five per cent. additional, for supplying such city or town with water, artificial light or sewers when the works for supplying such water, light and sewers shall be owned and controlled by the municipality."

The reference in this clause to a poll of tax- *The referendum.* payers on proposals for loans suggests another means of control, and that is the referendum. It is fairly common in the cities of the United States, and in the Canadian city of Toronto, resolutions involving expenditure out of loans can be passed finally by the city council only after they have been approved by the ratepayers at a poll—and the approval is by no means always given. The nearest approach to this in England is the poll of the ratepayers taken under the Borough Funds Act, on proposals to promote bills in Parliament.[1]

SECTION 3

We pass next to the second object of the *Administra-* control which is the restraint of legal expenditure *tive control.* within reasonable limits—reasonable, that is, in view of local conditions and the nature of the particular undertakings concerned. This has already been touched upon slightly, so far as there are restrictions imposed by statute, but there remains the large number of cases in which the only limitations are those imposed upon an authority by the discretion of a higher adminis-

---

[1] *Vide supra*, p. 318.

trative body whose approval it must obtain. We
have seen that the legislature has in some cases
fixed limits to the debts which may be incurred
by local councils, but even within these bounds
the borrowing power of the local authorities is
far from being unrestrained. All loans proposed
to be raised by them under general Acts need
the sanction of the Local Government Board,
and if that body (after holding a local enquiry,
if it thinks necessary, and hearing evidence)
authorises the loan it may impose any conditions
as to repayment, etc., which it believes to be
desirable. A Parliamentary Committee on Local
Loans reported in 1902 that:

" Each general statute which confers borrowing
powers upon local authorities specifies a maximum
period for the repayment of loans raised under
such powers. Within the limits thus established
a discretion is . . . as a rule, left with the
government department specially concerned with
the matter for which the loan is required, to
decide the exact term for the redemption of each
particular loan. . . . It is obvious that the discretion left to the government departments which
fix the actual period for the repayment of each
loan is a very wide one. . . . The Local Government Board, being charged with the general
supervision of local finance, takes into account
in fixing the period for redemption, not only the
probable useful life of each part of an undertaking
for which a loan is desired, but also the probable
future condition of localities with regard to debt,
in order that the ratepayers of the future may
not be unduly burdened, and so unable to

discharge efficiently the duties that may come
upon them."

The ideal thus set forth has not always been
attained by the Local Government Board, but
the department has seldom been willing to allow
to local authorities so long a period for the repayment of loans as Parliament itself would permit;
the maximum period allowed by the latter's
Standing Orders is sixty years (or eighty for
housing schemes), but the Board generally pre-
scribes a much shorter period. In the exceptional
case of London the metropolitan borough councils
can raise loans only by permission of the London
County Council, subject to appeal to the Local
Government Board; and the Council itself lends
the money if it approves the purpose.

One result of the moderately strict action of
the Local Government Board has been that local
authorities have preferred, whenever possible, to
go direct to the legislature by means of Private
Bills, since the Select Committees were much
less strict in their dealings with the financial
provisions.[1] Recently, however, there have been
distinct improvements in this respect, partly
because of the growing strictness of the legislature itself, and partly owing to the greater attention which is given by the Committees to the
reports of government departments upon the Bills.

Borrowing under Local Acts.

[1] The Committee of 1902 admitted its inability "to discover any
general principle by which the periods allowed by Local Acts are
fixed."

Moreover the actual amounts and conditions of loans authorised by Local Acts are now often left to be settled by the Local Government Board as the need for them arises ; and must be so left unless detailed estimates are set forth in the Bill itself.

Restraints upon borrowing abroad. The absence of "special" legislation of this kind upon the Continent, and the necessity for administrative approval of proposed action, leaves the control of loans entirely to the supervising authorities, and it is generally much more stringent than in England. In France, communal loans which exceed a million francs, or which raise the outstanding debt beyond that amount, require a special law, which proceeds as an ordinary Bill in the French Parliament. But with this exception loans need only the consent of the higher authorities—Prefect or Minister—and this is also the rule in Prussia.

Administrative approval of taxation. In France and Prussia the levying of taxes beyond a certain amount generally requires similar consent, as already noticed ; but this practice is very infrequent in England, though it exists for the rate for higher education in counties, which may not exceed twopence in the pound except with the consent of the Local Government Board. In view of the very rapid increase of local rates in England, mainly in the urban areas, some sort of check appears to be desirable, but it is by no means easy to see how one can be applied ; legislative limitation is unsatisfactory in practice, where large and important authorities, with varying

and growing needs, are concerned ; and it is in
those cases that there would also be the greatest
opposition to merely administrative checks.   It
may be that the only remedy is the pressure of
the ratepayers upon the councils, a consequent
change of financial policy on the part of the
latter, and their acquiescence in a slower rate of
municipal development.

CHAPTER XII

THE COURTS OF JUSTICE AND LOCAL ADMINISTRATION

SECTION 1

The task of the Courts.

THE task of the Courts of Justice in regard to the administration in any country is two-fold. They have to interpret the enactments of the legislature, or the rules of the common law, as to the powers and duties of the various public authorities; and also to enforce obedience to the law thus interpreted, either by compelling the authorities to carry out its positive commands or by restraining them from exceeding the powers which it has conferred upon them. The courts entrusted with this duty may be either the ordinary civil and criminal courts of the land, or special tribunals established to deal solely with a particular class of cases affecting the administration.

(i) The Civil Courts in England.

In England, where " the axiom of the equality and identity of all law, whether public or private, is rooted in the common law,"[1] this control of the action of public authorities, both central and local, is exercised by the ordinary

[1] Redlich and Hirst, II., p. 360.

courts of justice. As we have seen already, the
central departments have very little power of compelling local authorities to obey either the enactments of the legislature or departmental orders
made under legislative sanction, by administrative
action; and such small power as they have is
mostly left in abeyance. All they can do is to
apply to the King's Bench Division of the High
Court of Justice for a writ of *Mandamus*, which The "Mandamus."
is "a command, issuing in the King's name, and
directed to any person, corporation, or inferior
court of judicature within the King's dominions,
requiring them to do some particular thing therein
specified, which appertains to their office and duty."
The writ is granted on the application only of some
person or persons having a special right to call for
the duty in question; and this in practice means
the particular government department concerned,
acting either on its own initiative or at the instigation of interested citizens. The writ will be issued
only to compel the performance by a local authority
of an absolutely obligatory duty, and when there
is no other adequate remedy available.[1] Before
the writ is issued an opportunity is given to the
local authority whose conduct is in question to
show cause against it; and this enables any point
of law involved to be duly argued and determined,

---

[1] Thus application may not be made by a private citizen for a
Mandamus directed to a local authority under the Public Health Acts,
since sec. 299 of the Act of 1875 gives him the remedy of an appeal
to the Local Government Board, which can then take whatever
action it thinks necessary.

and thereby provides an effective safeguard against the giving of arbitrary directions by the central departments to the local authorities. If the *Mandamus* is issued and the local authority, to whom it is directed, still resists, the members become guilty of contempt of court, and may be imprisoned until they become willing to obey the law. It is not often necessary for the central departments to have recourse to this weapon— since the knowledge that it is in reserve is usually sufficient to induce the local council to yield to departmental representation; but cases of its use do occur from time to time.[1]

Against illegal action the remedies are more numerous, and are provided by both the civil and criminal courts.[2] The former act firstly by means of two writs. The writ of *Prohibition*, as its name implies, is an order issued by the King's Bench to inferior authorities directing them to refrain from doing particular acts which are beyond their competence; its use is, however, very infrequent, since the desired result can usually be obtained in other ways. The writ of *Certiorari* is a means of bringing up before the same tribunal the decision of any inferior court for review, in order that it may be either confirmed or quashed, and its use has been extended to all orders for

The writ of "Prohibition."

The writ of "Certiorari."

---

[1] Cf. the cases of the Leicester Board of Guardians, 1899 (as to the appointment of vaccination officers), and the Council of the West Riding of Yorkshire, 1906 (as to salaries of teachers in voluntary schools).

[2] Cf. Goodnow, II., pp. 148 *seq.*

payment out of the county or borough fund by a county or town council. For the detection and future prevention of illegal action there is the Local Government Board's audit, previously described; but where there is any doubt as to the validity of any allowance or disallowance made by the auditor the writ of *Certiorari* can be used to enable a decision to be obtained from the King's Bench.[1]

Secondly, the civil courts exercise a check upon arbitrary action on the part of authorities, both central and local, by their power to entertain suits against administrative officials for any damage (however nominal) caused by them in the doing of illegal acts. The theory of the English law, as previously pointed out, is that any official who in the discharge of his public functions does anything for which he has not lawful authority, is in respect of that particular action to be treated as an ordinary private citizen—however much he may have believed himself to be fulfilling his duty, either in obedience to orders or upon his own responsibility — and is therefore liable in the ordinary courts. In the civil courts an action for damages may be brought against him ;

Actions against officials.

---

[1] The Poor Law Amendment Act, 1844, directs that " any person aggrieved by any allowance, disallowance, or surcharge by an auditor of any union, district, or parish can make the auditor state his reasons in the book of account in which the allowance or disallowance was made and . . . may apply to the Court of the King's Bench for a writ of *Certiorari* to remove into the King's Bench the said allowance, disallowance, or surcharge in the same manner as if it were an order of the justices of the peace."

or alternatively he may be prosecuted in the criminal courts.[1]

The criminal courts act as a restraining power both in this way, and also by the very important fact that they alone are empowered to impose penalties upon citizens guilty of any violation of the law. Obedience to the law, whatever the matters may be to which it relates, is in England enforceable almost solely in the police courts, by fine or imprisonment; and therefore if a private citizen regards a bye-law or other order made by a local authority as being in any way *ultra vires*, he can simply decline to obey it, and then wait for the local authority to try to enforce it either by means of their own officials (in which case he could bring an action against those officials, or prosecute them), or by proceedings against him in the police courts or in petty cessions, where he can challenge the validity of their action. From the decision of the court he can appeal to Quarter Sessions, or by means of the writ of *Certiorari* to the Court of King's Bench. This writ is, however, now seldom employed, owing to the adoption of the simpler method of appeal to the same tribunal by means of a case stated by the police magistrate or bench of justices for the consideration of the High Court. It is an understood rule that the

---

[1] The Public Authorities Protection Act, 1893, consolidating provisions contained in previous statutes, simply directs that no action or prosecution against any person for any act done in the intended execution of his public duty may be instituted after six months have elapsed.

magistrates will "state a case" whenever there is any reasonable doubt; and, should they refuse, application may then be made for the writ.

Thus the general situation in England, as throughout the British Empire, is quite simple. The private citizen is protected against unlawful action on the part of any public authority, whatever that authority may be, by the ordinary courts of justice, which give him the same remedies as he could obtain against any other citizen; the powers and duties of public authorities as between themselves are decided, in cases of doubt, by the same tribunals, and the local councils are rendered secure from the tyranny or arbitrary action of the central departments by the fact that the latter are almost powerless without the aid of these same ordinary courts, which are concerned solely with questions of law, and are not influenced by what the departments may consider to be administrative expediency or political necessity.

SECTION 2

In France the judicial control of the adminis- *The courts in France.* tration is exercised not only by the ordinary civil and criminal courts as in England, but also by the special administrative tribunals. On the general nature of administrative law, with its admitted vagueness of content, enough has been said in a previous chapter; here it is necessary only to endeavour to indicate briefly the way in which the various sets of courts act in this matter. For the enforcement of obedience to the law on the part of the local authorities there is little or no judicial machinery — the power possessed by the central government of dismissing prefects and mayors, and of dissolving local councils, for non-fulfilment of their obligatory duties, does away with many of the difficulties which the *Mandamus* remedies in England. But for the prevention of illegal or improper action the aid of the Courts of Justice becomes necessary.

The prevention of illegal action.

(i) The civil courts. The ordinary civil or criminal courts may take cognisance of conscious violations of the law or deliberate abuse of powers by officials, just as the English courts may; but the action of these courts does not extend in France, as it does in this country, to unlawful acts done by officials in what they consider to be their duty (*fautes de service*). It may, of course, frequently be extremely difficult, and in fact almost impossible, to prove that an official was knowingly exceeding his legal authority, or making an improper use of it; and in any case such intentional faults must be comparatively rare. The most frequent faults are unconscious illegalities — mistakes by an authority as to the extent of its powers, or a mistaken application of them. These are checked first by the criminal courts. Just as in England, so also in France is it the general rule that the imposition of penalties for disobedience to bye-laws or other regulations made by local authorities, is a matter only for the police courts; and these, in deciding upon (ii) The police courts. a case, may take into consideration the validity of the bye-law or regulation in question, and may overrule it.[1] So that the citizen is protected against arbitrary action (to this extent at least) in the same way in both countries.

A further remedy against unlawful action is (iii) The administrative courts. provided by the administrative courts, whose jurisdiction falls into two divisions. These are:— (1) the *contentieux administratifs*, which are complaints as to the acts of authorities; in dealing with these the courts are concerned with questions of both law and expediency, and may overrule the decisions of an authority, or amend them. (2) The *recours pour l'excès de pouvoir*—actions for the annulling of the acts of any authority on the ground that they are *ultra vires*: in this group of cases, which go direct to the Council of State, the question is simply one of law, and the act of the authority must be either affirmed or annulled— there is no third alternative. In some instances there may be a difference of opinion between the police tribunals and the administrative courts; a police tribunal may decline to impose penalties for disobedience to a bye-law on the ground that the local authority had no power to make it, whilst an

---

[1] "Non pas en ce sens qu'ils pourront les annuller pour illégalité, mais en ce sens qu'ils pourront refuser de les appliquer s'il les jugent illégaux." Berthélemy, p. 856.

administrative court, on an application that the bye-law be annulled, may hold that it is perfectly valid. In such a conflict there seems to be no means, short of parliamentary enactment, of actually compelling a settlement of the question; and unfortunately for the citizens the various police courts may not take a uniform line. Usually, however, an agreement is reached as to the rule to be adopted, without recourse to the legislature.[1]

(a) The Prefectoral Councils.

The lower administrative courts are the Prefectoral Councils, whose composition and other functions have already been described.[2] They deal with appeals against assessments, disputes under the election laws, cases arising from the sale of domains and in connection with public works, some questions as to indirect taxes, and many other matters. In one case only—highways—do they act as police tribunals, with power to impose penalties for infractions of the law. There is an almost unlimited right of appeal (within two months) to the Council of State. The main defect of the Prefectoral Councils is that the members are badly paid, and consequently the standard of ability is not high; with the natural result that, whilst not under suspicion, they yet fail to

[1] "Comment sortir de cette impasse? En fait, on transigera: ou bien l'administration réformera son acte dans le sens réclamé par les tribunaux judiciaires, ou bien la jurisprudence des tribunaux judiciaires se réformera dans le sens indiqué par le conseil d'Etat; mais, en droit, il n'y a pas moyen d'exiger cette transaction. Les deux autorités demeurent maîtresses de leurs appreciations contradictoires, lesquelles valent chacune pour leur objet." Berthélemy, p. 857n.

[2] *Vide supra*, pp. 83-4.

command any pronounced public confidence. But
the great freedom of appeal to the Council of State
avoids many dangers which otherwise might arise.

The Council of State itself—or rather that (b) The
Council of
section of it which acts as an administrative court State.
—has a three-fold character.[1] It is a *tribunal de
cassation*, hearing appeals against final decisions of
administrative courts,[2] which it may annul on the
ground of the incompetence of any court to deal
with a particular case, and also deciding disputes
between administrative authorities as to their
respective spheres of action ; it is a *tribunal d'appel*,
hearing appeals from the prefectoral councils and
from the administrative courts of French colonies ;
and it is a *tribunal de premier et dernier ressort*,
on applications for the annulling of administrative
acts (including presidential decrees, decisions of
prefects refusing consent to resolutions of communal councils, etc.), and for disputes in regard to
elections to the councils-general. An administrative act may be annulled for *excès de pouvoir*,
when one administrative authority encroaches upon
the sphere of another, or when the formalities
required by law have not been observed, or when
an authority, acting within its competence and
with due formality " uses its discretionary power
for purposes other than those for which the
power was granted."[3]

[1] Bœuf, pp. 48-52.

[2] Including the *Cour des Comptes* and the Courts of Revision for
matters connected with recruiting.

[3] Goodnow, II., 229-30.

For the settlement of disputes as to whether
a particular case should or should not go to the
ordinary courts or to the administrative courts there
is a *tribunal des conflits*, consisting of the Keeper
of the Seals (who is also Minister of Justice), three
ordinary Councillors of State elected by their
colleagues, three members of the Supreme Court
of France (*Cour de Cassation*) also chosen by
their colleagues, and two persons elected by the
other seven. They all hold office for three years,
and five members form a *quorum*. The "conflict"
may be raised only by the Prefect in each department; if he finds that any case touching the
administration, unless specifically left to the
ordinary courts by legislative enactment, is being
taken to them, it is his duty to draw the attention
of the courts to the fact, and, if they persist in
hearing it, to appeal to the *tribunal des conflits*.

SECTION 3

The courts
in Prussia. In Prussia the general position, and the part
played by the ordinary civil and criminal courts
in the restraining of public authorities from
unlawful action, is much the same as in France,
and does not call for any special description. But
the working of the administrative courts is somewhat different.[1] There are three grades — the

---

[1] For a detailed account see Von Seydel, *Preussisches Staatsrecht*
(1894), pp. 199 *seq*. The general rules are laid down in the Landesverwaltungsgesetz, of 1875, amended in 1880.

Circle Committees, the District Committees, and
the Supreme Administrative Court; their composition has already been described,[1] and it will
be remembered that in the two lower courts the
unprofessional and indirectly elected members
predominate, whilst the members of the Supreme
Court hold office for life.   These arrangements
undoubtedly give the Prussian courts a far greater
feeling of independence than is possessed by the
French tribunals, and also enable them to secure
a larger amount of public confidence.   The
ordinary members of the lower courts are—so far
as they act as judges—altogether independent of
bureaucratic control, and so are the Landraths and
Government Presidents; though the fact that all
the members are subject to that control in their
other character of agents of the central government probably tends somewhat to make them
take the official view.   But the members of the
French Prefectoral Councils are in the same
position, and probably the ability of the Prussian
administrative courts as a whole, and certainly
of the District Committees, is superior to that
found in the corresponding tribunals in France.
Both have the theoretical defect, which is also
to some extent a real one, that in the lower
courts administrative and judicial functions in
regard to the same matters are combined in
the same hands : the " representative " element
in the Prussian courts, however, makes this less

---

[1] *Vide supra*, pp. 129-30, 140-2, and 148-9.

important and much less likely to be harmful than in France.

(i) The Circle Committees. The Circle Committee deals with disputes arising out of official-district and communal elections, boundaries, communal taxation assessments, the apportionment of circle expenses between the communes, education, highways, waterways, building laws, sanitation, etc. The cases in which these matters can give rise to actions before the administrative courts are all indicated in the various laws, and notably in the great " Competence Law,"[1] which states positively a large number of cases in which an action (*Klage*) may be brought against an authority, and therefore negatively that in all other cases the only remedy is a complaint (*Beschwerde*) to the appropriate controlling authority. In some instances, however, when a complaint has been unsuccessful, but not before, an action may be brought.[2] Where there is doubt as to which of the two courses is to be taken, the Supreme Administrative Court decides.

(ii) The District Committees. From the decisions of the Circle Committees appeal lies (in all cases where it is not expressly prohibited by law) to the District Committees. These are also courts of first instance for similar controversies arising in the Circles themselves; for " police " matters in communes of more than 10,000 inhabitants or in Town Circles; and also

---

[1] *Das Zustandigkeitsgesetz.*
[2] Cf. the *Zustandigkeitsgesetz*, secs. 10, 11, 18, 19, etc.

for actions brought by a Landrath challenging (on
the ground of incompetence or illegality) the
resolutions passed by the Assembly or Committee
of his Circle.

The Supreme Administrative Court (*Oberver-* (iii) The
Supreme
waltungsgericht) is (i) a court of revision, reviewing Administrative Court.
the decisions of the District Committees given
in second instance; (ii) a court of appeal from
the decisions of those tribunals given in other
cases; (iii) a court of first instance, hearing and
determining complaints by Circles against their
assessed shares of provincial taxation, by the
Chief Presidents against the decisions of the
Provincial Assemblies, Committees, and commissions of various kinds. The Supreme Court
has also power, if adequate cause is shown, to
order a new trial of a case in the court in which
it originated.

As to the general working of these courts there The working
of the courts
are several points which are worthy of notice.
The first is that any dispute between two courts of
equal rank as to jurisdiction is decided by the next
higher tribunal. Secondly, in the lower courts it
is not necessary for any formal trial to take place;
the parties may agree on the facts, and submit
them to the court for a legal ruling; and this
method, which is almost without cost and is also
very rapid, is greatly used. If either party, or
the court itself, so wishes, there must be a formal
hearing. Thirdly, it is a rule that the courts are
not limited to the evidence tendered by either

party, but may call for such other evidence as
they may think desirable; and in coming to their
decisions they are directed to take a broad view,
and may consequently bring into account considerations which have not appeared at all in the
arguments.   Finally, not only may either of the
parties to a case appeal against a judgment, but
a Landrath or Government President may appeal
" on the ground of the public interest," against
the decisions of the very court over which he
presides.   The general aim of the rules of
procedure is to secure that the cases shall be
disposed of as rapidly as possible, and with the
minimum of cost and trouble, to the parties concerned; and, so far as a foreign observer can judge,
the arrangements seem to meet with general
approval.

Conflicts of jurisdiction. For the settlement of conflicts of jurisdiction
between the ordinary and the special administrative
courts there is the Court of Conflicts at Berlin
(*Kompetenzkonflikts - Gerichthof*).   It consists of
eleven persons appointed by the King on the
nomination of the Ministry of State; six of them
must be members of the Supreme Civil Court
(*Oberlandesgericht*), and the other five must be
qualified for high administrative positions.   They
hold their post for life, or for the term of the
office which they held at the time of appointment to the Court of Conflicts.   There is only
a single tribunal — seven members forming a
quorum.

Finally it may be worth while to repeat here what has been said previously, that the administrative courts of both France and Prussia are *legal* tribunals. That means that under the direction and guidance of the Supreme Courts in particular there is being built up, in the two countries, a system of law relating to the public administration which, though very different in many respects from private law, is yet regular and definite, is as a rule (especially in the highest courts) little influenced by considerations of mere administrative expediency, or by any particular regard for the wishes of the executive authorities, is animated by the true legal spirit, and does on the whole give general satisfaction. The English student will probably still prefer his own national system, but that need not blind him to the merits of some at least of continental methods and ideas ; and in the actual working of the administrative courts he may find some incidental advantages.

General character of the administrative courts.

INDEX

PRINTED AT THE EDINBURGH PRESS, 9 AND 11 YOUNG STREET.